Copyright © 2023 by Raphael L. De'Veritas

Cover and back designed by Raphael L. De'Veritas. Photo on cover has an expired copyright but was taken by Walt Cisco of the Dallas Morning News on the day of Kennedy's Assassination.

The Big Event

Operation: Kill Kennedy

Created Reality, Theater, and Puppet Mastery in the Killing of Kennedy, Tippit, and Oswald

Why the Truth About JFK's Murder Still Matters 60 Years Later

by Raphael Luceri De'Veritas

Acknowledgments

This book took five years to research, and in that time, true friends showed their support and enthusiasm for this project, too many to list here, but the ones that deserve the most recognition are noted below.

My mother, Adela. She has shown me how faith is applied in everyday life and how it has allowed her to persevere through adversities. She is a much more courageous, patient, and caring person because of that faith and she inspires me.

My friend, William E. Lore. Aside from being a loyal and dear friend, he agreed to edit this book for me. His edits, comments, suggestions, and encouragement made this book much better and I cannot repay him for his time, talent, and kindness.

Finally, to the many fine and inspiring people I worked with throughout my challenging and satisfying career with the Department of Homeland Security. When you are surrounded by an incredible group of dedicated public servants, it becomes easy to be infected by their diligence and commitment to the truth.

Cover Photo

The photo on the cover was taken by Walt Cisco of the Dallas Morning News. The copyright expired in 1991. It is one of several photos that have become part of Kennedy's legacy and is frequently associated with the assassination on November 22, 1963.

The photo shows the President's limousine just before it arrived at the Texas School Book Depository. President Kennedy has less than two minutes to live.

President Kennedy and First Lady, Jacqueline Kennedy, are both clearly delighted by the public's response to their visit. Jacqueline Kennedy received a significant amount of attention from the public that morning in Dallas, by both men and women. Men whistled and gawked at her. Women stretched their necks to see what she looked like and what she was wearing. While Kennedy may have had pockets of people that hated him, the crowds that came to see the Kennedys that day were not among them. The young President and the First Lady exuded charm, charisma, and a genuine appreciation for the American public. Even Nellie Connally took notice of the crowd's affinity and admiration for the Kennedys. The last words the President heard came from Nellie Connally when she said "Mr. President, you can't say Dallas does not love you!" Sadly, just after Nellie Connally uttered those words, a cascade of bullets, I assert at least nine shots, were fired at and upon him from different kill zones.

Kennedy's purpose for his trip to Dallas was two-fold: 1) to garner precious southern votes to help him win the presidency in 1964; and 2) to repair a fractured relationship among Vice-President Johnson and Governor Connally with Senator Ralph Yarborough, a man despised and openly disrespected by both Johnson and Connally.

Vice-President Johnson had other plans for this trip to Dallas. It was to eliminate the biggest obstacle to his ascension to the Presidency and to quell all investigations of his criminal activities. November 22, 1963 was part of a covert, illegal operation to kill Kennedy. Internally, it was known as "The Big Event." I would like to think Kennedy's last minutes alive were happy ones, but he would not be leaving Dallas alive.

Preface

I tussled with the thought of writing a book about the JFK assassination in my mind over a thousand times and over the course of several years of my adult life. What could I contribute to the mass of books, articles, and websites that covered every aspect of this tragic event that many considered to be unsolved and a multi-party conspiracy? The "crime of the century" was a bold undertaking. The list of books alone has run the gamut from everything between a lone gunman to the *Illuminati, Voodoo,* and *Opus Dei* as having a role in this murder-conspiracy. Some books were very well researched, objective, and well cited – exceptional in their own right; others were dubious pieces of shoddy work not worth the paper they were printed on. It took a bit of courage to enter this realm, but, more than courageous, I was determined — or as my mother would say, hardheaded. I wanted to write about what really happened and why, and I wanted to draw on my years as an attorney in a wide array of legal specialties and as an advisor to senior federal government employees, including political appointees. My experience has allowed me to analyze issues and subjects with a strong sense of logic, but also to write succinctly and with certainty about exactly why entities such as the CIA, LBJ, Cuban exiles, rich Texas oil men, and the Mafia were motivated to assist in this complex and convoluted murder-conspiracy. I wanted to tell the best possible truth of how a beloved President was violently taken away from this country and the world.

But that was not my only problem. About 4 million people visit the Arlington National Cemetery, and most come to see the Eternal Flame at Kennedy's grave. How many people born after 1963 care about what happened to that beloved President or why he died? I surmise that whatever that number is, it is not enough. Aside from being a well-publicized murder, a very public person was taken away from us that day and the evidence of governmental involvement and a cover-up is overwhelming. It was a violent overthrow of power in our very own country, and it happened *only* sixty years ago! How can we be assured that this violent overthrow of power in our own country could not be repeated? I am eminently aware that there have been many reforms in the form of laws, regulations, and policies that have been changed, passed, or implemented, but if we do not know the entire truth, how effective can these changes be? Most importantly, when will the government be forthcoming about the assassination instead of leaving us to rely on private researchers and historians for versions of the truth?

I was born in 1974, so I have no actual live memories of President Kennedy. My mother and uncles spoke very fondly of him, and I cannot recall anyone ever saying a bad thing about him, including modern-day, middle-of-the-road Republicans. I never associated the horrific assassination with him until I watched the Zapruder film when I was 17. I simply heard very moving speeches by him, saw streets and schools named after him, and of course, saw him on half-dollars, which I enjoyed receiving, and spending even more. Once I saw the video of his death, I could not believe what I saw. Captured on film was the murder of a president, the goriness of his head exploding and the eruption of blood and brain matter, and then this beautiful, elegantly dressed woman, who I later learned was First Lady Jacqueline Kennedy, desperately jumping on the trunk of a moving vehicle in a futile effort to recover bits of her husband's brain and skull to put him back together. Then I saw a courageous Secret Service agent also jump on the trunk as the limousine sped off. It was surreal. Nevertheless, it really happened. That day would be forever etched in the memories not only of Americans, but of people all over the world. On that day, not only was a young, dynamic president's life taken from the world, but the hope that he brought to millions of people also died, and it was replaced with cynicism. That day was Friday, November 22, 1963, in Dallas.

Later in life, I became a lawyer and worked initially as a prosecutor for the Department of Justice, and then the Department of Homeland Security. I was diligent and hard-working. I rose quickly within the federal government, earning and maintaining a Top Secret-SCI (secret compartmented information) clearance, the highest clearance anyone can get. For almost twenty years, I handled national security cases, human persecutor cases, class-action cases, and media-interest cases. As I rose up in the federal government, my exposure and expertise in various legal fields increased. They included criminal law and procedure, immigration, naturalization, customs, habeas corpus, labor and employment, and tort law. I worked with many federal, state, tribal, and local agents and officers from numerous law enforcement and intelligence agencies, both domestically and internationally, in both civil and criminal matters. I was able to see how federal agencies work and how law enforcement agencies collaborate and compete with each other. I also provided advice abroad to national police and prosecutors that resulted in hundreds of arrests of human traffickers and smugglers in a multi-nation, multi-agency operation.

My curiosity about who really killed JFK and why began to peak around 2018, when I read several well-known books on this topic. Then it got complicated. The more books I read, the more confused I got. One book by a well-respected source said *X happened,* yet another book, by yet another well-respected source, stated *Y happened.* Some books I found to be baseless, illogical, and unfounded. Getting to the truth in an abyss of divergent thoughts, opinions, theories, and impressions was no easy task. In this case, the millions of discrete facts can be selectively used to support almost any theory. I was interested in all facts and where they objectively lead me and not where I led them.

As confusing as it was for me, consider how confusing and frustrating it must have been for the numerous committees that investigated the assassinations of prominent figures and the activities of intelligence agencies. Here, prominent political figures and their assistants came together under color of law and with a high authority to discover the truth, and they were lied to and deceived –- the truth never came, yet they issued a report with their best conclusions and recommendations and moved on.

In the meantime, the conspiracy train kept rolling. A significant number of credible "magic bullet" and "lone gunman" critics had voiced their concerns by the time the 1978 House Select Committee on Assassinations made the conclusion that there had been a conspiracy. By the time it reached its conclusions, the world had seen the Zapruder film. A great majority of Americans had suspected foul play *before* seeing it. But after its wide publication by Geraldo Rivera in 1975, the video confirmed their suspicions: Basic physics forces you to conclude that a shot came from the right front, near the grassy knoll, as Kennedy's head jerked violently back and to the left in response to that fatal head shot. Nevertheless, these committees were stymied and prevented from getting to the truth through lies, destruction of evidence and, on far too many occasions, the untimely and suspicious deaths of key witnesses.

With the premise that there was a conspiracy and more than one shooter accepted as fact, things were as murky as ever. There were still many pieces missing from this puzzle. I tried to read diverse books on this topic, including books about Mafia members, such as Jimmy Hoffa and Sam Giancana. I also read books about Watergate and what, if any, ties Nixon or the Watergate burglars may have had to the JFK assassination. I looked at this investigation in a fresh way. I initially tried to answer who would be found guilty based on *any* legal standard, even one of the lowest legal standards, *more likely than not,* and quickly learned that the evidence was far from solid and reliable. I gave up trying to find out who was really guilty based on what I can only describe as refutable, controverted, shoddy, and tampered evidence (and I had no visibility of the amount of destroyed evidence). Apparently, Hoover and others gave up trying to find the truth as well. When Oswald was shot by Jack Ruby two days after Kennedy's assassination, FBI Director Hoover hoped for a confession from Oswald before he died, and when that did not happen, he expressed an urgent desire "to have something issued so that we can convince the public that Oswald is the real assassin."

Additionally, Captain Fritz from the Dallas Police Department told the men in charge of Oswald's case to "make sure you can wrap up a good case on Oswald shooting Tippit because we're not too sure about this Kennedy business." The evidence against Oswald, even when fresh, was far less than "beyond a reasonable doubt."

With the passage of time, the intentional destruction of evidence, lies, manipulation, fading memories, and the deaths, sometimes intentional, of key witnesses, the evidence has been significantly compromised. In short, Oswald probably could not have been successfully tried for the murder of Kennedy or JD Tippit, assuming Oswald had survived, which is also why he had to be silenced, and assuming Oswald would have had a fair trial. But there was a bright side. Deathbed confessions, new evidence, and newly released documents shed more light on the assassination. Now the question became: Why? Who stood to gain the most, and how could sense be made of this multi-party, multi-faceted murder-conspiracy? Allowing the facts to guide me also allowed me to debunk several conspiracy theories and clarify many theories that have taken a life of their own.

Now you can read about how and why it happened with largely irrefutable evidence patched together in a single book, including the number and type of shots fired and the key people behind "the crime of the century." In this book, I lay out, with as much precision and granularity as possible, what happened that day *sans* the intelligence community's created reality. I logically build a case of factors and events and, in the end, tell you how things went down in Dallas. My goal was to tell this story as factually and succinctly as I could. I hope you find that it will answer many of your questions and eliminate many of your doubts.

Road Map

My goal was to try to summarize this murder-conspiracy as succinctly as possible and build, chapter-by-chapter, a story that peels away the created reality our intelligence community orchestrated, in order for us to get to the highest form of the truth. This book ends with "The Big Event" as it really happened and not as some wanted us to believe.

In my efforts to summarize the crime of the century, I felt the most important place to start was with the basic understanding of how the events transpired on that day according to the Warren Commission. It includes created reality, theater, and puppet mastery. In that regard, Chapter 1 is a summary of the official version of what happened.

Chapter 3 is a compilation of some legal terms, techniques, and an explanation of how evidence is weighed by lawyers and judges as well as an analysis of motive. Why? Because one of the most difficult aspects of this convoluted crime was assessing and getting to the truth, weighing evidence, including conflicting facts, and analyzing motive. For example, courts give great weight to deathbed confessions, and here we have many deathbed confessions, some of them inconsistent with others. We also have a vast number of motives from various entities, but many motives were attenuated, indirect, and simply factually improbable, so an explanation about motive, I felt, was necessary.

In my efforts to summarize the crime of the century, I felt the most important place to start was with a basic understanding of some legal terms and how evidence is weighed by lawyers and judges as well as an analysis of motive. Why? Because one of the most difficult aspects of this convoluted crime was assessing and getting to the truth, weighing evidence, including conflicting facts, and analyzing motive. For example, courts give great weight to deathbed confessions, and here, we have many deathbed confessions, some of them are inconsistent with others. We also have a vast number of motives from various entities, but many motives were attenuated, indirect, and simply factually improbable, so an explanation about motive, I felt, was necessary.

Next, I begin with the person that initially ordered the hit on Kennedy, his very own Vice-President, Lyndon B Johnson or LBJ. Chapter 4 is about LBJ's depraved mind and criminal culpability.

From there, I felt I had to summarize the numerous key figures involved in this murder conspiracy. In Chapters 5 and 6, I summarized the key figures that were involved in some form or fashion in this crime. With the exception of James Files, these figures have passed away and memories of them also tend to fade away, so these two chapters are a summary of *some* of the people involved. These two chapters also serve to refresh your memory about these figures and begin getting you up to speed about certain facts from this murder-conspiracy.

I excluded a few characters in order to maintain my goal of being succinct, but that does not mean they were not involved in some form or fashion in the assassination. For example, I decided to exclude probably the most mysterious character of all the characters in this assassination: the very handsome and elusive George de Mohrenschildt. A book can be written trying to find out just who de Mohrenschildt was and what role he played. He may have worked for one or all of the following companies, agencies, or professions: insurance salesman; film producer; newspaper correspondent; textile salesman, British intelligence; French intelligence; French counterintelligence, Nazi agents; Polish intelligence; Polish military;

Shell Oil, the Department of State, the CIA as an informant or operative or both; stamp collector, Swedish intelligence, and Rangely Oil Field in Colorado. He was known as Jerzy Sergius von Mohrenschildt, and then George de Mohrenschildt, and possibly Phillip Harbin. He has claimed Polish, Belgium, Swedish, and Russian origins. More relevant to the topic of the JFK assassination, the vast bulk of the information about George de Mohrenschildt's relationship with Lee Harvey Oswald is either controverted or lacks substance or both. The only consensus about their relationship is that it was odd because de Mohrenschildt was well-traveled, rich, extremely handsome, older, and well educated and Oswald was none of these things. In short, I excluded him because I could not find any evidence that de Mohrenschildt played a pivotal role in Oswald's life as it relates to the assassination, except for getting him the job at the map-making company, Jaggars-Chiles-Stovall, and being his babysitter for a short period of time until the Paine couple took over.

Chapter 7 is my attempt to understand Lee Harvey Oswald. He remains a complicated and enigmatic character, but this chapter highlights Oswald's fascination with intelligence and living a double life.

Chapter 8 goes into greater detail about the assassination. It builds upon Chapters 2, 5, and 6 but is far more granular.

The theory of an Oswald double and his role in this assassination is covered in Chapter 9.

Chapter 10 covers the details of Tippit's murder. Some books conclude that Oswald could not have killed JFK but leave open the possibility that Oswald may have killed Tippit. This chapter provides details about this murder and explains why Oswald could not have killed Tippit and explains who probably did.

The April 1963 attempted assassination of General Walker, an outspoken critic of JFK's policies, is covered in Chapter 11.

I underscore in Chapter 3 how important a *modus operandi* is for criminals, especially if they are successful. Chapter 12 covers the Mafia's successful use of a patsy in killing politicians and how things can go terribly wrong when a patsy is not employed.

The Mafia and the CIA began to work together officially in 1942 in an operation aptly called "Underworld." British intelligence began working with organized crime long before that. Years later, Vice-President Nixon permitted or ordered the CIA to work with the American Mafia in the planning of the Bay of Pigs invasion. By the time of the assassination, the Mafia and the CIA were so close, that their relationship has been described as incestuous. Chapter 13 is about this special relationship.

The context and order to kill Kennedy is provided in Chapter 14.

Chapter 15 further builds upon Chapter 12, the first chapter discussing the successful use of a patsy. The Mafia and the CIA further refined the use of a patsy by killing the patsy at the scene or shortly after the killing of a politician.

Chapter 16 discusses an operation that could be used to incorporate plausibility deniability, and thus deny the CIA's involvement in the Kennedy assassination— abort teams. The CIA is notorious for building numerous redundancies and distractions into their plans. Here, the CIA actually sent in men to Dealey Plaza that were intended to protect the President that day. The CIA created these covert and illegal teams to protect the President and relied on mostly military-trained officials. The purposes of having abort teams were to explain to senior government officials that the CIA actually wanted to protect the President just in case things went awry or if there were an investigation. It is another example of using plausible deniability to distract would-be investigators and oversight committees.

Oswald's assassin, Jack Ruby, was known as the Privileged Character because he was a notorious name-dropper. Chapter 17 is about him.

Chapter 18 goes into detail about six legends that were born on November 22, 1963, and persist to this day. The basis for the existence of these legends is answered in this chapter. This chapter is the last chapter to support the facts concerning The Big Event.

Chapter 19, the last chapter, is essentially a timeline of how things really went down on November 22, 1963. No smoke and mirrors. No created reality. No deception. It is based on all the previous chapters and the best information we have to this day.

Chapter 1: The Condensed Official Version, including Created Reality, Puppet Mastery, and Theater

I begin this book by summarizing the version that the American public and the world was expected to believe concerning the murder of President John F. Kennedy. It includes created reality, theater, and puppet mastery orchestrated by the CIA and military intelligence. This is a story that you may already be familiar, and while some swear it is a factual account of the President's death, it is a work of fiction made to look like reality. Please forgive me in advance for my cynicism.

According to the Warren Commission (sometimes abbreviated as WC or the Commission), Lee Harvey Oswald killed President Kennedy and acted alone. Oswald was born in New Orleans, Louisiana and was an ex-marine and defector of the United States that lived in Russia for three years and had ties to communism. He purchased a 1940 Italian Mannlicher-Carcano rifle and a .38 special revolver through the mail in March 1963 even though he could have easily purchased a better rifle and revolver locally without creating a paper trail.

According to a few key witnesses, on the morning of November 22, 1963, Oswald brought that rifle to his work at the Texas School Book Depository (or Depository or TSBD). He knew the President's motorcade was scheduled to pass in front of the Depository around 12:30pm Central Standard Time because the motorcade route was published in the local newspapers. After the President's limousine passed the Depository and as it approached the grassy knoll, Oswald fired three extremely difficult shots from the sixth floor of the Depository, fatally wounding the President and seriously injuring Texas Governor Connally even though it was reported that he had never practiced with his surplus rifle. The military in a number of countries including Mexico, Russia, Israel, and the United States have set up the exact position as Oswald's in reenactments.[1] No one has come close to making the shots as stated in the Warren Commission.

The Commission concluded that the first shot missed, but the second shot made a magical trajectory through President Kennedy and Governor Connally, piercing seven bones, tissue, and cartilage yet losing less than 2% of its weight. The magic bullet also suspended itself in midair for almost 1.5 seconds after exiting Kennedy's body and before entering Connally's body. A magic bullet indeed! This bullet caused severe bodily damage to Connally, who required four hours of surgery, yet the bullet came out in almost pristine condition. The bullet was discovered on a stretcher that was not used by either Connally or Kennedy, but the Commission nevertheless concluded that this bullet was the one used in this murder and assault. The third shot was a fatal headshot, made at a distance of 265 feet, which entered the rear of Kennedy's head and blew off the top portion of his skull. Many witnesses to the murder saw the right front of President Kennedy's face being blown apart and his head jerking violently to the left rear. Additionally, many witnesses, including trained police officers, ran almost immediately to the grassy knoll, to the right front of the President when he was fatally wounded, because they heard shots from there.

Oswald, unable to drive and without having been issued a driver's license, walked away from the Depository as it was being swarmed by police officers and fellow employees that had stepped out to see the President. Oswald then boarded a bus about five blocks away, but the bus was stuck in traffic. After advancing only about two blocks, Oswald decided to get off the bus. He walked to the nearby

Greyhound bus terminal and took a taxi to his room in a rooming house in the Oak Cliff neighborhood of Dallas, changed his clothes by putting on dark pants and a light grey Eisenhower or wind-breaker-style jacket popular at the time. He also retrieved his loaded .38 special revolver from his room. He then was able to walk about a mile in seven minutes or so without anyone seeing him. He was then approached by Officer J.D. Tippit in his patrol car. Oswald leaned in on the passenger-side vent window to speak to Tippit, placing his hand on the car window.

Officer J.D. Tippit exited his vehicle and Oswald walked toward the front of his patrol car. Oswald took out his revolver and shot Tippit three times in the chest. Once fallen, Oswald leaned over Tippit, placed his hand on the right front fender of Tippit's car, and shot him in the right temple. Oswald then sought refuge in the Texas Theater where he entered without paying for a .90¢ ticket even though Oswald, now the most wanted man in the world, had $13.87 on him when he was arrested. Oswald moved around suspiciously in the rear of the of the first-floor theater. Around 1:45pm CST, Oswald was arrested by 16 named Dallas police officers and a swarm of other officers.

Oswald was in Dallas police custody from Friday afternoon until Sunday morning, November 24, 1963. He was interrogated numerous times, including one 12-hour interrogation session. The Dallas Police Department had a policy of not tape-recording interrogations, but notes were kept by Captain Fritz and FBI Special Agent James Hosty and subsequently released.

Summaries of what Oswald told investigators were made after he was killed in police custody, consisting of the following: Like many criminals, Oswald immediately claimed he was innocent, but Oswald declared something far more interesting and peculiar than his mere innocence—he claimed to be a patsy. He also claimed that he did not kill anyone and that he did not own a rifle. Finally, upon being shown a photo of him in a yard holding a rifle and two communist newspapers with a gun in a holster, he immediately claimed that the photo was an alteration.[i] Oswald's only phone call, made late Saturday evening, was to a "John David Hurt" of Raleigh, North Carolina.[2] John Hurt worked in the Army Counterintelligence Corps in Europe and Japan from 1942 to 1946. The call was not allowed to go through and John Hurt later denied knowing Oswald or why Oswald had called him.[3]

In addition, Oswald was subjected to a paraffin gunshot residue test, which, even at the time, was not a conclusive test but was used more for interrogation purposes. The paraffin test showed no gun residue on Oswald's cheeks,[ii] which would have been evidence of the shots that fired at the President from the Depository, yet when a series of seven expert marksmen used the same model of rifle under similar, controlled circumstances, they all had substantial residue on their right cheeks.[4]

On Sunday, November 24, 1963, Oswald was scheduled to be transported from the Dallas police precinct to a more secure location. By this time, Oswald told the world through television news cameras that he was a patsy and that he did not kill anyone. At 11:21am CST, with about 80 armed police officers on watch as well as approximately 300 personnel from national and international news networks, Jack Ruby, a night club owner, snuck into the basement of the precinct, leaped from the crowd, and shot Lee Harvey Oswald once in the abdomen. While Ruby shot Oswald, he yelled "you killed my President, you rat." The term "rat" was, and still is, common parlance among Mafia and underworld figures.

It was the first murder captured live on television. The bullet pierced several of Oswald's major organs. Doctors call this a "shish kabob" shot. Dr. McClelland, the same doctor that treated President Kennedy just two days before, also treated Oswald, who died about 40 minutes later. He was 24 years old.

No fingerprints were immediately found on the rifle Oswald used to kill the President, but suddenly a clear palm print was discovered after Oswald's death.

Initial reports by news outlets stated that Oswald attempted to enter Cuba for unknown reasons, and, by implication, the assassination may have been a plot by Fidel Castro to kill Kennedy. The new President, LBJ, also initially expressed that the assassination may be part of a larger plot against America, stating "[w]e've all got to be careful ... [t]his could be a worldwide conspiracy to kill off all our leaders."[5] American military forces were put on high alert worldwide.[6] For four days, CBS, NBC and ABC provided non-stop coverage of the assassination and JFK's funeral. For four days, Americans gathered around their television sets. Days after the assassination, with the nation still in mourning and shock, the reports of Russia or Cuba involvement were quelled.

On November 29, 1963, new President Johnson issued an Executive Order creating the Warren Commission to investigate the assassination. Officially, it was called "The President's Commission on the Assassination of President Kennedy" but was commonly referred to as the Warren Commission because of its chairman, Chief Justice of the Supreme Court Earl Warren. Johnson appointed all seven members of the Commission. Johnson, in implying that the Warren Commission could not implicate the Soviet Union or Cuba, told Earl Warren in a manipulative manner, "was he [Earl Warren] willing to be responsible for World War III?"[7]

Fidel Castro immediately disavowed any involvement in the assassination and rightfully criticized the United States for allowing someone of the likes of Jack Ruby to enter a police precinct and kill the President's alleged assassin. Years later, the Soviet Union, after conducting its own internal investigation, also disavowed any involvement and even implicated Johnson in the assassination.

The Warren Commission, with its budget of $10 million dollars (or $96,500,000 in today's money), issued a 26-volume report on August 14, 1964. It stated: "[t]he assassination of John Fitzgerald Kennedy on November 22, 1963, was a cruel and shocking act of violence directed against a man, a family, a nation, and against all mankind." This statement, I believe, is one of the few statements from the 888-page report that is true, uncontroverted, and indisputable.

The Warren Commission could not identify a particular motive for Oswald's killing of President Kennedy. The Commission found that Oswald acted alone. The Commission painted Oswald as a frustrated loner that wanted attention, but it struggled to find any particular animosity toward President Kennedy or his policies other than Oswald's own alleged affinity for communism.

The Commission could not find a motive for Ruby's killing of Oswald either. The Commission found that Ruby was not tied to underworld figures and did not know Oswald prior to killing him. Ruby claimed his motive for killing Oswald was to obviate the need for Jacqueline Kennedy to go through the stress and anxiety of having to return to Dallas to testify against Oswald. Jack Ruby was willing to spend the rest of his life in prison or possibly be killed by death penalty in order to save Jaqueline Kennedy from testifying. Who knew Jack Ruby, the owner of a burlesque nightclub, could be so chivalrous?

From the time of the assassination until this very day, the majority of the American public, and many others worldwide, have always believed a conspiracy was at work. This book methodically peels away at the created reality, theater, and puppet mastery in the JFK killing and applies the most up-to-date information there is concerning this murder-conspiracy.

The murder of a beloved President was a highly orchestrated plan called "The Big Event" by the CIA, but many people in and out of the CIA were involved. The last chapter summarizes what actually happened, the reality, the non-fiction, and the highest truth we have until the government is forthcoming to the American public that on November 22, 1963, America suffered its only successful coup d'état in our history.

Chapter 2: Evidence of a Conspiracy

This chapter is a summary of the evidence of many aspects of this crime and delves into the unequivocal evidence of a conspiracy and cover-up. I begin with a description of the two victims and the facts concerning their murder and attempted murder. I also discuss the evidentiary weight of the Mannlicher-Carcano rifle, its bullets and shell cases, and how they could not be tied to Oswald.

Arguably, the victims of this murder-conspiracy include the American people, and, if not all of the American public, then certainly the large majority of Americans that held a favorably view of President Kennedy. Nevertheless, the victims for criminal law purposes are: 1) President John F. Kennedy; and 2) Texas Governor John Connally. I then summarize the damage done to the limousine and the alleged bullet fragments that were recovered from it. I cannot summarize all of the evidence of a conspiracy in this book without the risk of writing an encyclopedia, but that does not mean all or most of the evidence has not been considered. I simply underscore the most relevant and controverted pieces of evidence in this complex murder-conspiracy.

Victim #1: President John F. Kennedy:

President John F. Kennedy was the 35th President of the United States. He remains the youngest president in our history, taking the oath of office at the age of 43. Prior to becoming president, he was a Senator from Massachusetts. He was also a hero from the Navy where he saved many lives of the men under his charge. His torpedo patrol boat was rammed by a Japanese destroyer ship in the Solomon Islands.[8] To give you a sense of his heroism, he swam approximately three and a half miles to land while towing an injured man by a life-vest strap, which the President clinched with his teeth as he swam. For his heroic efforts, the President earned a Navy and Marine Corps Medal, and injuries suffered during the incident also qualified him for a Purple Heart.[9]

The President's time in the Navy and the death of his older brother, Joseph, informed the President's views about the ravaging effects of war in every regard, especially on the mental psyche. Some have called President Kennedy a peace president. I disagree. The hawkish President planned an invasion of Cuba that was slated to begin on December 1, 1963. This invasion was a clear violation of the agreement that Kennedy made to Russian Premier Khrushchev to not invade Cuba as a solution to the Cuban-missile crisis. The preparations for this top-secret invasion, some argue, provided a training platform for the Mafia to learn many assassination-related tricks and employ them in JFK's assassination. I did not write this book to underscore all of President Kennedy's hypocrisies, management deficiencies, and defects. This

book focuses on the murder-conspiracy. The Cuba invasion is related to this crime insofar as it may have given the Mafia a significant edge that they exploited in killing the beloved President.

While I do not believe JFK was necessarily a peace president largely because of his private actions, his commencement speech at American University on June 10, 1963, clearly distinguished him from all other presidents in terms of his tone and attitude toward peace. In other words, publicly, he was a peace president that envisioned the world by ending the Cold War instead of winning it; he spoke of love for fellow man, including the courageous Russian people, and how every human deserved peace. That powerful commencement speech about future peace became part of his legacy, and so it is understandable why many believe him to be a peace President, but more relevant to this murder-conspiracy, why he may have been perceived to be a threat to the CIA, the military industrial complex, and the national security network. Unfortunately, by the time JFK made his now-famous commencement speech, he was already declared to be a *persona non-grata* by certain key members of his own government, his own Vice-President, and the Mafia.

The President made his trip to Dallas because it was a key state in the upcoming presidential elections. On November 22, 1963, at 12:30p.m. CST (all times are central standard time until the President's body was shipped to the greater Washington DC area), while riding through Dealey Plaza, the President was assassinated. The more precise location of the crime was an open area of Elm Street, just before the entrance to the Stemmons Freeway, just after the Texas School Book Depository, and immediately to the left of a grassy knoll of the plaza.

President Kennedy was riding in the right rear-most seat of his presidential limousine, which had three forward-facing rows of seats. The first row had two secret service agents; the second row had Governor Connally and his wife, Nellie; and the last row is where the President sat with the First Lady, Jacqueline Kennedy, to his left. The presidential limousine was an unarmored convertible with a clear, bubble top, but the bubble top was not used that day and its use was disfavored by the charismatic President.

Immediately after the assassination, the presidential limousine rushed to Parkland Hospital, a leading national trauma and training center at the time and one that had extensive experience with gunshot wounds given the large amount of gun owners in the state.[10] At the time, it averaged 1,200 gunshot wounds per year, or about three gunshot wounds per day. The presidential limousine arrived at Parkland Hospital at 12:43pm. Later that same day, the

President's body also underwent an autopsy at the Bethesda Navy Medical Center.

Please keep in mind that Navy-related wounds are seldom gunshot wounds, but more often are injuries that are job-related or illnesses. The experience of the doctors at Bethesda to conduct an autopsy is a source of controversy, as noted in more detail below. Additionally, and also explained below, there is great speculation that the President's body was altered or tampered with to ensure that all bullet trajectories appeared to have come from the rear in the direction of the Texas School Book Depository.

Efforts to resuscitate the President at Parkland Hospital were futile. While he had a faint heartbeat upon arriving at the hospital, his wounds were too severe to treat. Every time doctors forced air into his lungs, blood and brain matter would seep out of the back of his head due to excessive vascular bleeding and brain trauma.[11] His breathing was slow, spasmodic and without any coordination. This is typically known as agonal breathing. His eyes were open; the pupils were dilated and did not react to light. He had no pulse. A few chest sounds, thought to be heart beats, could be heard.[12]

Dr. McClelland noted the back of Kennedy's head and exclaimed, "My God, have you seen the back of his head? ...It's gone!" and just as he said that the right half of the President's cerebellum fell out of his skull and onto the stretcher he was laying on.[13] He knew no one could survive this wound. Dr. McClelland described the massive head would as being five inches in diameter in the back of the President's skull.[14]

He was pronounced dead by Parkland Hospital doctors at 12:50pm, but his official death was delayed by ten minutes so that the Roman

Catholic President could receive his last rites. He was 46-years old at the time.

Later that same day, the President's body was illegally shipped out of the state by the Secret Service to Bethesda Naval Medical Center, or Bethesda for short. The official autopsy conducted at Bethesda did not dissect the bullet wounds in Kennedy's body to determine their depth or trajectory. The failure to dissect the bullet wounds was a clear deviation of standard medical practice even in 1963. In fact, the 1978 House Select Committee on Assassinations Forensic Pathology Panel concluded that the autopsy doctors in Bethesda made "extensive failings" and that the pathologists made multiple procedural errors, such as:

- failing to confer with the Parkland doctors prior to the autopsy;
- failing to examine clothing, which could have indicated bullet trajectories;
- failing to determine the exact exit point of the head bullet;
- failing to determine the angles of gunshot injuries relative to body axis;
- failing to take proper and sufficient photographs; and
- failing to properly examine the brain.

The forensic panel concluded that the three pathologists were not qualified to have conducted a quality autopsy. Panel member Dr. Milton Helpern, Chief Medical Examiner for New York City, went so far as to say that selecting Dr. Humes (who had only taken a single course on forensic pathology) to lead the autopsy was "like sending a seven-year-old boy who has taken three lessons on the violin over to the New York Philharmonic and expecting him to perform a Tchaikovsky symphony."[15] To their credit, the two doctors in Bethesda were assisted by ballistics wound expert, Pierre Finck, of the Armed Forces Institute of Pathology.

I also wish to underscore that, while the experience of these doctors may be questionable, I do not believe they were part of the conspiracy. I believe they tried to do the best they could under what can best be described as chaotic circumstances. The autopsy room, a relatively small room, was filled with civilian officers, military officers, intelligence officers, and members of the FBI and Secret Service. The military officers in the room were Admirals and others with much higher ranks than the doctors. When the doctors tried to examine, and possibly dissect the neck wound, they were told that it was where a tracheostomy tube had been inserted and to leave it alone. I am very sympathetic to these three doctors. The President of the United States was killed just a few hours ago. They were conducting an autopsy that would be hyper-analyzed by not just highly experienced forensic pathologists, but the world. And while all the unknown men in the room were intimidating, several of those men were far above the three doctors' ranks. This was a no-win situation. It would be very easy to say that the doctors should have collectively protested, stopped the procedure, asked to speak to the man in charge, and have him order all non-essential personnel out of the autopsy room so that they could, for the sake of the President's family and the American people, and for their own satisfaction as medical experts to conduct a competent autopsy. They certainly would have been overruled and ordered to focus on the back of Kennedy's head. Regardless, this autopsy had a preordained result: conclude that the fatal head shot came from rear and blew the top of the President's head off.

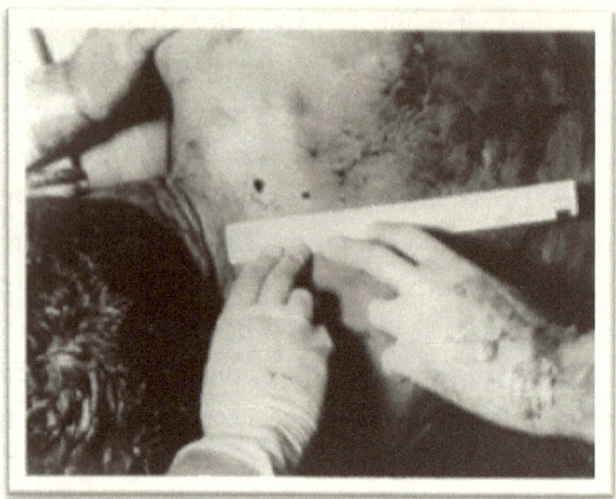

The doctors at Parkland Hospital and Bethesda both concluded that the cause of death was a fatal head shot. With a large degree of certainty, the President had four bullet wounds on his body, with the third and fourth wounds to the head being the most controverted and part of a classified and covert surgery.

Autopsy face sheet noting where Bethesda doctors marked location of

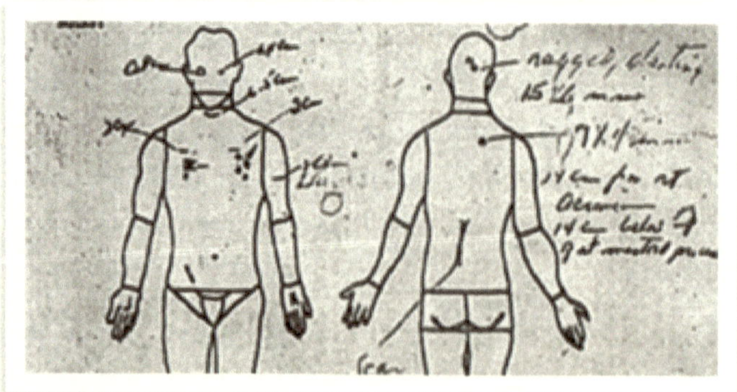

First, an entry wound in his right back that, according to the Bethesda doctors, bruised his right, top lung. The bruising indicates the President was alive at the time he suffered this wound. This

non-fatal wound is over the shoulder blade as seen in the picture, yet, the autopsy doctor, James Humes, identified the back wound as "a wound in the low posterior neck of the President."[16] The coat and shirt worn by the president at the time of the shooting provide corroboration for the location of the back wound being 5 to 6 inches down from the collar, and not at the base of the back of the neck, as stated in the autopsy report.[17] FBI expert Robert Frazier testified that "there was located on the rear of the coat 5-3/8 inches below the top of the collar, a hole, further located as 1-3/4 inches to the right of the midline or the seam down the center.[18]

In this photo, you can see the President's jacket is not meaningfully bunched up except for the upper shoulders, which are slightly bunched left to right, but not up.

Some lone gunman apologists claim that the President's suitcoat and shirt were bunched up, but there is no evidence of this in the Zapruder film or in any other photos taken just before his assassination. (*See, e.g.,* the attached photo taken while the presidential limousine travels through downtown Dallas, above).

As noted above, the doctors in Bethesda were prevented from adequately tracking the trajectories of this bullet, as well as the bullet in the throat.[19] While they probed the holes by inserting their fingers up to the first or second knuckle and with a metal rod, they were not allowed to explore beyond that or create an incision that would reveal the wounds' depth.[20] In other words, they were prevented from doing their jobs in a thorough manner and in compliance with medical norms at the time. Another deviation from standard medical norms in the autopsy is the lack of examination of organs, which the doctors in Bethesda were forbidden to examine.[21]

As a side note, in 1977, President Gerald Ford confessed to altering the location of this back wound by raising its location on a diagram used by the WC in order to make the "magic bullet" theory more viable.[22] Why would Ford do this? According to Bobby Baker, in 1963, the FBI was investigating a lobbyist for tax evasion and installed listening devices in a suite of the Sheraton-Carlton Hotel in Washington DC.[23] Bobby Baker and Gerald Ford had access to this room. The FBI picked up incriminating information about Ford and this information was passed on to Hoover and Johnson, which, Bobby Baker asserts, was used to blackmail Ford.

The second non-fatal wound was an entry would in Kennedy's throat, just below the Adam's apple.[24] The doctors at Parkland Hospital believed this wound to be an entry wound of about 4 to 5mm wide with rounded, inverted edges. It injured his windpipe but otherwise did not cause much damage. On three separate occasions during the press conference, while his memory was still fresh, Dr. Perry of Parkland Hospital described the bullet wound in the throat as an "entrance wound." He further stated that this bullet "appeared to come at him," meaning it came from the front, and not the back. It was later learned that Dr. Perry was phoned at home that night by a local Secret Service agent named Elmer Moore, who explained that the doctor had to have seen an exit wound in the throat and berated him for holding an opinion that would cause the government trouble. Imagine the audacity it took to have a Secret Service agent, untrained in the medical field, to question the judgment of a savvy, experienced doctor from a hospital in a major city known for high incidences of gunshot wounds? Not only was this doctor experienced, but he was one of the first medical professionals to lay eyes on the dying president. The doctors in Bethesda, however, concluded that the throat wound was an exit wound that did not pass through any bony structures.[25]

The third wound was in the back of the President's head known as the rear occipital region of the skull where most people have a slight bump or protuberance. This wound is a source of significant controversy.

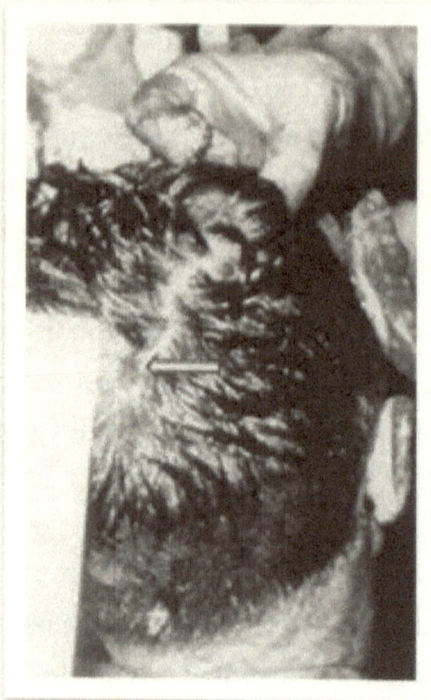

This is the altered, small entry wound
after the President's skull went through
a covert surgery.

The doctors at Parkland Hospital noted that the rear head wound was about 5 inches in diameter, but the doctors in Bethesda noted it was a small entry wound. This is part of the controversy concerning this wound—was it an exit wound or was it an entry wound. According to the WC, it could not have been an exit wound because this would mean the shot came from the front. The doctors in Parkland noted the large wound and that cerebellum, the rear portion of the brain, leaked out of this rear wound.[iii] They knew this shot was fatal and no one could survive it. This wound in the back of the head was determined by the doctors at Parkland to be an exit wound, meaning that the entry point was from the front.[26] When a bullet enters a person's body, the wound is going to be very small, essentially the size of the bullet. As it proceeds through the body, however, it is pushing mass in front of it and the bullet may tumble, thus causing a larger exit wound.[27] In the case of a head shot, it is pushing thicker, more viscous, brain mass in front of it. Thus, when the bullet exits on the other side of the skull, it does so with a "blow-out," or a much larger wound. Thus, the large 5-inch hole in the back of Kennedy's head seen by Parkland doctors also implied that a shot had been fired from the front.[28] The doctors at Parkland were focused on major wounds, and their focus was the back of the President's head, but they knew nothing could be done.

The damage was too great. Between Parkland and Bethesda, however, the five-inch hole cha

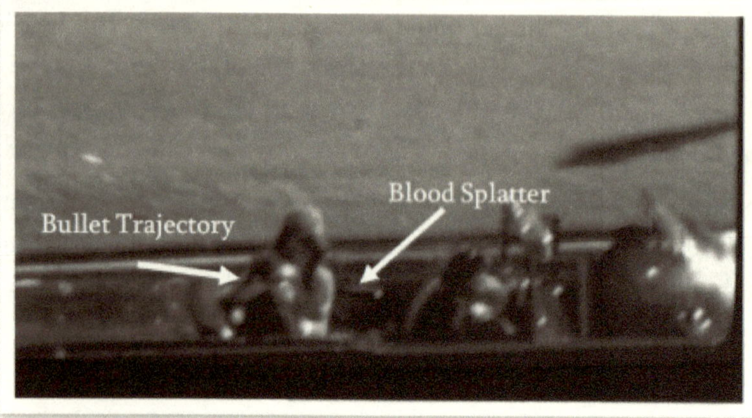

Zapruder Frame # 329, above and 330, below. After the fatal front head shot, evidence of a rear shot can be seen in these frames. The blood splatter is moving forward in front of President Kennedy as a causal reaction to a bullet being fired from behind. Governor Connally described seeing blood and brain matter splatter on the dashboard and interior of the limousine at this

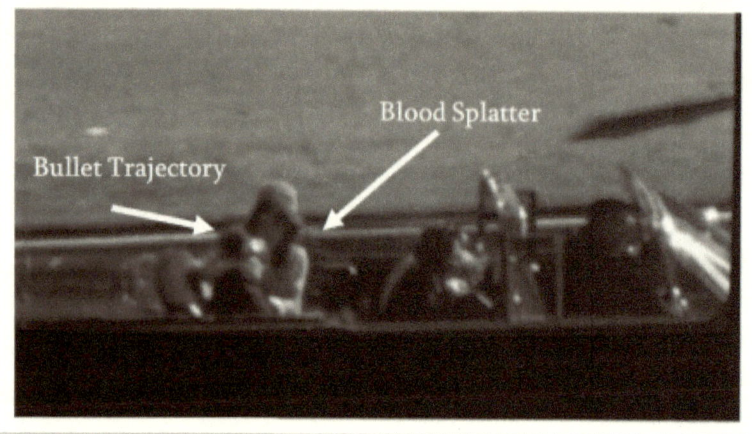

nged to a small entry wound.

A day after the assassination, a medical student found a piece of bone in Dealey Plaza, and it was conclusively determined to be a piece from the occipital bone region.[29] The piece of bone was fairly large, consistent with the large hole Parkland doctors saw at the back of the President's head, and was found on the grass twenty five feet to the left or south of where the fatal head shot was fired, which could only mean that the shot came from the right of the President, where the grassy knoll was. This piece of bone went missing after it was turned over to federal officials.[30] Why? Because, as you will read further, a "surgery" conducted on the President's head at Walter Reed Hospital, sealed or closed the large back head wound so that it can appear as though a bullet entered it, thus suggesting that the projectile came from the rear, when it actually came from the front.

Zapruder Frame # 313. Note the abundance of blood and blood trajectory coming from the right front part of the President's head.

The entry wound on the President's neck was compromised by the insertion of the tracheostomy tube, thus it became hard to determine scientifically whether it was ultimately an entrance wound or an exit wound without dissection. This third wound was near the President's right temple, just in front of and slightly above his right ear, partly damaging his face. The attached image from frame # 313 of the Zapruder film shows the fatal head shot just before JFK's head had violently jerked back and to the left. The core of that explosion is on the right side of his face. The motorcycle officers on the left of the president's limousine were spattered with blood, flesh, and brain matter. The officers riding to the right of the presidential limousine were not splattered at all.

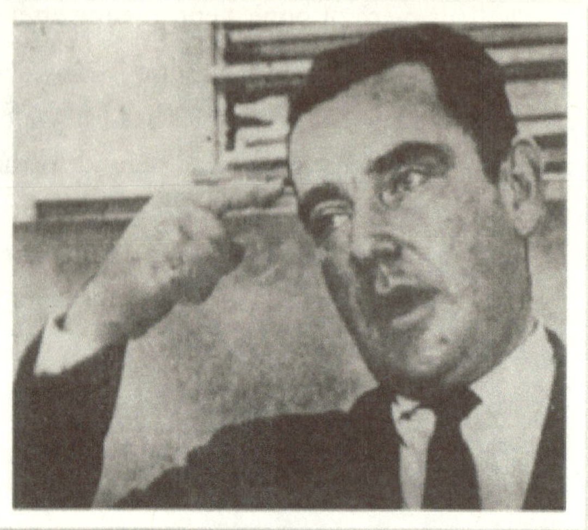

The man in this photo is White House Press Secretary Malcolm "Mac" Kilduff. While in Parkland Hospital, he was asked by reporters where the bullet struck the President and his index finger is clearly pointing to the right temple. In response to reporters questions, Mac states that Connally was hit twice—once in the wrist and once in the thigh. He also states the President was hit once in the head. Mac, at times, had difficult maintaining his composure.

There is more supporting evidence of a head shot to the right front of the President's face. In a 1966 interview, Marilyn Sitzman, Abraham Zapruder's secretary, told researcher Josiah Thompson that when she was standing with Zapruder, the President was almost directly in front of them when she saw the shot *"that hit him on the side of his face. . . between the eye and the ear"* (emphasis added). In a report made on the day of the assassination, Secret Service Agent George Hickey, riding in the left rear seat of the Secret Service follow-up car directly behind the President's car, stated: that after hearing an explosion, he turned to the rear, and then on turning back toward the President's car, he heard two more shots *"and it seemed as if the right side of his head was hit."*[31] Hickey, as so many others did, later amended his initial and fresh-from-memory report to state that the President appeared to be hit from the right-upper rear of his head.[32] Hickey was not called to testify before the WC along with a long list of others that claimed the President was hit from the right front. A partial list of the people not called by the WC to give testimony about a frontal shot are:

- Secret Service Agent Sam Kinney (I saw one shot strike the President on the right side);

- Assistant to the Special Agent in Charge of the Secret Service, Emory Roberts (*...felt that shots came from right*);

- Officer B.J. Martin, motorcycle patrolman riding to the president's left (*noticed blood stains on his helmet and on the windshield of his motorcycle*);

- Douglas Jackson, motorcycle patrolman riding on the outside right rear of the Presidential car (...heard first two shots, Jackson "turned to look at the Presidential car, [and] he heard a third shot and observed President Kennedy struck *above the right ear and the top of his head exploded to the left of the Presidential car*";

- Witness William Eugene Newman (saw the President "jump up" in his seat, and then when the President was directly in front of me, "I was looking directly at him when he was hit in the side of the head. . . . *I thought the shot had come from the garden directly behind me.*")[33]

The list of witnesses that saw the president being shot from the right and towards his front continues, yet they were not called. In fact, Douglas Jackson, above, was not called until 1975. A navy hospital corpsman, Paul O'Connor, and x-ray technician, Jerrol Custer, both confirmed that when they saw the President's body, it was nude except for a sheet wrapped only around the head; that there was a huge hole (4" × 7") in the back and top of the head; and the brain was almost completely gone except for residual tissue.[34] Custer told author David Lifton that "the President's head wound was enormous—I can put both my hands in the wound."

The fourth wound is also controversial. This wound was determined to be the fatal head wound according to the doctors at Bethesda, but they concluded that it was an entry wound coming from the rear of the President. According to the Bethesda doctors, the fatal missile entered the skull above and to the right of the external occipital protuberance.[35] The five-inch hole seen by Parkland doctors was now a smaller hole made to look like an entry wound. This is the quintessential created reality of JFK's assassination. Only upon a very close inspection of the Zapruder film and careful inspection of the frames can it be determined that there was in fact a shot from the rear, but that shot came after the fatal front shot. Zapruder frame numbers 329 and 330, above, clearly show blood splatter moving forward from the front of Kennedy's face. Based on basic principles of physics, the blood splatter reacts to a bullet that enters from the rear of the President's head. This bullet comes only about 16 frames after the fatal frontal head shot, or about .9 seconds later. The idea of having a cluster of shots being fired at about the same time was to make is appear and sound as if there were only three shots being fired at the President, but in reality, there were at least nine shots fired at or upon the President, with some shots completely missing their target.

Compare Frame 313 (above) to this frame (321) and notice how far back the President's head moved backward in merely 8 frames or slightly less than .49 seconds.

Zapruder Frame # 313. Note the abundance of blood and blood trajectory coming from the right front part of the President's head.

So how did the four or five-inch hole in the back of the President's head where viscous cerebellum fluid leaked out of turn into a small diameter bullet would? David Lifton, author of *Best Evidence*, interviewed James Curtis Jenkins, a laboratory technician at the autopsy table "touching elbows" with Dr. Finck, who said he saw a "huge hole" in Kennedy's head, "'at least one-third of the skull was gone when Kennedy was brought in ... a hole which extended toward the rear, and with fragments that seemed to be hanging on, and which seemed to have been exploded toward the rear, Jenkins formed the opinion that President Kennedy had been shot in the head from the front ... But then, the next day, said Jenkins, 'I found out that supposedly he was shot from the back. I just, you know, I just couldn't believe it, and have never been able to believe it.'"[36]

More importantly, in David Lifton's book, he found evidence of a prior head surgery that had been conducted after the President left Parkland and before his body arrived in Bethesda in an FBI report dated November 26, 1963.[37] Lifton calls this the Pre-Autopsy Autopsy. Additionally, Lifton was able to track down Dennis D. David, a retired Naval Lieutenant Commander from the Medical Corps, who was there that day during the Bethesda autopsy.[38] David was "Chief of the Day" in the Bethesda Medical Center when the assassination occurred.

He stated that he doubted "that all the necessary information was forwarded to the commission or made available to experts."[39] David said that Kennedy's body was brought in through a back door in an unmarked black Cadillac hearse where there was a landing stage or jetty, but there was an ambulance with an empty, bronze casket that entered through the front door facing Wisconsin Avenue, which arrived about fifteen minutes *after* the unmarked black Cadillac hearse that had entered through the rear jetty.[40] The casket in the black Cadillac hearse was grey, simple, and made of metal.[41] The second ambulance had the ornate casket that was acquired when Kennedy was still in Dallas.[42]

David wrote a contemporaneous memo on orders from a Secret Service Agent, which stated "...that four large pieces of lead were removed from Kennedy. They were not separate bullets but had jagged edges like shrapnel. *There was more material than would come from one bullet, but maybe not enough for two...*"[43] In summary, the surgery that was conducted was to remove any evidence of a bullet entering the front and probably involved patching the president's right front facial structures and the large exit wound in the back of the President's head. When the Zapruder frames from 313 to 330 are examined closely, coupled with David's contemporaneous report of removed bullet fragments that totaled more than one bullet, then one has to concluded that two bullets entered the President's skull—one from the front, at around Zapruder frame number 313, and one from the rear, at around Zapruder frame 329. This explains why there was such a large variation of the size of the hole in Kennedy's head between the Parkland doctors and the Bethesda doctors as well as the change in caskets and the placement of the president's body in a body-bag.

The attached color photo shows the bronze casket in a yellow Army airport cargo lift truck and the marked ambulance, which is a Pontiac Bonneville station wagon retrofitted as an ambulance, waiting for the casket to be loaded onto it. Although the vehicle looks blue in the photo, it is more of a grey blue.[44] (*See* photo below from Barret-Jackson Auctions website). The black Cadillac hearse had a driver and an attendant in white smocks, according to David.[45] In the back of the black hearse were six to eight men in civilian suits that David assumed to be secret service agents.[46] They carried the simple metal casket and, based on how the men handled the casket, it appeared heavy.[47]

Although the House Select Committee on Assassinations dismissed allegations of a prior surgery as a mistake, it made the terrible mistake of noting that Kennedy's body was delivered to Bethesda in a body bag,[48] yet there was clear evidence that Kennedy's body left Dallas wrapped only in a bedsheet. How could this be?

I assert, like others, that Kennedy's body was removed from the bronze casket *before* it was loaded onto Air Force One, or shortly after it was loaded onto Air Force One and placed in Air force Two (the Vice-President's airplane, identical to Air Force One). There is support for this assertion. The bronze casket was delivered empty, in which case, it would have still weighed around 300 pounds.

This is the famous swearing-in ceremony aboard Air Force One. Jackie Kennedy refused to change her blood-splattered dress because she wanted the world "to see what they did to my husband."

The President's body was placed in the bronze, ornate casket at Parkland Hospital with only a bed sheet around the President's head. The First Lady, Jaqueline Kennedy, stayed close to the bronze casket from the time it was loaded onto Air Force One until it arrived at Bethesda, even riding in the same Pontiac Bonneville ambulance on which the casket was loaded. The only time she was away from the casket was when Johnson asked her to join him in a swearing-in ceremony to assume the oath of office. Some researchers and critics further speculate that Kennedy's body was probably removed while all passengers in Air Force One went to the front of the plane to watch Johnson's swearing-in ceremony. Philip Nelson, author of *"LBJ: The Mastermind of the JFK Assassination,"* states that Kennedy's body was taken from the ornate bronze coffin and put into a light shipping casket then moved to the "backup" aircraft formerly designated by LBJ as "Air Force Two," during a fourteen-minute period when the casket was unattended, as Mrs. Kennedy was forced to attend Lyndon's swearing-in ceremony. At this point, both airplanes were parked next to each other, and the passengers had already been seated and were waiting to take off.[49]

Above is a 1963 Cadillac Hearse. Below is the actual 1963 Pontiac Bonneville Ambulance, or an exact replica, which carried JFK's body along with Jacqueline and Bobby Kennedy.

This was certainly possible. Kennedy's body would have been sent ahead arriving in time to conduct the covert surgery and still arrive at Bethesda fifteen minutes before Jaqueline Kennedy, Bobby Kennedy, and the bronze casket. In fact, while Air Force One took off before Air Force Two, Air Force Two, carrying Kennedy's body, passed Air Force One in the air, arriving well-before Air Force One. The "leapfrogging" had been a common practice so that the vice president would arrive first in order to greet the president, and while there was no Vice President, the practice would be used to ensure

Kennedy's body made it to Walter Reed Hospital. Air Force Two passing Air Force One was confirmed by the FBI agents who interviewed the head of the Secret Service White House Detail, Gerald Behn, who stated that "Air Force Two passed Air Force One in flight." The official Secret Service reports indicate that Air Force Two arrived at Andrews after Air Force One; however, the two contradictory statements cannot be reconciled. Given that Behn's statement indicated that Air Force Two passed Air Force One in flight, it implicitly means that Air Force Two landed first. Moreover, this switching of Kennedy's body and having it arrive ahead of Air Force One was part of Johnson's responsibilities in this phase of the conspiracy, so the Secret Service reports indicating that Air Force One arrived first was an intentional fabrication.

Once Air Force Two landed at Andrews Air Force Base, JFK's body was immediately removed and taken by helicopter to Walter Reed Army Hospital, which could have been reached within five to eight minutes, allowing for at least forty-five minutes for pre-autopsy "surgery"—as inadvertently verified in the FBI report discovered by Lifton—before being sent on to Bethesda in a black Cadillac hearse and delivered to the rear door at 6:35pm, consistent with the testimony of three witnesses.[50]

After the U.S. military completed its autopsy on Kennedy's body, everyone who participated in the autopsy was sworn to secrecy.[51] The participants were told that everything they had witnessed was "classified." Participants were presented with "letters of secrecy," which they were required to sign. Military officials threatened them with court martial or criminal prosecution if they ever told anyone what they had seen. As one participant put it, they put "the fear of God" in them.

Why would the autopsy of a public figure be classified? It would be understandable to prevent certain details of the autopsy being released, such as gruesome pictures of Kennedy's body, or evidence of his pre-existing medical issues in order to prevent damaging his reputation, but the cause and manner of death of persons are generally public information that is releasable upon request. The fact that the subject of the autopsy was the President of the United States, a public figure, begs the need to make as many aspects as possible of the autopsy public. Instead, it was immediately classified and those involved were told to not discuss the issue under penalty of court martial or criminal prosecution. Even today, viewing autopsy photos requires permission from a Kennedy representative and must come from a forensics doctor only. Why? Because upon the death of President Kennedy, LBJ was issuing all orders because he, after all, was the first person to order Kennedy's assassination, as explained in greater detail in Chapter 14.

<u>Victim #2: John Connally</u>:

Governor Connally is the second victim in this murder-conspiracy. There is controversy as to when he was struck by a bullet and even whether he was struck by one or two bullets.

Prior to being Governor, Connally worked as a campaign aide to Johnson. Connally supported Johnson in his 1960 presidential bid and stated that because of Kennedy's Addison's disease and dependence on cortisone, he was unfit to be president. After Johnson became Vice-President, he requested that Connally be given the position of Secretary of the Navy, which was granted. Eleven months later, Connally left the Navy position to run for Governor of Texas, which he won. On this particular day in November 1963, Connally was 46-years old and otherwise healthy. Later in his political career, Connally became Treasury Secretary under Nixon's administration. He stepped down from that position to become head of "Democrats for Nixon," a Republican-funded campaign to promote Democratic support for Nixon in the 1972 presidential election. Connally also made a failed Presidential bid in 1980.

Connally sat in front of President Kennedy in the second-row jump seats of the limousine with his wife, Nellie, sitting directly to his left. He underwent nearly four hours of surgery to repair wounds to his chest, wrist, and thigh.[52] The high-velocity bullet that hit the governor was a full-metal jacketed missile designed not to fragment or expand. It entered his back under the right armpit. Then it went through his body, tore through four inches of rib, ruptured his lung, and exited his chest, about two inches below and to the left of his right nipple. The bullet continued through the back side of his right wrist and finally landed in his left thigh. No bullet fragments were recovered from his chest. Connally's thoracic injuries consisted of a comminuted, or multiple, fracture of the fifth rib, lacerations of the middle lobe, and hematoma of the lower lobe of the right lung. Dr. Shaw told the WC that the patient had a "sucking wound of the chest" that would not have allowed him to breathe or talk in a normal manner. This calls into question exactly how and when Connally was able to shout out, "Oh my God, they're going to kill us all," as Connally and his wife, Nellie,

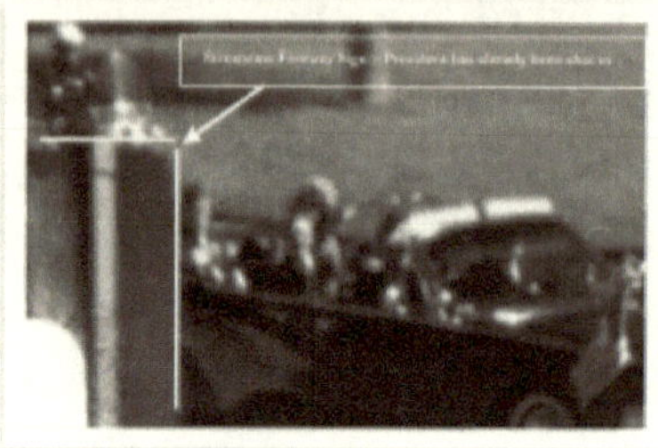

On the left is Zapruder frame #225. It shows that Kennedy has already been hit in the throat, but Connally has not. On the right is Zapruder frame #238. It shows Connally is hit as his shoulder drops suddenly and he grabs at it (see arrow).

stated.[53]

According to the WC, Connally was struck by the second bullet that was fired from the Texas School Book Depository. This is the same bullet that allegedly made the magical trajectory from Kennedy's body, yet a close examination of the Zapruder film, Nellie and Governor Connally's own testimony, and FBI Hoover's own assessment are contrary to this position.

Compare Zapruder frame 225, which shows that the President was already hit and is desperately clutching at his throat. Connally is seen looking slightly to the right but does not show any reaction. Thirteen frames later, Connally is hit, dropping his shoulder suddenly. Thirteen frames is the equivalent of .49 seconds or almost half-second but remember that Kennedy was hit *before* the limousine passed the freeway sign. Some say Kennedy was hit as early as frame 210, which would make a difference of 1.53 seconds between the time of Kennedy's reaction to his throat shot and Connally's reaction to a chest shot. Below is Nellie Connally's summary of events:

> I heard a noise that I didn't think of as a gunshot. I just heard a disturbing noise and turned to my right from where I thought the noise had come and looked in the back and saw the President clutch his neck with both hands. He said nothing. He just sort of slumped down in the seat. John had turned to his right also when we heard that first noise and shouted, "No, no, no," and in the process of turning back around so that he could look back and see the president. I don't think he could see him when he turned to his right – *the second shot was fired and hit him. He was in the process of turning, so it hit him through his shoulder*, and came out right about here. His hand was either right in front of him or on his knee as he turned to look, so that the bullet went through him, crushed his wrist, and lodged in his leg. And then he just recoiled and just sort of slumped in the seat. I thought he was dead.[54]

Below is a portion of a transcript taken during an interview of Governor Connally by C-Span in 1991:

> I heard this sound ... that I thought was a rifle shot. I turned to look over my right shoulder because that's where the sound came from ... to see if I could see anything. I didn't. *And I was in the process of turning to look over my left shoulder when I felt an impact as if someone hit me with a closed fist right in the middle of my back.* The force was strong enough to where it knocked me over. And I saw that I was covered with blood, so... frankly I thought I had been fatally hit. My wife pulled me down in her lap ...she was seated in the jump seat on my left and I was seated in the jump seat directly in front of the President. She pulled me down in her lap and about that time I heard another shot, a smack, and my eyes were open, and I was conscious, and I saw the blue velour interior of this presidential limousine covered with blood and brain tissue ....[55]

Finally, in a taped telephone conversation with Johnson on November 29, 1963, FBI Director Hoover told Johnson that there were three shots: The first shot hit Kennedy, the second shot hit

Connally, and the third shot hit Kennedy. What follows is a verbatim transcription of their conversation:

Johnson: How many...how many shots were fired?

Hoover: Three.

Johnson: Any of them fired at me?

Hoover: No. All three at the President...and we have them. Two of the shots fired at the President were splintered...but they had characteristics on them so that our ballistics experts were able to prove that they were fired by this gun...*the third shot which hit the President...he was hit by the first and the third...second shot hit the Governor*. The third shot is a complete bullet...and that ruled [sic] out of the President's head...it tore a large part of the President's head off...and, in trying to massage his heart at the hospital...on the way to the hospital...they apparently loosened that and it fell on to the stretcher. And we recovered that. And we have that. And we have the gun here also.[56]

Hoover is telling Johnson that the almost pristine bullet that tore off the President's head, the third bullet, fell out of somewhere when the President's heart was being massaged. If this were not such a tragic event, it would be comical. In summary, it was well known that a separate bullet injured Connally by the time the WC issued its report in 1964; thus, disproving the magic bullet theory.

Connally's surgery took four hours. While he was in the operating room, LBJ-aid, Cliff Carter, obtained Connally's suit and clothing and had them dry-cleaned. As you can note, the cover-up began immediately.

The bullet fragments that were removed from Connally's wrist belie the almost pristine magic bullet theory. Dr. Gregory removed the most significant bullet fragments from the governor's wrist and gave them to a scrub nurse who handed them to Nurse Audrey Bell.[57]

She described the "four or five" fragments as grayish in color and "anywhere from three to four millimeters in length and a couple of millimeters wide." The smallest fragment was about the size of the striking portion of a match, she indicated. The largest piece was twice that size. She then labeled, sealed, and initialed a manila envelope and turned it over to a federal agent named Mr. Sorrels (Forest Sorrels was the Secret Service Special Agent in Charge of the Dallas Office and the one that obtained copies of the Zapruder film). Once these bullet fragments were in the hands of federal agents, they ironically disappeared. Remember, the bullet fragments in Connally's lung cavity were never recovered, so more bullet fragments were unaccounted for, underscoring how ridiculous and baseless the magic bullet theory is. More evidence of a conspiracy and created reality. The total fragments removed from Connally's wrist were far greater in size and weight than the slight dent of the "almost" pristine magic bullet. Bullets going through empty plastic bottles have more destruction to them than the almost pristine magic bullet. The magic bullet was undoubtedly fired from the Mannlicher-Carcano before the assassination, but it was fired into a water tank to capture the lands and grooves from the barrel. It would then be planted inadvertently on the wrong stretcher in Parkland Hospital. Once the Mannlicher-Carcano was tied to Oswald, the case had been solved.

Additionally, legitimate steps were taken to disprove the magic bullet theory when they surfaced, but these endeavors were futile in order to keep secret this highly orchestrated murder-conspiracy. In early June 1993, for example, the JFK community began hearing that ex-governor John Connally was having serious medical issues from pulmonary fibrosis and was not expected to live much longer.[58] Famous WC critic, Cyril Wecht, and several other well-known forensics pathologists drafted a letter to then U.S. Attorney General

Janet Reno to explain that the governor had metallic fragments or shavings in his body that might have evidentiary value in the assassination investigation. The letter stated: "Subjected to neutron activation analysis and other scientific procedures, these fragments may be able to resolve the controversy as to whether President Kennedy was assassinated as the result of a conspiracy." The doctors collectively recommended that the Justice Department issue an order to allow a qualified forensic pathologist to remove any metallic pieces that could then be sent to a metallurgy lab to see if there was a match to the magic bullet that was supposedly found on the Parkland stretcher. The Attorney General reacted with lightning speed and said she would send an FBI agent to speak with Nellie Connally because it would be necessary to obtain her permission before any further action could be taken. Mrs. Connally, however, turned down the request, and her husband was buried with his metal fragments intact.[59] Governor Connally died on June 15, 1993, from pulmonary fibrosis, which ironically, may have been caused by growing and thickening scar tissue from the remaining bullet fragments in his lung.[60] He was 76 years old.

One contextual issue that is important to note. Kennedy's trip to Texas was for political reasons in every sense of the word. Kennedy believed he needed to win Texas in 1964 if he were to be re-elected President. But there was also another purpose of the trip. Kennedy had to show solidarity among Texas Democrats. Part of the trip was to try and smooth things over between the feud and infighting between Texas Senator Yarborough, a liberal, and Vice-President Johnson and Governor Connally. Although Connally and Johnson were democrats, they were also closely associated with conservative businessmen from the oil, construction, military industrial complex, and whatever entity financially supported them. These Texas conservative democrats wanted to keep the old-boys network intact.[61] Connally and Yarborough barely spoke to each other. Johnson hated Senator Ralph Yarborough and did everything he could to undermine him and render him powerless. Somehow Johnson convinced Kennedy to allow him to make all recommendations for political appointments in Texas, which is a privilege often reserved to Senators.[62] Additionally, Johnson even blocked Yarborough from being permitted to be a delegate to the 1960 Convention.[63]

For several days prior to the trip to Dallas, including the night before and the morning of the assassination, Vice-President Johnson urged Kennedy to sit in the presidential limousine with Senator Yarborough. On the previous evening in Fort Worth, Johnson and Kennedy had an argument about this very issue.[64] Johnson wanted Governor Connally, his friend and ally in his home state, to ride with him in the Vice President's car.[65] Kennedy forbade it; the Governor's place was with the President. They argued loudly enough to be heard outside.[66] On the morning of the assassination, Kennedy reads in the newspaper that the focus of the Texas trip is to repair the political feuding among the Texas politicians accompanying him on this trip (Connally and Yarborough).[67] The headline in the Dallas Morning News also reads: "Nixon Predicts Kennedy May Drop Johnson,"[68] which Johnson certainly read or had read to him.

On the morning of the assassination, there is yet another argument between Kennedy and Johnson, again, about the seating arrangements. Earlier that morning, Johnson, on his own initiative and as a surprising act of generosity, offers Yarborough a seat in the presidential limousine, a gesture over which he lacks authority.[69] Johnson then walks into Kennedy's suite and suddenly demands that the motorcade seating arrangements be changed; this led quickly to back and forth shouting between the two men that was overheard by the hotel staff outside in the hallway.[70] Johnson wanted Governor Connally to ride with him and wanted Senator Yarborough, his longtime political enemy, to ride with JFK in the presidential limousine, which he continued pointing out, was an unusually generous gesture on his part to his long-time enemy. The hotel servants were in and out of the suite and heard Yarborough's name mentioned several times; their impressions were consistent—that Kennedy felt the senator was not being treated fairly by Johnson and Connally and their staffs and that he expressed himself emphatically. Kennedy refused to change those arrangements and ordered Johnson to "make up" with Yarborough for the good of the party and the 1964 elections. The hotel staff and caterers also said that Johnson had tried to control his famous temper in JFK's presence, but that when he exited, "he left that suite like a pistol," said Max Peck, who watched him lurch down the corridor, "long legs pumping and looking furious." Jackie asked JFK what the argument was about, and he said, "That's just Lyndon. He's having a bad day." Kennedy had also told his wife that Johnson is "incapable of telling the truth."

After Johnson left, Kennedy rang for his aide, Kenny O'Donnell, and tells him that the bickering must end right now. O'Donnell explains how the liberal Texas Senator Ralph Yarborough refused to ride in LBJ's car the day before. Kennedy speaks very evenly. Today, the president says, will be different. "You tell him it's ride with Lyndon—or walk."[71] On the morning of November 22, Kennedy angrily ordered aide Lawrence O'Brien: "I don't care if you have to throw Yarborough into the car with Lyndon. But get him in there."[72]

Yarborough begrudgingly rode with Johnson that fateful day. Yarborough later claimed that Johnson threw himself to the floor of the limousine well *before* the shots were fired and was listening to a walkie-talkie. Yarborough also claimed that he smelled gun smoke as he passed the grassy knoll. A wide-angle photo from Associated Press photojournalist, Ike Altgens, clearly shows Texas Senator Yarborough and Lady Bird Johnson in the back seat of the vice-presidential limousine, but the tall and lanky LBJ is clearly not visible at all because he is hiding on the floor.

Madeleine Duncan Brown, Johnson's long-time lover and mother of Johnson's son, is famously remembered for revealing Johnson's assassination-eve confession: "After tomorrow, those goddamn Kennedys will never embarrass me again. That's no threat. That's a promise." That confession is often eclipsed by her conversation with Johnson on the morning of the assassination. She claims that "I had barely eked out the words, 'About last night...' when his rage virtually went ballistic. His snarling voice jolted me as never before – "That son-of-a-b——crazy *Yarborough* and that g- - - - - - f - - - ing Irish Mafia bastard Kennedy will never embarrass me again!"[73]

Why all the fuss about seating arrangements? Lyndon could certainly be childish and petty, but he nagged Kennedy endlessly about seating arrangements. I assert that Lyndon not only ordered Kennedy's murder, but Yarborough's as well. Yarborough, in fact, was the target of the bullet that ultimately wounded Connally. I believe LBJ did not have enough time to communicate to the assassination teams about Yarborough not being where he was supposed to be. Although the bullet or bullets that hit Connally were not fatal, they were serious and could have been fatal by a few more inches to the left. It appears that most body shots fired on Kennedy and Connally were off the mark by a few inches, for example, Kennedy's throat shot should have been a shot to his heart or his head; the shot in Kennedy's and Connally's back should have been to their hearts—both shots should have been over to the left and into their respective hearts through their backs.

Yes, this was a two-person murder conspiracy, but the word to the assassins on the ground did not reach them in time. The very manipulating Johnson tried until the very last minute to convince Kennedy to have Yarborough sit with him, and then, once the motorcade started, Johnson could not pass on word about canceling Yarborough's death warrant with Yarborough sitting right there with Johnson in his vehicle. Johnson could not communicate in any clear manner to the command center with Yarborough sitting right next to him. Johnson holding a walkie-talkie when he was surrounded by secret service and Dallas police officers is also very telling.

<u>The Presidential Limousine</u>:

The president's limousine was a midnight-blue custom-built 1961 Lincoln Continental convertible.[74] The car weighed nearly four tons and is over twenty feet long. It averaged less than five miles per gallon. The Lincoln was leased from Ford for only $500 per year but was modified by elite custom coachbuilder Hess and Eisenhardt in Cincinnati, Ohio at an astronomical cost of $200,000 (or two million dollars in today's dollars, and it was still not armored).

While the limousine was parked outside of Parkland hospital, secret service agents placed the hard top on and washed away the blood stains with buckets of water they requested from hospital staff. The hospital staff also noticed the cracked windshield.

The limousine was flown to Washington DC on the evening of the assassination.[75] Two bullet fragments were apparently discovered.[76] One bullet fragment appears to be a nose piece; and the other appears to be a base piece. The two fragments could have come from one bullet or two. It is unknown where the bullet fragments were found other than the front seats. It is unknown who found these bullet fragments. It is unknown when the bullet fragments were found. The best we can ascertain about the origins of these bullet fragments is from testimony from Special Agent Robert Frazier. He testified before the WC that he determined definitely, by analysis of microscopic markings on the fragments and on the rifle barrel, that both fragments were fired in the [Mannlicher-Carcano] rifle. Establishing a chain of possession proved to be difficult as noted below by Arlen Specter's questioning of Frazier:

> *Specter*: Now, where, according to information provided to you then, was the fragment found?

> *Frazier*: That was found by the Secret Service upon their examination of the limousine here in Washington when it first arrived from Dallas, and the fragments [were] delivered by Deputy Chief Paul Paterni and by a White House detail chief, Floyd M. Boring, to a liaison agent of the FBI, Orrin Bartlett, who delivered them to me in the laboratory at 11:50 p.m. on November 22, 1963."

> *Specter: Does that constitute the total chain of possession then from the finder with the Secret Service into your hands, as reflected on the records of the FBI?*

> *Frazier: Yes, sir.*[77]

Frazier cannot state with any certainty who initially found the bullet fragments; instead, he says the Secret Service found them. Frazier states that the Secret Service found the fragments after the limousine arrived in Washington DC but cannot explain the gap between the time the limousine was in the emergency room parking lot of Parkland Hospital and its arrival in Washington DC, thus he cannot establish a chain of possession. There is no way to tell who may have had access to the car during the hours between the assassination and their discovery as the limousine made its way back to Washington. Also, there is no way of determining how many people handled the bullet fragments before they reached Deputy Chief Paul Paterni. As of today, it is unknown who found these fragments, when they were found, and how they were maintained, and whose hands they passed through, before Paul Paterni received them.[78]

The FBI, realizing that they could not establish a chain of possession, issued a letter dated July 7, 1964, stating who found the bullets and where.[79] Unfortunately, this is not a contemporaneous report and merely tries to establish a chain of possession *after the fact*, thus it has diminished credibility and evidentiary weight. Additionally, whoever initially found the bullet fragments never properly marked them, so we can never be sure about their origins.

Why is this important? Well forget about the legal requirements of establishing a chain of possession in a court of law–that certainly did not happen here. Instead, so many aspects of this murder-conspiracy seem so irregular and controverted. Take, for example, the magic bullet—it was "placed" and later discovered on the wrong stretcher and the WC, despite hearing testimony to the contrary, concluded on its own that the bullet was found on Connolly's stretcher. Another example is Oswald's revolver. It was never tested by either the Dallas Police Department or the FBI, yet the Commission concluded that it was the revolver used to kill Tippit. These conclusions by the WC are not only absurd, but they also lack a factual basis.

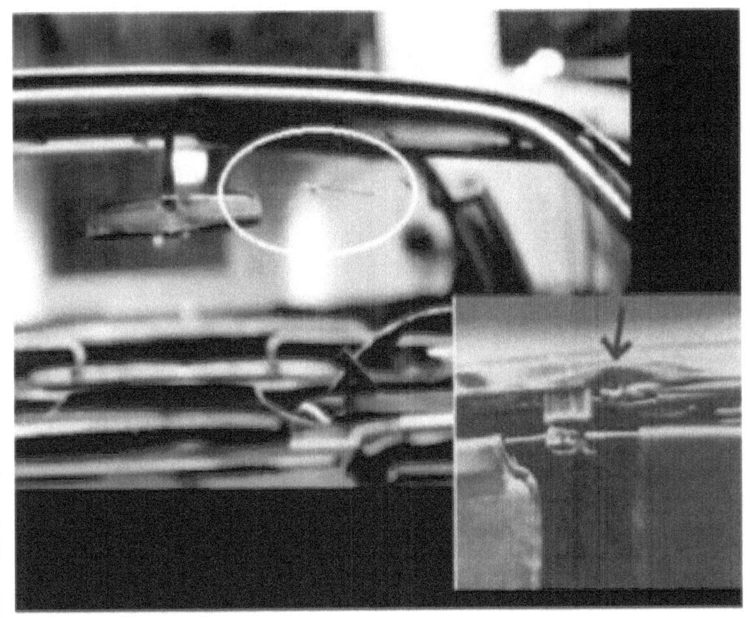

The limousine had a hole in the windshield and a dent in the chrome above the windshield between the visors. This ballistic evidence was destroyed when the limousine was refurbished.

Aside from not being able to determine the chain of possession of the two bullet fragments, the limousine itself was a piece of evidence that could have provided additional information, such as bullet trajectory.

Ultimately, the limousine was quickly refurbished by the original coach builder in Ohio under the operation name "Quick Fix." The fix destroyed ballistic evidence in the form of two bullets holes, as shown in the picture. The name "quick fix" is ambiguous, and implies a cover-up, but the reality is that this was the only limousine available because the acquisition of another limousine would have taken years.

Evidence Casts Doubt and Shows a Cover-Up Locally and Nationally:

As you know, Oswald was killed and therefore silenced two days after allegedly assassinating the President. In that regard, there was no criminal trial; therefore, the rules of evidence, namely, establishing a foundation and a chain of possession were not established. Weapons, bullets, and other key evidence must have an origin that is tied back to criminal defendants; otherwise, the evidence is excluded. As noted above, I gave up trying to show who would be guilty in a court of law in this murder-conspiracy. I merely underscore how poor the evidence was, and even how evidence had been altered, tampered with, and compromised. I submit that Oswald was framed by our government, by a few corrupt members of the Dallas police department, by the Secret Service, by Hoover's FBI, and by our intelligence agencies. It is a serious indictment, I know, but the evidence of a cover-up is equally massive and formidable. I further submit that if Oswald had lived, the government would not be able to prove its case of murder for Kennedy and Tippit and attempted murder for Walker and Connally, at least not in a fair trial.

This inventory sheet describes only two (2) 6.5 bullet hulls and one (1) live round.

To be sure, there was no chain of evidence for the Mannlicher-Carcano Oswald allegedly used. In fact, no one at the Post Office remembers Oswald picking up a parcel as large as a gun or any other parcel for that matter. A person with an ID in the name of A. Hidell, Oswald's alias, could not pick up a parcel there because that name would have had to be on the registration form, and it was not.[80] Additionally, Marina Oswald was shown a photo of the rifle Oswald allegedly used yet she emphasized she could not distinguish a rifle from a shotgun.[81]

There was no chain of evidence for the magic bullet that was found on a stretcher. In fact, what really makes the magic bullet magical is that it was found on a stretcher that was not used by Kennedy or

Connally. The WC made it jump to Connally's stretcher so it can be claimed to have made its magical trajectory of piercing seven bones, tissue, and cartilage and lose less than 2% of its weight. According to Darrell C. Tomlinson, who was the senior engineer at Parkland Hospital, he testified that he had found the bullet.[82] He said he saw a man whom he could not identify in contact with a stretcher and that when that person pushed the stretcher, a bullet rolled out. He said that it did not come from the stretcher that had been used for Connally.[83] The only witness who testified about the stretcher was Tomlinson. The Commission concluded that "the bullet came from the governor's stretcher," relying on the only witness to the event who said that it had not. This is one of many examples where the WC—in its mission to derive at one conclusion—dismissed, discredited, rejected, coerced, and even failed to call people that had a contrary opinion of the Commission's preconceived theory—that Lee Harvey Oswald was the lone-nut gunman.

On the left is the initial evidence sheet. On the right is the altered sheet that was part of the Warren Commission's Exhibit CE2003. Shaw, Gary J and Harris, Larry Ray, *Cover-Up*. (Thomas Investigative Publications, 2013), 160.

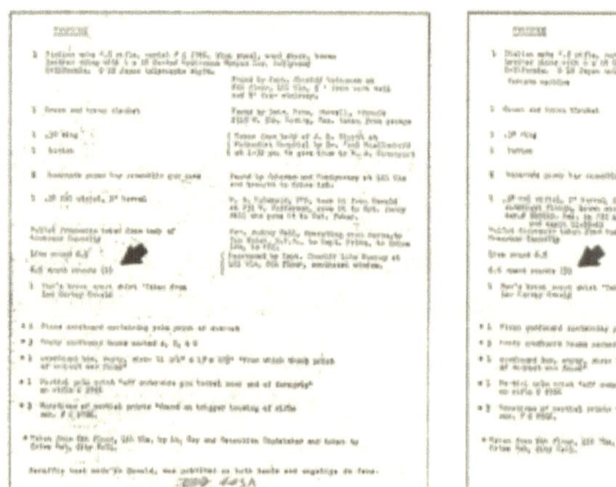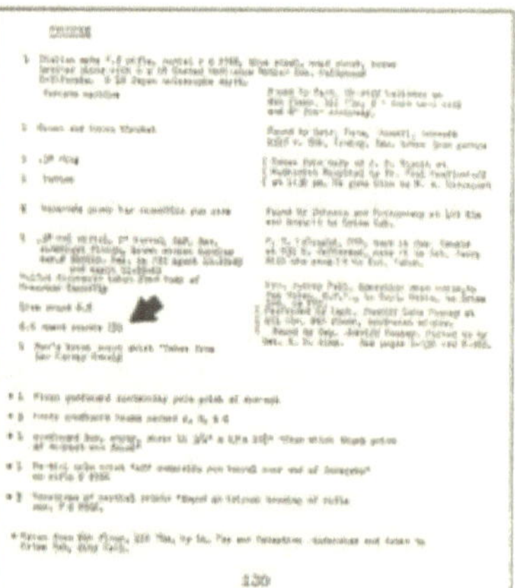

Further, there was even doubt as to the number of empty shell casings found in the sniper's nest.[84] The discrepancy between two shell casings and three was initially discovered by Anna Marie in the National Archives. There, she found in an evidence envelope signed by FBI Special Agent J. Doyle Williams of the Dallas Field Office. The envelope is dated November 22, 1963, and the description states: 2 negatives and 4 prints of each of *two 6.5 bullet hulls & 1 live round of 6.5 ammunition* from rifle found on 6th floor of Texas School Book Depository, Dallas, on 11-22-63. The photographs in the envelope consisted of eight prints, all showing two empty cartridges and one round of live ammunition.[85] This evidence envelope was never shown to the WC. This clearly shows that there were indicia of only two shots being fired, unless they were planted or placed there, in which case, no shots were fired, at least not from the Mannlicher rifle. It gets even better. What was shown to the WC appears to be two alterations made after Williams mailed the evidence to FBI Headquarters in Washington DC. The first is an FBI Evidence Sheet with the original showing *two* 6.5mm spent shells, but the altered evidence sheet shows three spent shells with the number # 3 being handwritten. *See above.* The second alteration is a crime scene photo taken of the sniper's nest. The original photo shows two spent shells (B & C) and a live round (A), consistent with the original evidence sheet. But the altered photo clearly shows a poor forgery of (A) to make it look like a third spent shell. *See below.* The two spent shells and the live round are also pictured neatly on top of a desk. The WC needed three spent shells to explain its ludicrous magic bullet theory and eliminate the appearance of a conspiracy.

The photo on the left came with a set that was taken from the crime scene. The middle photo shows what is seen in the first photo: two bullet casings and one unspent cartridge. The third photo shows three spent casings and one unfired round. The third photo is an obvious alteration showing three spent casings. That photo was submitted as an exhibit in the Warren Commission. It became part of the "story" that Oswald fired three shots.

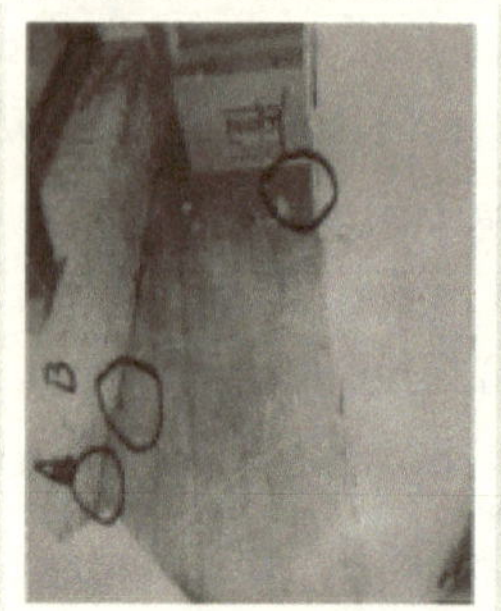

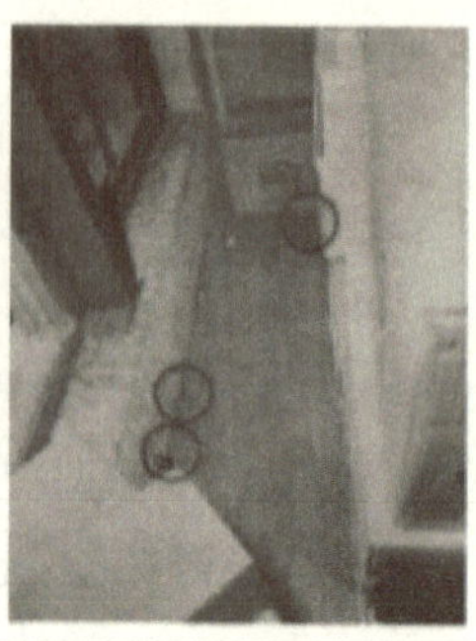

Lastly, there is even evidence that all shell casings were either planted or were recreated. Dallas Morning News photographer, Tom Alyea, states in no uncertain terms, all still photographs of the shell casings and their positions on the sixth floor are re-creations.[86] Alyea, the first newsman on the sixth floor after the assassination, states he took newsreel footage of the shell casings in their original positions and that Captain Will Fritz, then, picked them up to show Alyea.[87] Alyea also states the casings shown in the still photographs are not only in different positions but are not the casings first recovered.[88]

Ruth Paine and Marina Oswald (as well as Wesley Buell Frazier) are one of the few people that have survived this ordeal, at a significant cost to them, I am sure. One of the most difficult aspects in researching this story was determining the credibility of Ruth Paine and Marina Oswald. I will discuss them in more detail below.

<u>Manipulated Witnesses</u>:

As to Marina Oswald, many alleged that she was a KGB agent, or a honey trap (a prostitute) and these assertions are largely based on her uncle's membership with the communist party. Marina's uncle was a lieutenant colonel in the Ministry of Internal Affairs (MVD), which had responsibility for internal security in Russia.[89] The MVD was also responsible for paying Oswald a monthly stipend while he was in Minsk. I do not believe Marina was an agent of the KGB or a honey trap. I believe that the KGB had no interest in either Oswald or Marina, and they were issued exit visas in an incredibly short period of time, despite Oswald's feigned allegations that Marina was being harassed by Russian officials ostensibly because of her association with Oswald. I do believe that Oswald's primary mission in going to Russia was to marry a Russian woman and bring her to the United States. This may explain why they had a courtship of less than three weeks. The very end of Oswald's stay in Russia was delayed mostly by U.S. immigration paperwork. Both Oswald and Marina were deemed unimportant to the KGB and were happily sent off to the United States.

I further believe that Marina was threatened with deportation if she did not relate a story that was consistent with the WC's ultimate conclusion. It was very common for mostly U.S. citizen males and law-enforcement officials to exploit foreign-born females by using the threat of deportation. Laws, such as the Violence Against Women's Act and immigration-related policies now protect vulnerable women from deportation, now called removal, in cases where they are being exploited because of their lack of immigration status, but in the 1960s, this was not the case. Marina came to the United States as a preferred immigrant, subject to deportation until she naturalized in 1989. She was undoubtedly coerced by federal officials to maintain a narrative consistent with the WC and to follow the WC and FBI's lead in the investigation. With her lack of fluency and the overwhelming force of the federal government, she must have been terrified. Marina had no security in Oswald. He could barely hold down a job and he remained an enigma to Marina. The only security she may have had was to tell a story that the WC wanted to hear. I believe Marina was an innocent, often naïve, spectator in this convoluted plot to kill a President, a police officer, a U.S. Senator (but resulted in harming Governor Connally instead), and an innocent patsy. Others that were unduly influenced by the WC and the FBI were:

- Housekeeper Earlene Roberts who was told, among other things, to say she never saw Oswald leave his room outside of work and weekend visits to Irving. Roberts was also asked leading questions to confirm the identity of the wrong-sized jacket discovered by the DPD at a parking lot, which was used to tie him to the Tippit murder;

- Wesley Buell Frazier,[iv] Oswald's co-worker at the TSBD, along with his sister, who were told to say that they saw Oswald with a long, bulky bag on the morning of the assassination even though no one else saw this long bag, including Oswald's depository co-workers. In fact, Wesley Buell Frazier was initially arrested and handcuffed for the murder of President Kennedy, scaring him into submission. Wesley Frazier's mother reported to the FBI that she never saw Oswald with a long bag on the morning of the assassination. The notion of the long bag is more theater to explain how Oswald managed to get the rifle into the TSBD.

As to Marina's coerced testimonies, there are many, but here is a summary:

- To state Oswald had a rifle, even though she never saw him bring a rifle home nor saw the packaging that the rifle came in. Marina also could not distinguish a rifle from a shotgun, yet the WC was satisfied that she identified Oswald's rifle;

- To state that they lived on 214 W. Neely Street, where the famous enlarged photo of Oswald holding his rifle, having his revolver in a holster, and two diametrically opposed Communist newspapers. The holster was never recovered. There are no rent receipts, utility records, testimonies from neighbors, or any other records that corroborate the Oswalds ever lived there. The only evidence to prove that Oswald lived at 214 W. Neely for seven weeks is an affidavit dated June 12, 1964, in which an M. Waldo George, claiming to be the office manager of the Tucker Manning Insurance Company of Dallas, stated that he owns the Neely Street duplex and rented the upper floor to Oswald on March 2, 1963, but you would think a lease or rent receipts, or proof of payment of rent would have accompanied a property management company's oversight of such a property;

- To state that Oswald admitted to trying to kill General Walker and was expected to board at least two city busses with his 40" rifle without being seen; and

- To state that Oswald beat her when there was also evidence that Marina intentionally provoked Oswald by scratching him and evidence that she wanted to have bruises so that she could form a solid basis for divorce.

The first picture above and to the left is the yard of 212-214 W. Neely St and the second picture is the famous picture of Oswald with his guns and two communist newspapers in that same yard. Oswald claimed the photo was altered upon seeing it. The

Today, Marina believes Oswald was in fact a patsy despite her damaging testimony that the WC used to make its findings and conclusions. Marina did nothing wrong under the very unique and stressful circumstances in which she found herself. This operation was much bigger than she was. Despite these incredible and tragic events, she has made a wonderful life for herself and her children.

<u>A Key CIA Puppet</u>:

As to Ruth Paine, was she a humble, attentive, well-intentioned Quaker that was sincere in wanting to assist Marina, a young Russian mother in a new country? Or was there something more sinister, Machiavellian, and manipulating about Ruth Paine and her Bell helicopter employee husband? Two basic tenets of the Quaker lifestyle are integrity and stewardship of the earth, which includes helping others. She had a long history of befriending Russians and assisting them assimilate to this country. She also has a long history of being active in Civil Rights. Later in her life, she became a pacifist and withheld 40% of her federal income taxes to protest military funding, which she then donated to charity. So, was she a sincere Quaker or a puppet for American intelligence, or was she both?

Honestly, I avoided writing about Ruth Paine for the longest time. One of the reasons that I avoided writing about Ruth Paine is that most of the factors concerning her role, like George de Mohrenschildt, were largely circumstantial except her garage was able to put out very damaging evidence against Oswald at just the right time. As far as circumstantial evidence goes, lawyers always prefer direct evidence over circumstantial evidence even though circumstantial evidence is enough for a conviction. But then again, this murder-conspiracy is largely based on circumstantial evidence, associations, and factors.

Parenthetically, as further support of a strong intelligence relationship, the Dallas Police Department found a small Minox miniature camera, known as a spy camera, which had 5 serial numbers, which meant it was not commercially available. The FBI tried to get the Dallas Police Department to change their inventory report to read that Oswald had a Minox light meter, but even the then-largely corrupt Dallas PD refused. Who really owned that camera? Oswald or the Paines? If it were Oswald's, it would be strong indicia of his intelligence ties. If it were the Paine's, then it would demonstrate their ties to the intelligence community.

The factors concerning Ruth Paine's life, as circumstantial as they might be, also bely her humble, simple, well-intentioned, Quaker background. Those factors are too many to write about, and in fact, other books are dedicated to the Paine couple and the discoveries in their mystical garage.[90] In an effort to be succinct, I have enumerated some of those factors about Ruth Paine here:

- Ruth Paine was born in New York City and was well educated. She was not born into a simple Quaker family but became one later in life. Was this transition a natural evolution of her sincere beliefs, or was it a perfect cover for her future employment?

- Ruth Paine was already a teacher of the Russian language before she met Marina, but according to Ruth Paine, her primary purpose in befriending Marina was to learn Russian;

- Ruth Paine's father, William Avery Hyde, was under consideration for a covert CIA assignment in Vietnam in 1957 described as a cooperative education center, but was not considered because he could not pass a security background.[91] Ruth Paine said she was surprised to learn this, but even if true, she said her father would not have accepted such a position, yet a background check is not initiated until after a conditional offer of employment is accepted. In other words, he applied for the job and accepted it. He nevertheless worked for the Agency for International Development in a capacity that provided cover for many CIA operatives working as insurance and credit union representatives;[92]

- Ruth Paine's sister, Silvia Hyde Hoke, was a CIA employee;[93]

- The mother of Michael Paine, Ruth's husband, was a close friend of Mary Bancroft, who was the mistress of former CIA Director Allen Dulles for over twenty years;

- Michael and Ruth Paine's IRS income tax records were classified secret, probably because the sources of income had to be kept confidential, and it was certainly not because of Michael Paine's employment with Bell Helicopter. How many simple, altruistic Quakers have classified income tax records?

Ruth Paine, a pivotal witness providing the longest testimony to the WC, wants the world to believe she kept a very watchful eye on both Marina and Oswald since they returned from New Orleans and right up until the assassination out of her noble and altruistic

Quaker culture. She also wants us to disbelieve evidence from other eyewitnesses that: Marina and Oswald were seen in a furniture store; Oswald was at a car dealership test driving a Mercury Comet; and Oswald was seen at a firing range on numerous occasions. Ruth Paine had to testify that these other sightings were not credible in order to belie and discredit any sightings of the real Oswald and his double. The absurdity of all this is that Oswald and Marina had been estranged, with Marina living with Ruth Paine half an hour away in Irving. Ruth Paine had no way of knowing, and therefore testifying, about Oswald's whereabouts half an hour away in Dallas, especially during the weekday and even on some weekends as Oswald visited Marina on *some* weekends. I say some weekends because I am quite skeptical when people use absolutes, *e.g.,* Oswald *always* went home after work or Oswald *always* went to Irving on the weekends. Prior to staying with Marina and Ruth Paine for the last time on Thursday night, he had not seen Marina for 10 days,[94] which means he skipped an Irving visit the weekend before the assassination, so he did not visit *every* weekend. Even the WC stated Oswald *generally* would go to Irving on Friday afternoon and return to Dallas Monday morning.[95]

I assert that Ruth Paine ordered the rifle from Klein's Sporting Goods, picked it up, and hid it in her garage and loaned it out to intelligence officials to procure the magic bullet and the other bullet fragments planted in the Presidential limousine.

Ruth Paine marked on her personal calendar "LHO purchase of rifle" on March 20, 1963. Nevertheless, before the WC, Ruth Paine testified that she never saw the rifle until the police showed it to her at the station on the day of the assassination.[96]

A more probative fact that demonstrates Ruth and Michael Paine's complicity in this murder-conspiracy is a telephone call made only

30 minutes after the shots rang out in Dealey Plaza. At 1:00pm, according to telephone company records, Michael Paine placed a collect call to Ruth Paine's home from his work number.[97] Ruth Paine received the collect call and began talking with her now-estranged husband while the telephone operator remained on the line. The operator told the FBI, the man on the phone said he, "Felt sure Lee Harvey Oswald had killed the President but did not feel Oswald was responsible." Michael Paine then told his wife, "We both know who is responsible."

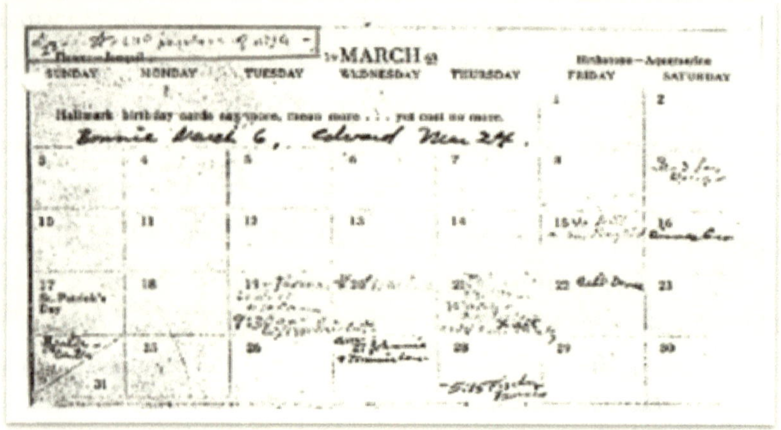

This is Ruth Paine's personal calendar noting Oswald's purchase of a rifle on March 20, 1963.

Who was responsible if they were not referring to Oswald? Cliff Shasteen, a barber shop owner in Irving, cut the person's hair that he believed to be Lee Harvey Oswald almost every other week for several weeks. He saw this same person at Ruth Paine's house.[98] When Michael Paine says "we both know who is responsible [for the President's murder], he is referring to Oswald's double.

Chapter 3: Legal Terms and How to Assess and Analyze Conflicting Evidence

This chapter is a framework of legal terms and how evidence is weighed by judges and lawyers. There were many aspects to this case that were technical, and I did not want to assume were common knowledge. There were many aspects to this case that were technical, and I did not want to assume they were common knowledge. I felt that an explanation of some legal terms and analysis was important. In that regard, I decided to lay out factors that played significantly into my analysis and factors that I hope will add clarity and meaning to this investigation.

Judges must weigh factors properly to come to an informed and just conclusion. Sometimes it is not always clear what weight should be given to different types of statements. For example, what weight should be given to an after-the-fact report over a contemporaneous one, or to a sworn statement versus a deathbed confession? This chapter hopes to answer those very basic, yet important, analytical questions. I begin with the legal definition of conspiracy and later explain how evidence is weighed by courts and how motive is properly analyzed.

One other important note: There are two common methods of conducting an investigation, scientific or otherwise. The scientific method begins with a hypothesis, for example, "I believe Oswald was an agent of Fidel Castro." From there, I study the evidence to determine if there is support for the hypothesis. The critical thinking method, on the other hand, involves thinking in a manner that seeks to eschew biases and attempt to be as neutral and objective as possible. More specifically, lawyers, prosecutors, and criminal investigators do not make an initial conclusion when conducting an objective investigation. Instead, they look to the facts to determine whether those facts "fit" into an element of a crime, a larger criminal scheme, a *modus operandi*, and a psychological profile. The facts must lead the investigator to a conclusion, and not the other way around. This is the analytical method I followed. With that out of the way, let us begin with the definition of conspiracy.

Conspiracy: A conspiracy, in legal or judicial contexts, is an agreement between two or more people to commit a crime. To prove a conspiracy, there must be some kind of agreement to commit that crime, and in most cases, one of the individual members must take some affirmative step toward committing it. A conspiracy is also secret. Conspiracy laws were designed to deter the planning of criminal behavior. Not all countries have conspiracy laws or punish a conspiracy. In the United States, a person can be punished simply for making the agreement and taking some affirmative step toward completing the conspiracy, such as purchasing a gun, but need not complete the crime itself. Conspiracy laws fall under a class of crimes called "inchoate crimes," because they do not need to be completed in order to be punished. Other inchoate crimes include solicitation (*e.g.*, solicitation to commit murder), and attempt (*e.g.*, attempt to commit murder), both punishable without having actually committed the murder. Again, the idea is to punish the planning (without having to wait for the damage to be done by the actual commission of the crime). Here, the people that killed Kennedy were not only part of a conspiracy; they would have been convicted of first-degree murder because they completed the conspiracy. In the case of Governor John Connally, as you will see later in this book, there was a conspiracy to commit murder and there was an assault with a deadly weapon (called, under Texas law at the time, "assault to murder").

All the people that *knowingly* assisted in the conspiracy, but did not pull the trigger, would be guilty of conspiracy to commit murder if they knew the objective of the conspiracy (*i.e.,* killing the President). In short, all the parties must know and agree to the criminal goal. So, if I buy a guy from a gun dealer and later shoot and kill someone, the gun dealer, assuming he followed all relevant laws in selling the gun to me, would not be criminally liable for the death I caused with that gun he sold me. If the person did not know the President would be killed, then that person is not part of the conspiracy. If you believe the Warren Commission that Oswald acted alone, then there would not be a conspiracy because there was no arrangement or agreement between two or more people to commit an unlawful act. I would like to use a Mafia and CIA technique here called compartmentalization, which means that assets and operatives only know what they need to know to complete their mission or assigned task and nothing more. They may not know the exact locations of other shooters or the person that may be planting evidence elsewhere. This technique not only makes it difficult to prove a conspiracy of knowing actors, but it also makes it difficult for one actor to "squeal" about another actor's complicity.

Conspiracies are not always easy to prove. In fact, conspiracies are, as noted above, inherently secret—very few criminals record the details of the conspiracy and the roles each of their co-conspirators are responsible for carrying out or announce them prior to their commission.

Co-conspirators, including people that assisted before the crime was committed, in some states known as accessories before the fact, and those that assisted in the cover-up, sometimes known as accessories after-the-fact, must know about the underlying crime, in this case, murder. But in this case, many more people played an unknowing role in the assassination. The planners of this crime programmed a cover up as well as the assassination, and it involved people from within and out of the federal government that would simply take orders and not ask questions because they belonged to a military or para-military structure, such as the Dallas Police Department, the doctors, nurses, and medical staff responsible for the autopsy at Bethesda Medical Center, and the FBI. There were also people that were paid in cash to do certain jobs before, during, and after the assassination. As far as documents go, there are hundreds of thousands of documents related to this event, but some key documents were destroyed, such as the reports and briefings by Oswald to the FBI about plots to kill the president. Proving knowledge or intent is often the most difficult aspect of prosecuting a crime. Take, for example, Jimmy Hoffa. He was no fan of the Kennedys. Some well-respected researchers assert he had nothing to do with the JFK assassination.[99] Nevertheless, Hoffa was notorious for throwing large sums of money at his problems, and his close ties to the underworld are very instructive and informative in determining whether he *may have known beforehand* of a plot to kill the President, and if he did, and he financially supported it, then he would be a co-conspirator.

As far as witnesses go, there are plenty of those too. There were witnesses on the grassy knoll, witnesses to Officer Tippit's murder, witnesses that saw Lee Harvey Oswald with Jack Ruby and CIA man David Atlee Phillips, and witnesses to the men on the sixth floor of the Texas School Book Depository. Some witnesses were unduly influenced by investigators to give testimony consistent with a certain narrative, and some witnesses were simply told to shut up and to never discuss this event with anyone. Randall Carr, for example, distinctly remembers seeing Mac Wallace, Johnson's personal hitman, on the sixth floor and then enter the famous light-colored Nash Rambler station wagon with other men.[100] He was told by the FBI effectively to keep his mouth shut. There is also a long list of people that may have had inside information about the assassination, and those people unexpectedly found themselves dead,[101] such as Chicago Outfit boss Sam Giancana and many other Mafia figures. Finding proof of a conspiracy did not turn so much on the vast amount of information that was already in existence. Instead, solving this crime required an anatomy of motive and weighing the abundance of evidence carefully. Additionally, many people involved in this multi-faceted murder-conspiracy committed other crimes that were punishable under federal and state law, such as: obstruction of justice, perjury, destruction of evidence, evidence tampering, witness tampering, destruction of government property, uttering false statement to a government official, among others.

<u>Motive</u>: Motive is the reason a person commits a criminal act. It may surprise you to know that motive is not necessary to prove crimes in our American criminal justice system. Take murder, for example. Murder essentially has three elements or ingredients that the prosecution must prove beyond a reasonable doubt: 1) the intentional (not accidental or reckless); 2) killing of another; 3) with malice aforethought (meaning the defendants thought about the killing before they actually killed and formed the idea to kill in their minds even mere seconds before the actual killing). That is all the prosecution must prove. Motives, such as jealousy, greed, revenge are not part of the essential elements of murder, but in our American judicial system, a jury is more likely to see intent if it understands why a person acted. A prosecutor often focuses more on motive after establishing the elements of the crime because motive is what juries can appreciate and factor into their analysis. We also seem to understand rage, greed, and jealousy to some extent or degree. Greed, for example, better explains a defendant's actions than the actual three elements of proving intentional murder: 1) the intentional; 2) killing of another; 3) with malice aforethought. In the case of Lee Harvey Oswald and Jack Ruby, the Warren Commission could not define a clear motive for their respective actions, which is very unusual, but again, not technically necessary under our criminal justice system.

In order to solve this crime, I used motive as a jury would, to better determine whether there was a viable motive, and if none, then the conspiracy was discarded, diminished, or otherwise not pursued. For example, many people believe that the military industrial complex was responsible for JFK's assassination because Kennedy supported a withdrawal of American troops in Vietnam, and, as the theory goes, there is no money in peace. Accordingly, the leaders of the military industrial complex were not making money from Kennedy's peace talks, so they conspired to kill the President. I will stop right now and say this motive is too remote and comes closer to being absurd than logically sound or even plausible. Still, I researched it and further found that the facts did not support the assertion that Kennedy wanted to get out of Vietnam. On Walter Cronkite's nationally televised show that aired on CBS in September 1963, President Kennedy told Cronkite that it would be great mistake for America to withdraw from Vietnam. The following week, Kennedy told Chet Huntley and David Brinkley on NBC that "I think we should stay [in Vietnam]. We should use our influence in as effective way as we can, but we should not withdraw." President Kennedy's brother, Bobby Kennedy, said there was never any consideration given to pulling out [of Vietnam.] [The President] had a strong, overwhelming reason for being in Vietnam and that we should win the war in Vietnam because if Vietnam were lost, then the loss of Southeast Asia would be next. If that happened, it could then mean India, the Middle East, Indonesia ... [102] I am aware that Kennedy withdrew advisors from Vietnam, and I am aware Kennedy wanted a permanent solution to the Vietnam problem, but what Kennedy stated publicly supported remaining engaged in Vietnam.

Even if the military industrial complex wrongly inferred a withdrawal from Vietnam by Kennedy, there still remained one problem. Motive is not just what drives people to commit a crime, but in their minds, by killing JFK their problems would be over. How could the military industrial complex, assuming it formed the grand, extreme, and dangerous idea to kill Kennedy, be guaranteed that Johnson would be different from Kennedy in regard to Vietnam? The military industrial complex as a killer, like so many other entities, individually or collectively, did not fit the motive analysis very well unless we answer that question.

In short, pulling out of Vietnam was not even a possibility under Kennedy, and even if it were, the motive of wanting to assassinate a President because of an inferred pull-out simply does not fit into a proper, causal motive. The military industrial complex lacked a precise motive even if you assume it may have incorrectly believed Kennedy wanted to pull out of Vietnam altogether. It simply does not follow that because they perceived an imminent pull-out from Vietnam that they would conspire to kill a President. At a minimum, the military industrial complex, guided by former military officers, would certainly have liked Kennedy to increase resources dedicated to Vietnam and certainly called into question his leadership when he spoke publicly about peace, but I do not believe the military industrial complex played a role in the assassination.

Another person that many conspiracy theorists assign responsibility for Kennedy's assassination is Allen Dulles. Many sources say Kennedy fired Allen Dulles as head of the CIA. Kennedy did not, in fact, fire Dulles. He allowed him to resign, probably so that Dulles could keep his government pension, and then rewarded Dulles with an optional National Security medal. Many assert that Dulles and several other senior CIA and military intelligence officials were fired because of the Bay of Pigs fiasco. The Bay of Pigs invasion occurred in April 1962, but Allen Dulles was allowed to resign in November 1962, almost eight months later. In addition, Dulles and Kennedy displayed mutual admiration in farewell thank-you letters that neither of them was obliged to write.[103] Additionally, Allen Dulles is on record as voluntarily stating how fond he was of President Kennedy; how brave he thought he was as he laid down on a sofa in his Massachusetts home in excruciating pain in the 1950s as he recovered from his back injuries, yet managed to focus on learning from Dulles' vast worldly experience; and how surprised he was that Kennedy wanted him to stay on as CIA Director because Dulles had expected to happily retire after serving nine Presidents.[104] Finally, although Dulles denied it, Dulles likely briefed Kennedy about the Bay of Pigs invasion as the Democratic Presidential nominee, which Kennedy then used in the famous debate to underscore Nixon's weakness on communist Cuba.[v] In short, Allen Dulles' motives to kill President Kennedy seemed, based on the totality of circumstances, unfounded, and thus were not pursued.

Allen Dulles was, however, part of a cover-up as a committee member of the Warren Commission. Dulles' allegiance to the agency that he effectively created was greater than his allegiance to Kennedy, and so ensuring the CIA's reputation was protected was an essential part of his role on the Warren Commission. And LBJ knew that. Ostensibly, Dulles was placed on the Warren Commission to explain and clarify the cryptic documents from the CIA and to explain how the secret agency worked. The reality is that Dulles, along with FBI Director Hoover, and other senior government officials protected their respective agencies from harm, accusations, and embarrassment by intentionally destroying documents, including reports of Oswald's activities and Oswald's briefings about Presidential assassination plots.

Finally, many have assigned to "the deep state" the primary responsibility for the assassination of President Kennedy. In fact, President Eisenhower, a five-star General himself, warned the American public about the dangers of the military industrial complex before he left office. The deep state, for most people, includes military intelligence and, particularly, the CIA. The CIA, however, did not formulate the idea to kill President Kennedy. Lyndon Johnson did. Johnson gave the order. The CIA along with the Mafia and Jack Ruby's strong ties to corrupt Dallas officers, and Johnson's hit man, Mac Wallace, and partner in crime, Cliff Carter, orchestrated the created reality, theater, and puppet mastery. The CIA played a key operational role in planning Kennedy's assassination, in the coverup, and most importantly, in implicating Oswald in a pro-Castro scheme in order to stoke an international crisis. Lee Harvey Oswald's alleged trip to Mexico City in an effort to get into Cuba became a thorny subject when it came time to cover up the assassination.[105] The day after the assassination, J Edgar Hoover and Deputy Attorney General Katzenbach reviewed an audio tape and photographs that had been flown in from Mexico City to Washington DC on the night of the assassination. The audio tape and photographs were purportedly of a "Lee Harvey Oswald" entering the Russian embassy in Mexico City and speaking to Russian embassy employees. The photos were later identified as being of Ralph Geb, a high school friend of Malcolm Wallace, Johnson's personal hitman.[106]

Hoover and Katzenbach immediately knew Oswald was set up as a patsy. Hoover told Johnson that tapes of Oswald contacting the

Soviet Embassy in Mexico City did not match the voice of the living Oswald.[107] Hoover said, "[i]t appears that there is a second person who was at the Soviet Embassy down there." This impersonation of Oswald "had to be suppressed in order to maintain the lone nut façade called for in the Katzenbach directive. There was a more sinister purpose for suppressing the tapes and photos of an Oswald imposter. As long as the tapes survived, the story in them was undermined by the fact that Oswald's voice was not on them. The cover-up of the Mexico tapes began three hours after Hoover told Johnson that the voice on them was not Oswald's. Johnson, as a brand-new President via violent overthrow, did not want a war. The lone nut assassin theory had to dominate the assassination explanation. This is part of the created reality, theater, and puppet mastery of the JFK assassination.

***Modus Operandi* or MO**: MO is a distinct pattern or manner of working that comes to be associated with a particular criminal. It is a method or procedure. A *modus operandi* is very important to criminals because they are almost immediately rewarded when things go right in the form of getting away with a crime and almost immediately punished when things go wrong in the form of being arrested and convicted. When things go wrong, they find themselves sitting in prison with an abundance of time, rethinking almost continuously about what went wrong and how to avoid it in the future. Many actually do learn from their mistakes and follow what has worked in the past and avoid what went wrong. I will provide MOs that the Mafia, the CIA, and associates of Lyndon B. Johnson have used in the past and show how they applied these motives in the assassination of President Kennedy and Lee Harvey Oswald.

Lie once, lie forever: In Latin, the term is: *falsus in uno, falsus in omnibus*. Essentially, it is the legal maxim that a witness who testifies[1]

---

1. https://en.wikipedia.org/wiki/Testimony

falsely about one matter is not credible to testify about any other matter. The maxim is based on primitive psychology that claims that once a mind is depraved enough to lie once, it is always a depraved mind. We now know this is not true. Nevertheless, this maxim is still applied in our American judicial system, albeit, in a more relaxed fashion, and most famously, was applied in the O.J. Simpson trial, where Judge Lance Ito applied the doctrine to instruct the jury that "[a] witness who is willfully false in one material part of his or her testimony is to be distrusted in others." Courts have even held that if a person lied in one claim, say a civil case for injuries related to a car accident, then that adverse credibility finding can be used in a separate claim, such as being the victim of a violent crime. The law is very arcane and outdated in this regard. Even Satan is said to have mixed lies with the truth.

In a case like this where many witnesses provided testimony both contemporaneously and years after the fact, this principle naturally comes into play. Consider, for example, James Files. He confessed to being the grassy knoll shooter. Most criminals never confess. He claims to have found God as he sat in prison for the attempted murders of two detectives. He also has a long criminal history. Is James Files telling the truth about being the grassy knoll shooter? If you plainly and fully apply the maxim, *falsus in uno, falsus in omnibus,* he cannot be believed because of his criminal background, but I disagree. James Files confirms many facts that were only suspected before, such as John Roselli's participation in the assassination and even Roselli's location in the Dal-Tex building on that day along with Charles Nicoletti.

Another example of this maxim are the claims provided by Rose Cherami or Cheramie. Rose Cheramie worked for Jack Ruby in his burlesque club. She testified that two days before the assassination, she was thrown out of a car by two Latin-looking gangsters that worked for Jack Ruby. She claimed that the two men were involved in a plot to assassinate Kennedy in a few days in Dallas. She also said that Jack Ruby and Lee Harvey Oswald were lovers. Her testimony was largely ignored because she was a drug addict and a drug courier and had an arrest record. Vincent Bugliosi, a well-trained lawyer and the formidable prosecutor of Charles Manson and his murdering clan, effectively applied this maxim to completely disregard and disparage Cheramie. He said "[t]here is nothing to the Cheramie thing. She's a drugged out narcotic addict with no credibility. A pathetic figure who's been exploited by conspiracy theorists throughout the years." I have a great deal of respect for the late Mr. Bugliosi, but I disagree with his assessment. Bugliosi's 1,600-page book about the JFK assassination, *Reclaiming History: The Assassination of President John F. Kennedy*, goes out of its way to discount conspiracy theories on this subject despite probative and substantial evidence to the contrary. Bugliosi's book, along with Gerald Posner's book, *Case Closed*, engages in the same faults as highly conspiratorial books on this matter: They dismiss facts that are inconsistent with their narrative; they over-value facts that support their narrative; and they spin neutral facts to support their narrative. This is called advocacy, and it is very effective in the court room, but not when one engages in objective, balanced research, or what Posner claims to be – an investigative author. In fact, both Posner's *Case Closed* and Bugliosi's *Reclaiming History* can be said to have harbored a preconceived battle plan. They read like prosecution briefs instead.

Obviously, Mr. Bugliosi would not call Rose Cheramie to the stand to testify about what she heard and saw assuming she were alive because any good lawyer on the other side would impeach her credibility. As a former prosecutor, Bugliosi should know that law enforcement successfully utilizes informants with less than stellar backgrounds all the time, but it does not render their information incredible or valueless. In fact, some of those informants are paid by law enforcement agencies, have perjured themselves in the past, and have often committed heinous crimes. Prosecutors nevertheless use them all the time in an effort to catch bigger fish.

Finally, Roger Stone was convicted of obstruction of justice, witness tampering, and making false statements. Based on the maxim, *falsus in uno, falsus in omnibus,* Stone's book, *The Man Who Killed Kennedy*, should be discredited even though his book was written before his legal troubles. I find his book to be well cited and, surprisingly, quite balanced despite Stone's passionate ideologies and profession as a conservative political consultant. Parenthetically, Nixon told Roger Stone the following: "Lyndon and I both wanted to be president. The difference was I wouldn't kill for it."[108] In summary, I have taken people's account of events and weighed them against other evidence to make a conclusion, and I seldom applied this maxim in its entirety because it is too rigid and would lead to discrediting otherwise probative and useful information.

The Weight of Evidence, Including Conflicting Evidence: In researching and investigating this crime, there was no shortage of information from a wide array of sources. All were accorded different weights and values. The numerous books written about this topic, including books written by lawyers, have weighed and appraised these varying facts and bits of information yet come to different conclusions. It is understandable but allow me to express my understanding of how conflicting bits of evidence should be weighed.

Take, for example, eyewitness statements. Under our American judicial system, a statement made under oath and subject to cross examination carries greater evidentiary weight than an unsworn statement, such as one made over dinner or in passing. The idea is that being sworn in or taking an oath awakens a person's duty to tell the truth, so sworn testimony is given greater weight. Cross-examination further gets to the truth by targeting issues with specificity and gives the opposing party an opportunity to point out the weaknesses of a witness's testimony, like holes in their story or a lack of credibility. Accordingly, testimony that is also subjected to cross-examination is given even greater weight.

Dying Declarations: Many of the men involved with the JFK assassination have made dying declarations, also known as deathbed confessions. Unlike most police reports, which are deemed to be inherently reliable because they are regularly and contemporaneously made soon after an incident, dying declarations are often made years after an incident, and many people naturally question their credibility and what, if any, weight should be accorded to them. In the eyes of the law, dying declarations are generally given great weight. Like a sworn statement, a deathbed confession generally carries more credibility under rules of evidence than a statement made in passing or over dinner. Dying declarations have a very long history in our judicial system as well as under English common law. In medieval English courts, the principle originated from *nemo moriturus praesumitur mentiri* — "no-one on the point of death should be presumed to be lying." An incident in which a dying declaration was admitted as evidence has been found in a case from 1202. In the law of evidence, a dying declaration is testimony that would normally be barred as hearsay but may nonetheless be admitted as evidence in criminal law trials because it constitutes the last words of a dying person and thus has indicia of reliability, truthfulness, and credibility, as people inherently want to clear their conscious before their deaths. In my professional experience, when it comes to dying declarations, individuals that are humble or ashamed of having been part of a crime tend to downplay or diminish their participation in a criminal scheme, such as Loy Factor. Those that have big egos, have no shame, or are narcissists tend to exaggerate, overplay, or amplify their role in a criminal scheme, such as Santo Trafficante or Carlos Marcello. Please keep this in mind when we later discuss dying declarations by several people involved in or with knowledge of the assassination. In summary, dying declarations are inherently truthful and thus were given greater weight than they deserve, in my analysis.

In looking at a wide body of evidence, I, like so many others before me, had to make the call as to what is credible and logical based on the totality of the circumstances and what is not. For example, famous spy and Watergate burglar, E. Howard Hunt, made a deathbed confession claiming that he was asked to be a bench warmer in the assassination of JFK; a small group of CIA operatives were responsible for the planning of the assassination; and French Corsican mobster Lucien Sarti was brought in by William Harvey and was the grassy knoll killer. Nevertheless, in Hunt's last book, *American Spy,* which was published in January of 2007, only a few months before his death, Hunt denies any involvement in a conspiracy; denies he was there in Dealey Plaza, or even in Texas at all; denies any knowledge about any plot to kill the president; denies being in Mexico City in 1963; and claims that Frank Sturgis, another Watergate Burglar, could not have been involved in the assassination because of his room-temperature IQ and inability to keep a secret.[109] So which version do I believe? I believe part of Hunt's deathbed confession. I believe he played a role in the assassination as opposed to simply being asked to be a bench warmer for several reasons. First, Hunt lost a civil defamation case because he could not prove he was not in Dallas on November 22, 1963.[110] Second, an eyewitness claims to have seen him in Dallas handing out envelopes of cash to Frank Sturgis and others.[111] Third, there is a photo of a person closely resembling Hunt with his fedora hat and raincoat in

Dealey Plaza. Fourth, Hunt's wife told her son, Saint John Hunt, that "Papa was in Dallas."[112] As to Lucien Sarti, while William Harvey did in fact contact and recruit French Corsicans, Lucien Sarti was allegedly in a French prison during the assassination.

Hunt has claimed that he was in a Chinese grocery store in Washington DC when he first heard of JFK's assassination.[113] I also express doubt about Hunt's deathbed confession where he refutes being involved in the assassination of JFK and claims to have been only asked to be a benchwarmer to "the Big Event." Instead, I believe Hunt was responsible for moving arms to Dallas and paying off co-conspirators in cash. In Hunt's mind, he mollified and justified his role by calling himself a bench warmer perhaps because he did not play a larger role in the assassination like others within the CIA. As a final note, in *American Spy*, Hunt states: "If LBJ had anything to do with the operation, he would have used Harvey, because he was available and corrupt. LBJ had the money and the connections to manipulate the scenario in Dallas and is on record as having convinced JFK to make the appearance in the first place. He further tried unsuccessfully to engineer the passengers of each vehicle, trying to get his good buddy Governor Connally to ride with him instead of in JFK's car—where theorists observe he would have been out of danger."[114] I definitely believe this aspect of Hunt's deathbed confession as well and it will be discussed in greater detail in future chapters.

Properly Weighing the Warren Commission Report: Finally, while I believe the Warren Commission Report is a results-oriented product that is more fictional than factual, there are several things about it that readers should know from a legal analysis. The Warren Commission was born from an Executive Order issued by Johnson, and Johnson reviewed all major pieces of evidence or issues before it reached the Warren Commission members. It was not created by elected government officials, but by people Johnson himself appointed, mostly his cronies. It was never subject to rules of evidence despite having the Chief of the Supreme Court as its chairman. In that regard, there was no cross-examination of the government's expert witnesses and no presentation of defense experts to challenge the government's interpretation of the evidence.[115] Many tactics which would have been ruled impermissible in a criminal trial were permitted in the Commission's proceedings, such as leading questions, the assumption of facts not in evidence, the acceptance of hearsay, and the lack of a proper foundation for evidence it considered.[116] Many witnesses whose testimony was inconsistent with the government's portrayal of Oswald as the lone assassin were either ignored or selectively quoted in the Warren Commission Report.[117] In this book, I cite to the Warren Commission several times only to underscore its many shortcomings and selective use of witnesses and evidence.

Plausible Deniability: Plausible deniability is the ability to deny any involvement in illegal or unethical activities because there is no clear evidence to prove involvement.[118] The lack of evidence makes the denial credible, or plausible. The use of the tactic implies forethought, such as intentionally setting up the conditions to plausibly avoid responsibility for one's future actions. The term is used both in law and in politics, but it originated in espionage. In politics, plausible deniability usually applies to the practice of keeping the leadership of a large organization uninformed about illicit actions that the organization is carrying out. The CIA is notorious for employing plausible deniability. Many of the covert operations approved by the CIA frustrated Kennedy's policies, such as supporting the independence of Algeria and supporting the government of Patrice Lumumba in the Congo. More importantly, the CIA's planned assassinations, sabotage operations, and coups were not always shared with senior leadership, including CIA leadership. This was the arrogant and rogue nature of the CIA at the time.[vi] Practically speaking, plausible deniability is very frustrating to prosecutors because they must now prove the intentional planning of the use of plausible deniability, a much more difficult step in their burden of proof. Plausible deniability allows those involved to say: "I was not there that day," or "I do not know him," or even the all-too-familiar "I don't remember." For example, in the case of the many CIA operatives and assets there that day in Dallas, there is no official evidence that can tie them to Dallas beyond photos and eyewitnesses. In other words, you will not find travel authorizations for Frank Sturgis, George H.W. Bush, or E. Howard Hunt, to name a few. Why? Because their travel was paid for in cash and they used aliases. They also may have used chartered flights and rented cars to get to Dallas. More relevantly, they were working covertly, and CIA and military intelligence would not only have covers but are trained to deny involvement even in the face of duress, torture, and death. Accordingly, lying to Congress was part of their job and all too easy. Another example of plausible deniability is to deny the existence of a relationship. For example, Lyndon Johnson denied knowing his very good friend, Billie Sol Estes, when he was in hot water with the feds by stating that he had only met him one time and that was when he invited him to a party in his Washington home during inaugural week of January 1961.[119] The truth of the matter is that Billie Sol Estes and LBJ were close partners in crime for many years and Estes knew of at least seven murders where LBJ was directly implicated. You will read more about this cozy criminal relationship in Chapter 4.

Who Stands To Gain The Most From a Crime: In Latin, the term in *cui bono* or who stands, or stood, to gain from a crime, and so might have been responsible for it? Applying *cui bono*, as well as an analysis of motive, allows me to conclude that the CIA alone was not the primary driver or instigator of this crime, but instead allows me to conclude, and forces me to conclude, that LBJ was in the better — and arguably, best — position to benefit from this crime. Johnson was under investigation for a wide ranging, highly orchestrated scheme of corruption for several years leading up to JFK's assassination. Those investigations ended upon JFK's death and Johnson's ascension to the presidency. Johnson, a power-hungry politician, desperately wanted the presidency to satiate his narcissism, but to also quell the pending investigations against him. Finally, Johnson hated the Kennedy brothers, who were nothing like him, being very well educated, born into wealth, disruptive of cronyism, cynical towards the deep state, and idealistic.

Cui bono, coupled with LBJ's longstanding proclivity to commit crimes, including murder, compels me to conclude that Johnson was the driver of JFK's assassination. The CIA, the Mafia, Cuban exiles still harboring anger about the lack of air support for the Bay of Pigs, military intelligence as well as the military industrial complex, possibly rich oil men that may have contributed money for this operation, the Secret Service, and J Edgar Hoover, were secondary co-conspirators that happily went along because they too held disdain and contempt for Kennedy and stood to gain something with Kennedy being out of the picture. But Johnson had the most to gain. If the CIA was the principal driver of this assassination, it would not have guaranteed that Kennedy's replacement, Johnson, or Congress, would have returned the CIA's covert authority unless Johnson made an agreement to do so, and he did. In fact, Johnson agreed to: 1) return covert authority to the CIA; 2) increase the number of troops in Vietnam; 3) maintain the oil depletion allowance for his rich Texas oil friends; 4) keep J Edgar Hoover on as FBI Director even though he was well beyond the mandatory retirement age; 5) put out Bobby Kennedy's fire against organized crime; and 6) actively cover up the assassination upon JFK's death, among other things. That was all the CIA, the military industrial complex, Hoover, the Mafia, oil men and others needed to hear to agree to join the conspiracy in some form or fashion.

RAPHAEL LUCERI DE'VERITAS

Chapter 4: The Epitome of Ruthlessness

Landslide Lyndon, Lyin' Lyndon – this chapter is dedicated to "the master of the Senate" – Lyndon Baines Johnson. His mastery came through extortion, cronyism, blackmail, and special favors. I begin this chapter by whetting your curiosity concerning the extent of Johnson's depravity and criminal culpability. Below is a letter written by Billie Sol Estes' attorney that was part of a back-and-forth negotiation about what Estes knew about at least nine murders, illegal schemes, and illegal payoffs, and whether he would receive immunity, have the restrictions lifted off his current parole, or a pardon, presumably, a Presidential pardon. The letter, as well as other correspondence, is in the excellent book: *The Men on the Sixth Floor,* by Glen Sample and Mark Collom. This particular letter is dated August 8, 1984, long after Johnson died, and is addressed to the criminal division of the US Attorney's Office in Washington DC:

My client, Mr. Estes, has authorized me to make this reply to your letter of May 29, 1984. Mr. Estes was a member of a four-member group, headed by Lyndon Johnson, which committed criminal acts in Texas in the 1960's. The other two, besides Mr. Estes and LBJ, were Cliff Carter and Mack Wallace. Mr. Estes is willing to disclose his knowledge concerning the following criminal offenses:

I. Murders:

1. The killing of Henry Marshall

2. The killing of George Krutilek

3. The killing of Ike Rogers and his secretary

4. The killing of Harold Orr

5. The killing of Coleman Wade

6. The killing of Josefa Johnson

7. The killing of John Kinser

8. The killing of President J. F. Kennedy.

Mr. Estes is willing to testify that LBJ ordered these killings, and that he transmitted his orders through Cliff Carter to Mack (Mac) Wallace, who executed the murders. In the cases of murders nos. 1-7, Mr. Estes' knowledge of the precise details concerning the way the murders were executed stems from conversations he had shortly after each event with Cliff Carter and Mack Wallace. In addition, a short time after Mr. Estes was released from prison in 1971, he met with Cliff Carter and they reminisced about what had occurred in the past, including the murders. During their conversation, Carter orally compiled a list of 17 murders which had been committed, some of which Mr. Estes was unfamiliar [with]. A living witness was present at that meeting and should be willing to testify about it. He is Kyle Brown, recently of Houston and now living in Brady, Texas. Mr. Estes states that Mack Wallace, whom he describes as a "stone killer" with a communist background, recruited Jack Ruby, who in turn recruited Lee Harvey Oswald. Mr. Estes says that Cliff Carter told him that Mack Wallace fired a shot from the grassy knoll in Dallas, which hit JFK from the front during the assassination. Mr. Estes declares that Cliff Carter told him the day Kennedy was killed, Fidel Castro also was supposed to be assassinated and that Robert Kennedy, awaiting word of Castro's death, instead received news of his brother's killing. Mr. Estes says that the Mafia did not participate in the Kennedy assassination but that its possible participation was discussed prior to the event, but rejected by LBJ, who believed if the Mafia were involved, he would never be out from under its blackmail.[120]

In that same letter, Estes, through his attorney, professes: 1) a detailed knowledge of the JFK assassination and claims a mutual associate met with Jack Ruby in Las Vegas a few days before the assassination to discuss the details; 2) that discussions were had with Jimmy Hoffa concerning having his aide, Larry Cabell, kill Robert Kennedy; 3) that Estes has records of his phone calls during the relevant years to key persons mentioned in the foregoing account;

4) knowledge of Johnson's illegal scheme of combining cotton allotments in order to defraud the federal government, including tape recordings made at the time of LBJ, Cliff Carter and himself discussing the scheme; and 5) knowledge of millions of dollars in payoffs, including Estes' collection of payoff money on more than one occasion from George and Herman Brown of Brown & Root, which was delivered to LBJ.[121] In response, DOJ states that a debriefing with Estes was necessary and required, as a matter of DOJ policy in qualifying an informant, that Estes be completely candid and honest, and if he were not honest, evidence could be used against him.

When two FBI agents showed up for a meeting at Estes' homes in Pecos, Texas, Estes abruptly canceled the meeting without explanation, much to the shock of Estes' lawyer and daughter.[122] No reason was given for the sudden cancellation of the meeting, but I ask you to draw your own conclusions. Mac Wallace, Cliff Carter, and LBJ had already died when Billie Sol Estes, through his attorney, communicated with DOJ's Criminal Division in 1984, but LBJ's attorney, Ed Clark, was still alive. Ed Clark was an extremely powerful person. Note that Ed Clark's name is left out in Estes' letter to DOJ and only includes Cliff Carter and Mac Wallace. Johnson, using the veil of attorney-client privilege, effectively communicated his orders to kill to Ed Clark and left much of the details up to Clark to sort out, including calling upon Wallace to kill individuals that stood in Johnson's way, such as Henry Marshall, a DOA employee investigating Billie Sol Estes for an illegal cotton allotment scheme.

Johnson ordered the killing of John Kinser when Kinser approached Johnson's sister, Josefa, about a loan from Johnson. Johnson interpreted this loan request as blackmail and ordered Wallace to do the killing. It seems reasonable that Lyndon Johnson and J Edgar

Hoover could have been involved in the plot in a similar, deliberate manner without their knowing the details of the plot. They would know only that it was going to happen and be given only the briefest outline of what their potential roles would become in the event certain items needed to be covered up. Many items needed to be covered up.

Throughout LBJ's adult life, Ed Clark was his personal attorney and Mr. Fix-it. And Mr. Fix-it in every regard. In Barr McClellan's excellent book, *Blood, Money & Power – How LBJ Killed JFK*, McClellan describes how Johnson and Clark used the attorney-client privilege to commit and carry out a bounty of crimes, from "mere" tax evasion to murder. As an attorney, I know firsthand how prosecutors and judges are reluctant to pierce the thick veil of attorney-client privilege. This privilege works to keep confidential communications between an attorney[1] and their client private. Its purpose is to encourage and protect frank and full communication between attorney and client so that the attorney can be in the best position to zealously represent the client. During criminal investigations, agents and officers are trained to stay clear of recording or otherwise "listen-in" on attorney-client privileged communications. In court, judges encourage parties to use alternative evidence instead of invoking the attorney-client privilege or its limited exceptions. As a general matter, and in the practice of law and criminal investigations, the government must prove a conspiracy or a crime without using attorney-client privileged communications. The Mafia is also known to use and exploit the attorney-client privilege when they speak to *il consigliere* of a *Cosa Nostra* family. LBJ, a prolific user of the telephone from early on, exploited the attorney-client privilege to communicate his criminal schemes, including his order to kill JFK. I am convinced Estes left

---

1. https://www.law.cornell.edu/wex/attorney

out Ed Clark because he feared him and knew Clark had the resources to cause Estes harm.

I also wish to return to the maxim of *falsus in uno, falsus in omnibus* as applied to what Estes would have testified. First, Estes had been convicted twice by the federal government. That alone makes his credibility suspect, and if the maxim is applied plainly, he could not be trusted. Second, Estes wanted to talk about LBJ's involvement in several murders, including JFK's, but only after Johnson died. Which way does this cut concerning Estes' overall credibility? On the one hand, Estes may have legitimately feared Johnson and his associates, so speaking about Johnson's criminal activities after his death seems logical. On the other hand, Johnson was no longer around to defend himself. Third, Estes states that Johnson did not want the Mafia involved because he was afraid he would be indebted to the Mafia through extortion. Here, I have come to a crossroads. Do I believe Estes, and if so, do I believe all of or part of what Estes says? I believe Estes was telling the truth, but he may not have had ultimate knowledge of Mafia involvement in JFK's assassination for several reasons. While it may have been true that Johnson expressed his desire that the Mafia not be involved, senior CIA officials were involved, and when the CIA is involved, especially in an assassination, the Mafia is necessarily involved. It is that very *incestuous relationship* – two sides of the same coin – that makes it difficult to separate the CIA and the Mafia from one another, especially when it comes to assassination attempts. Additionally, it seems reasonable that Lyndon Johnson could have been involved in the plot in a similar, deliberate manner without their knowing the details of the plot. He, like J Edgar Hoover, would know only that it was going to happen and be given only the briefest outline of what his potential role could become in the event certain items needed to be covered up.[123] Furthermore, why were Sam Giancana, John

Roselli, and Charles Nicoletti killed? I believe they were killed because they were about to spill the beans about their roles in the assassination as well as their numerous roles in other CIA covert operations, particularly, a highly classified palace coup that was slated to happen on December 1, 1963, where Castro would have been killed by the general of his army. That palace coup plan was overseen by Bobby Kennedy and approved by JFK, and if information about it had been leaked, it would have caused an international scandal for Cuba, Russia, and the United States that might even have led to World War III. Third, what about Carlos Marcello's confession to his cellmate in Operation CAMTEX and Santo Trafficante's deathbed confession? Fourth, what about E. Howard Hunt's deathbed confession linking CIA officials to the assassination, with Johnson on top? Fifth, the prosecution of Mafia figures significantly decreased during Johnson's time in office, which suggests a *quid pro* quo arrangement and does not show Johnson was extorted in any way—the Mafia got what they wanted, at least from Johnson. Lastly, of the many entities that had a reason to kill JFK, the Mafia is inherently the most violent, malicious, and rancorous. The Mafia also wanted Bobby Kennedy gone as well. In summary, Johnson tried to keep his hands as clean as possible without knowing details of murder-ploys in order to invoke plausible-deniability and left all the details to Ed Clark and others. In the end, you will have to determine the extent of Este's credibility.

For now, I return to Lyndon Johnson's proclivity to commit crimes, including murder. Johnson also had long-time associates that were much more loyal to him than any Mafia soldier could be to a Mafia boss. I also want to state that Johnson's crimes were so vast that I cannot write about them in detail without running the risk of making this a 1,000-page-or-more tome. If you wish to read about his criminal activities in more detail, I suggest the following books: 1) *Bloody Treason, The Assassination of John F. Kennedy,* by Noel

Twyman, Laurel Publishing, 1997; 2) *Blood, Money, and Power—How LBJ Killed JFK,* by Barr McClellan, Skyhorse Publishing, 2011; 3) *LBJ—The Mastermind of the JFK Assassination,* by Philip F. Nelson, Skyhorse Publishing, 2011; 4) *The Men on The Sixth Floor,* by Glen Sample and Mark Collom, Sample Graphics, 2011; 5) *The Man Who Killed Kennedy,* by Roger Stone, MJF Books, 2013; 6) *JFK—An American Coup D'Etat,* Colonel John Hughes-Wilson, John Blake Publishing, 2016; and 7) *Faustian Bargains—Lyndon Johnson and Mac Wallace In The Robber Baron Culture of Texas,* by Joan Mellen, Bloomsbury Publishing, 2016. If you believe allegations of Johnson's criminal side flourished only after his death, then think again by reading: *The Dark Side of Lyndon Baines Johnson,* by Joaquim Joesten, Icon Classics, 1968 and *A Texan Looks At Lyndon,* by J. Evetts Haley, Palo Duro Press, 1964. The evidence of LBJ's depravity in the form of criminal schemes and murders is nothing short of overwhelming.

Lyndon B. Johnson is the missing link to the many well-researched books that conclude the deep state or others killed Kennedy. Without Johnson, none of those entities would be guaranteed success in the form of a cover up and their motives would not be perfect or causal (*e.g.,* the CIA: Let's kill Kennedy because he hates us (with no clue about whether Johnson may feel the same way)... *vs.* Let's kill Kennedy *because* Johnson will give us our covert authorities back, will give us war in Vietnam, will dole out billion-dollar government contracts for our friends, will maintain the oil depletion allowance, etc.). Johnson is the person that stood to gain the most from Kennedy's death, or *cui bono.* Without Johnson, things simply do not add up, particularly motive.

Johnson is described as being crude, vicious, duplicitous, and cowardly with a proclivity to lie when telling the truth would have been easier.[124] Another word to describe him: ambitious. But ambitious in a bad way. That ambition included lying, cheating, exaggeration, and an almost uncontrollable obsession to appear greater than what he really was. By age twelve, he voiced his desire to be President of the United States.[125] His grandmother on his mother's side, Ruth Baines, regarded him as a disobedient delinquent and had considerable skepticism about Lyndon's future.[126] "More than once," Lyndon's brother, Sam Houston Johnson, recalled, "she told my folks and anyone else who would listen, 'That boy is going to wind up in the penitentiary—just mark my words.'" Lyndon apparently did not disagree with her, saying as he recalled his youth, "I was only a hair's breadth away from going to jail." This nascent criminality grew stronger until it was LBJ's central attribute. Johnson's entry into politics was largely during the time of Franklin Delano Roosevelt.

Johnson's lying began early. He grew up in Johnson City and claimed it was named after his family, though it was not. He would often introduce himself as "Lyndon Johnson from Johnson City," his way of implicitly communicating the status accorded to his family for being founders of the town; after he left Texas for Washington, he would use the same technique, yet stretch the lie even further to leave the impression not only that his family founded the town but that they were of some special aristocratic lineage. As Johnson's most prolific biographer Robert Caro confirmed, if anyone asked Johnson directly whether there was a connection, "he would confirm that impression, saying that Johnson City had been founded by his grandfather, a statement that was, of course, not true."

Johnson's Problems With the IRS and His Solution:

In addition to becoming more conservative, his other problem was getting some income. After all, his supporters were all getting wealthy.[127] LBJ was not. The money issue arose in a classic way. The first serious threat to expose his illegal election efforts centered on the 1941 Senate race. An Internal Revenue Service audit of Brown & Root's illegal contributions of corporate money through individuals had commenced. The criminal charges against Brown & Root were serious and necessarily involved LBJ. Despite an all-out legal battle, the IRS refused to drop the charges. Finally, after much internal maneuvering, the claim was killed in 1944. A private request to the White House got the vital help Johnson needed. FDR himself ordered the case dropped. Johnson, of course, learned another important lesson in his early political career: The White House controlled the criminal justice system. He also had a far better understanding of the power exercised by the IRS.

Johnson "Wins" A Senate Seat in a Runoff:

The final count in the primary poll, held on July 24, 1948, showed Johnson's adversary, Coke Stevenson, with 477,077 votes to 405,617 for Johnson, far out in the lead by a seemingly safe margin. However, since Stevenson's lead of 71,460 votes did not constitute a majority over the entire field, a run-off became necessary under the law at that time. The run-off was set for August 28, 1948. The wily Johnson quickly spotted his chance to reverse the comfortable majority his opponent had piled up on the first ballot. In the southwestern portion of Texas, where many people of Mexican parentage live, for the most part in primitive conditions, the master of an entrenched political machine can easily swing a large 'controlled vote' one way or the other. Some of these Latin-populated counties were ruled in almost medieval fashion by 'dukes' who lord it over vast areas by means of a well-established hierarchy of ward-heelers and *jefes politicos*.[128]

LBJ turned to George Parr for help in the 1948 runoff. At the time, Parr was both county judge and sheriff in Duval County.[129] In the rural counties of Texas, this was often all the power needed to be boss. George Parr was the boss, "*El Jefe.*"

When the count from the run-off election was in, Parr had delivered for LBJ. But though he had dallied in sending his returns while Lyndon kept in close touch by telephone, it finally turned out that they had closed their own count prematurely. Stevenson was ahead by 113 votes. Johnson made another frantic telephone call to Parr, who indicated that he might pick up what they needed in Precinct 13 at Alice (county seat of Jim Wells). Thereupon his henchmen "re-canvassed the returns," reporting on September 3 the "corrected" total of 202 additional votes for Johnson and one for Stevenson. Thus, Lyndon went into the lead by 87 votes out of nearly a million actually cast.

How were these votes found? Parr's political machines in the six counties he controlled engaged in blatant voter fraud. The precinct leader manipulated the vote of the Hispanic majority.[130] Few understood English. They simply did as they were told. In exchange for cash payments to vote for Parr's candidate, the precinct chairman would pay the poll taxes, make up the voting list, write the names on a checklist, and vote for the paying candidate. Usually the "voter" would never even have to vote.

Johnson Finds a Son – LBJ and Lyndon Jr.:

Bobby Baker was known as the 101st Senator because of the abundance of power he exerted. He is also known as the sole representative in Washington of the key state in the Union: Lobbyland. In reality, Bobby Baker was actually a mere Senate employee, an aide, and what we know today as an intern.[131] Bobby Baker started in the United States Senate as a pageboy, running errands for the members of the Senate.[132] Known then as the most exclusive men's club in the world, the members of the Senate insisted on the very best perquisites and benefits possible. In the Senate, ego was never an issue; it was an accepted fact. Most senators had huge egos and wanted everything. Baker would be in charge of satisfying those egos. But to many other Senators, he was much more than that. He is said to have brought three unique and valuable talents: a nimble mind, Southern charm, and a total lack of scruples.[133]

Young Bobby Baker contrived to be on good sides with two very powerful Senators: LBJ of Texas and the elderly Robert Kerr of Oklahoma. Besides being both Southern Democrats, the aging Senator Kerr and the then still youthful Senator Johnson were held together by a far more potent bond: their common allegiance to the oil industry, the greatest single force in U.S. politics as well as U.S. business in general. Senator Kerr amassed a wealth of over $20 million dollars.

One of the few solid disclosures of the Baker investigation has been that the enterprising young man, working for the government at an annual salary of $19,612, was able to amass a fortune of at least two million dollars.[134] Two of Baker's children, Lynda and Lyndon, were named after Johnson, according to those who knew them.[135] In 1963, Baker resigned during an investigation by the Democratic-controlled Senate into Baker's business and political activities. The investigation included allegations of bribery and arranging sexual favors in exchange for Congressional votes and government contracts. The Senate investigation looked into the financial activities of Baker and Lyndon Johnson during the 1950s. The investigation of Lyndon Johnson as part of the Baker investigation was later dropped after President Kennedy's assassination and Johnson's ascension to the presidency.

The hard fact of the matter, however, is that both Johnson and Baker served the oil interests faithfully and well over a period of many years and that they have, in turn, handsomely benefited from the oilmen's benevolence.

One good thing Bobby Baker had learned in the exercise of his official functions was that automatic vending machines were a booming business—especially if you knew how to get them installed in defense plants, NASA establishments and other places where the government has a big say.[136] With the easily-earned cash from the MAGIC or Mortgage Guarantee Insurance Corporation, stock deals tingling in his pocket, and his good friend and protector Lyndon B. Johnson installed in the office that is just one heart-beat away from the presidency, Baker, in 1961, launched his biggest and most successful business operation, a vending machine company called the 'Serv-U Corporation'. When Serv-U was formed in December 1961 as a Maryland corporation, Baker prudently kept in the background. As president he installed Eugene Hancock of Miami, a vending machine operator with considerable experience in this type of business. One of Bobby's brothers, Charles Baker, became a vice-president, and Bobby's wife, Dorothy, was made an assistant secretary of the corporation. Even more interesting than the list of executives of Serv-U was the roster of the corporation's stockholders. It included Bobby Baker himself, of course, even though he at first denied that he was an owner after the spotlight had fallen on his own complex affairs.

There never was an ethics code in the world of lobbyists, nor do the normal rules concerning conflict of interests apply to them (or to the lawmakers on whom they feed). It is not surprising, therefore, that Black, after having become a major stockholder of Serv-U, should have fruitfully worked both sides of the street. As a lobbyist for North American Aviation, he obtained lucrative government contracts for that firm. As Bobby Baker's partner in Serv-U, he saw to it that this company's vending-machines were favored by plant managers of North American Aviation. As a matter of fact, this company became Serv-U's principal customer and the source of its most lucrative contracts. Other aerospace industries with whom they did major business included the Northrop Technology Laboratories. With such sponsors as these, it's hardly surprising that Serv-U, starting from scratch on a shoestring, should have been able, by the end of 1961, to build a business that grossed more than $3.5 million in less than two years.

Fate caught up with Bobby's business partner faster than with himself. Baker was indicted on income tax evasion charges a few weeks after the Baker scandal broke in the fall of 1963. On June 18, 1964, Baker was given a 15-month-to-four-year prison sentence and fined $10,000, after having been convicted on three counts of evading $91,000 in Federal income taxes over a three-year period beginning in 1956.

<u>The Murder of John Kinser</u>:

John Douglas Kinser was the owner of a miniature golf course in Austin, Texas. He was also having an affair with Josefa Johnson, the sister of Lyndon B. Johnson, as well as Mac Wallace's estranged wife. Josefa was also having a relationship with Mac Wallace, who worked for Johnson at the DOA at this time. Not one to discriminate, Josefa was also having a sexual relationship with Mac Wallace's wife. This was indeed quite the circle and Mac Wallace understandably felt left out.

According to Barr McClellan, the author of *Blood, Money & Power: How LBJ Killed JFK*, Kinser asked Josefa if she could arrange for her brother to lend him some money. Johnson interpreted this as a blackmail threat because Josefa had told Kinser about some of her brother's corrupt activities. On October 22, 1951, Mac Wallace went to Kinser's miniature golf course. After finding Kinser in his golf shop, he shot him several times before escaping in his station wagon. A customer at the golf course had heard the shooting and managed to make a note of Wallace's license plate. The local police were able to use this information to arrest Wallace. Wallace was charged with murder but was released on bail after Edward Clark arranged for two of Johnson's financial supporters to post bonds on behalf of the defendant. Johnson's attorney, John Cofer, also agreed to represent Wallace. On February 1, 1952, Wallace resigned from his job at the DOA in order to distance himself from LBJ. His trial began seventeen days later. Wallace did not testify. Cofer admitted his client's guilt but claimed it was an act of revenge as Kinser had been sleeping with Wallace's wife.

The jury found Wallace guilty of murder with malice aforethought. Eleven of the jurors wanted the death penalty. The twelfth argued for life imprisonment. Judge Charles O. Betts overruled the jury and announced a sentence of five years' imprisonment. Then he suspended that sentence, and Wallace was immediately freed, never spending a day in jail for Kinser's murder. This was Texas justice with the right connections.

After his murder conviction, Mac Wallace went to work for Ling-Temco (later Ling-Temco-Vought, and then LTV), a conglomerate with substantial defense contracts. Wallace held supervisory jobs in manufacturing control and long-range programming.[137] It is inconceivable that Wallace could have operated in these spheres without a security clearance. In fact, files showed that he did indeed have clearance right up until September 18, 1964, when the Defense Department's Industrial Personnel Access Authorization Screening Board stripped Wallace of the clearance on grounds of "criminal, infamous, immoral and notoriously disgraceful conduct." The reasons stated were: the murder conviction, two drunk driving convictions, indications that Wallace was a communist as well as a homosexual. Johnson got Wallace the job at Ling-Temco and his security clearance was approved in the same way Wallace got away with murder—connections, and money to grease the wheels.

The Murder of Henry Marshall:

Henry Marshall, a Texas native, began working for the DOA in 1934. In 1960, he was asked to investigate Billie Sol Estes' acquisition of over 130 cotton allotments that violated DOA rules.

The DOA wanted to control cotton demand and avoid harmful surpluses.[138] Because of the success of cotton farming during the 1950s, production exceeded market demand. As in the oil business, cotton had to be controlled. Enforcement of cotton production was the job for the DOA, and this was done with allotments telling the cotton farmers how much they could and could not plant. Since Estes wanted his farmers to grow more cotton, he needed ever more allotments until they simply ran out. In desperation, he found an unusual niche. Some allotments were available for farmers displaced by the interstate highway program. Estes began acquiring these allotments to help with his financing needs. The practice was prohibited, but Estes used a loophole that allowed the transfer in a complicated exchange program for other land. Farmers in financial trouble were pleased. Estes continued to prosper. Not surprisingly, additional contributions went to Johnson. Estes financially supported Johnson, and Johnson returned numerous favors. In this case, the favor returned was the killing of the investigator looking into Estes' criminal scheme, and to make it look that Johnson had clean hands.

Billie Sol Estes said that illegal cotton allotments and other business deals he arranged with Lyndon B. Johnson's help in the early 1960's generated $21 million a year, with part of the money going to a slush fund controlled by LBJ.[139] Estes stated that in January 1961 – the same month LBJ became vice president – Estes and two other men met with Johnson at LBJ's Washington home to discuss Henry Harvey Marshall, an Agriculture Department official who was questioning the legality of Estes' cotton allotments. After Johnson authorized the DOA to offer Marshall a promotion and transfer to Washington DC to end his investigation, which Marshall turned down, Estes quoted LBJ as saying, "Get rid of him," referring to Marshall. Estes later said that four men were involved in planning the murder of Marshall—Estes, Johnson's troubleshooter and close aide, Clifton C. Carter, triggerman Malcolm Everett (Mac) Wallace, and Johnson himself.

What happened to Henry Marshall is barbaric. Mac Wallace was told to meet with Marshall and try to make the man see reason, but Marshall would not be dissuaded. If it meant a payoff, okay. Just get him to quit stirring up trouble. On June 3, 1961, Wallace arrived at Marshall's small ranch near Bryan, Texas.[140] The confrontation took place in Robertson County, an agricultural area north and west of Bryan. Wallace had driven to the meeting, stopping at a filling station to ask for directions. He then went to the ranch where the two men met in a quiet, isolated place. They had to get to the heart of the matter at a location where they could talk freely — meaning, without witnesses. Wallace was not successful in bringing an end to the investigation.[141] Marshall refused to cooperate. During the heated argument that resulted, acting pursuant to his vague instructions, Wallace attacked. Angered at an inability to get Marshall to cooperate at all, Wallace viciously hit the man with a pistol. Marshall fell to the ground, the side of his head cut and his eye badly bruised. Since Marshall was unconscious, Wallace felt he had time to stage a suicide. Rigging a plastic liner to the exhaust and starting Marshall's truck, Wallace counted on carbon monoxide poisoning to kill. Marshall inhaled a substantial amount of exhaust fumes, almost a fatal dose, but not quite. While the poisoning was underway, Wallace removed Marshall's personal belongings and placed them on the seat of the pickup. Then Wallace panicked. The exhaust was taking too long. He reportedly heard a truck driving nearby. Although he saw no one and no one saw the crime, Wallace had to get out of there. There was a bolt-action rifle in Marshall's truck, so Wallace used the man's own weapon to shoot him five times in the side of his lower torso. Three of the shots were sufficient to kill him. Finally convinced, after a fifth shot, that Marshall was dead, Wallace left.

At the first phone he could find, Wallace called Carter to let him know what happened. Carter told Wallace to stick around, to see if anything else needed to be done. They had to get word from Clark. Later that afternoon, Marshall's cousin discovered the body. He was with a man from Cliff Carter's Pepsi Cola bottling company in nearby Bryan. The body was near the exhaust, the rifle nearby. Personal effects were on the seat of the pickup. There was no suicide note. The next day, the coroner ruled the death was a suicide. Working with Carter, the local authorities took quick action to cover up the crime. There was no need for an investigation. Somehow, it was accepted that a nearly dead man could work a bolt-action rifle several times, and fire bullets into his own body. Only a fix with the justice of the peace could do it, and, as we have seen, that just happened to be Clark's *modus operandi*. Wallace, believing everything was okay, incredulously went back to the filling station the next morning, to tell the attendant he had not really needed to go to the Marshall ranch and had not gone there. He then returned to California, his perfect cover, out of reach of Texas criminal authorities.

Estes later testified in great detail about this and other murders under a grant of immunity. He also stated that Carter met him at his Pecos home after Marshall's death and that Carter commented that Wallace "sure did botch it up."

Other Murders:

As if the murders of Kinser and Marshall were not bad enough, there were more and they were all committed with the goal of protecting Johnson from scandal. Below is a summary of those murders:

- The murder of George Krutilek – Krutilek was Billie Sol Estes' accountant. On April 4, 1962, Krutilek was found dead. Despite a severe bruise on Krutilek's head, the coroner decided that he had also committed suicide. The next day, Estes, and three business associates were indicted by a federal grand jury on 57 counts of fraud. Two of these men, Harold Orr and Coleman Wade, later died under suspicious circumstances. Mac Wallace is believed to have killed Krutilek;
- The murder of Harold Orr – Orr was a business associate of Billie Sol Estes. After Estes was indicted, Harold Orr was also arrested and was eventually given a ten-year prison sentence. He was allowed to go home, and rumors began to circulate that Orr was planning to provide information on the case to the authorities. On February 28, 1964, Orr was found dead in his garage. The Justice of the Peace pronounced it

accidental death by carbon monoxide poisoning. Beginning to see a pattern? If the death is a suicide, then there is no suspect;

- The murder of Coleman Wade — Wade became a business associate of Billie Sol Estes. This included building storage facilities for Billie Sol Enterprises. Coleman Wade was arrested for his role in the Billie Sol Estes fraud. Wade died in 1963 when his plane crashed after attending a meeting with Estes in Pecos. J. Evetts Haley published *A Texan Looks at Lyndon* in 1964. In the book, Haley suggested that Lyndon B. Johnson had employed Mac Wallace to murder Wade, along with a long list of others;

As you can see, the bulk of the murders were associated with Billie Sol Estes' criminal scheme relating to cotton allotments, but all the murders were designed to protect LBJ, because after all, Estes was convicted and sentenced. The criminal group included Ed Clark, who handled legal issues, such as finding top-notch criminal defense attorneys and bribing judges, Cliff Carter, Mac Wallace, Billie Sol Estes, and Johnson, who always gave the orders to kill in Johnson's own way, saying things like "go talk to him," or on other occasions, such as in the case of Henry Marshall, saying "get rid of him." Also note that the murder of Kinser, which resulted in no jail time for Wallace even though the evidence of his guilt was clear, emboldened this group's audacity and proclivity to commit murder with impunity. When Jack Ruby was arrested for the killing of Oswald, Ruby said, *inter alia,* that the true facts will never be known because of people in very high positions.

Suspicions of how Johnson became so wealthy began to flourish as he ran for President in 1964. In *The New York Times* (International Edition) of August 13, 1964, the noted columnist James Reston took a critical look at 'Johnson's Money: An Underground Issue' and wrote: "President and Mrs. Johnson, according to published reports, seem to be getting richer and richer." In May, *U.S. News and World Report* estimated their net holdings at over $7 million. In June, the *Washington Star* made it $9 million, and *Life* magazine put it at "approximately $14 million." Just to put things into perspective, $9 million in 1964 would be valued at almost $85 million today after inflation. Keep in mind that LBJ came from poverty, worked briefly as a high-school teacher, then became a Congressional aide, and from then on, he had a career in the federal government. How he amassed such a fortune must raise eyebrows. The reality is that LBJ, through his partner and lawyer, Ed Clark, created a slush fund and scheme to launder illegal campaign contributions, bribes, and hundreds of thousands of dollars for awarding billion-dollar contracts to mostly Texas-based companies and ordered murders to prevent investigations into the origins of all that money.

Chapter 5: Key Assassination Figures (non-Mafia)

This Chapter summarizes the non-Mafia characters involved in the Big Event. It serves as general background and to bring you up to speed about how they are associated with this crime. The chapter that follows this one is dedicated to the Mafia characters, who played a larger role in the "dirty work."

Please note that those who worked for the Mafia and who worked for intelligence may be one and the same. I placed all long-term Mafia figures in Chapter 3. Here, some characters may have worked off and on with the Mafia, such as Dave Ferrie and Frank Sturgis.

Key CIA Figures:

E. Howard Hunt: Also known as Eduardo, Hunt was a master spy for the CIA. Hunt was pivotal in the American involvement in regime change in Latin America, including the 1954 Guatemalan coup d'état and the 1961 Bay of Pigs invasion. Along with G. Gordon Liddy, Frank Sturgis, and others, Hunt was one of the Nixon administration's "plumbers," a team of operatives charged with identifying government sources of national security information "leaks" to outside parties. Ultimately, Hunt was convicted as a Watergate burglar and was sentenced to 30 months to 8 years in prison and spent 33 months in prison before being released. More relevantly, Hunt made a deathbed confession to his son concerning the Kennedy assassination.[vii] In that deathbed confession, Hunt allegedly implicated Lyndon B. Johnson, Cord Meyer, David Atlee Phillips, Frank Sturgis, David Morales, Antonio Veciana, William Harvey, and an assassin he termed "French gunman grassy knoll" who many presume is Lucien Sarti, though

Sarti was purportedly in a French prison at the time of the assassination. I believe Hunt was there in Dealey Plaza that day and was responsible for making cash payments to assets involved in the assassination. I also believe that Hunt was responsible for bringing certain weapons and ammunition to Dallas.

This is what Nixon had to say about Hunt according to H.R. Haldeman, Nixon's White House Chief of Staff: "This fellow, Hunt, he knows too damn much ... If it gets out that this Cuba thing is a;; involved, it could be a fiasco. It would make the CIA look bad ...Hunt look bad and it is likely to blow the whole Bay of Pigs thing, which we think to be very unfortunate for the CIA and the country at this time."[142] H.R. Haldeman wrote in his memoir, "The Ends of Power," that when Nixon referred to "the Bay of Pigs thing," he was in reality, referring to the Kennedy assassination

Although Hunt is widely suspected of being one of the three tramps arrested and later released by the Dallas Police Department on the day of the assassination, he was not. The person believed to be Hunt in the famous "three tramps" pictures is actually Chauncy Marvin Holt, a backup to the Big Event, who delivered fifteen fake secret service credentials and badges.

Parenthetically, American labor official Frank Sheeran, who claimed later in life to killing Jimmy Hoffa, also claimed to having met a "big-eared" E. Howard Hunt in Florida when he drove a truck trailer full of munitions. At the time, he did not know Hunt's name, but years later, when Sheeran saw Hunt on television testifying before Congress about the Watergate affair, he instantly recognized him as the person with big ears that took his truckload of munitions. We now know Hunt was involved in the Bay of Pigs planning and these munitions may have been used in support of that operation.

Hunt died in 2007 at the age of 88.

David Atlee Phillips: Also known as Maurice Bishop. Oswald occasionally referred to him as Mr. B. He was also a senior CIA official and was probably the most prolific in this assassination as his name has been implicated by his CIA colleagues, the Mafia, and many highly regarded researchers. He was responsible for a psychological warfare campaign in the US coup d'état of Guatemalan President Jacobo Arbenz. He later became head of Western Hemisphere Operations, primarily serving in Mexico and Latin America. From 1958 to 1961, Phillips' cover was owning a public relations firm in his own name. The firm was so good that it attracted private clients seeking his expertise, whom Phillips had to turn down. He was also assigned to Mexico from 1961 to 1965 and undoubtedly played a role in attempting to frame Oswald by having a double play the role of Oswald trying to get into Cuba.

Phillips was the CIA-assigned handler of James Files and Lee Harvey Oswald, among others. According to James Files, Phillips told Oswald to go to the Texas Theater if he encountered any problems. He then told Oswald he would be transported to Redbird Airport and eventually flown into Mexico. David Atlee Phillips was the CIA man on the ground directing Lee Harvey Oswald and others, such as Antonio Veciana. Veciana, the leader of the anti-Castro sabotage and assassination group, Alpha 66, finally admitted that Philips is the person he dealt with for Cuba-related operations, and also admitted seeing Phillips meeting with Oswald in August 1963, in the building that housed the office of H. L. Hunt in Dallas.

David Atlee Phillips died in 1988 at the age of 65.

Cord Meyer Jr.: Cord Meyer was implicated by Howard Hunt in his deathbed confession. He was a senior Central Intelligence Agency (CIA) senior operative. He was brought into the OSS (the precursor to the CIA) by Allen Dulles and was soon put in charge of overseeing Operation Mockingbird, a plan to secretly influence domestic and foreign media. From 1954 until 1962, Meyer led the agency's International Organizations Division. Meyer headed the Covert Action Staff of the Directorate of Plans from 1962. Cord Meyer and his wife were divorced in 1958. His wife, Mary Meyer-Pinchot, became one of many of Kennedy's lovers, and their relationship was quite intimate rather than fleeting. In fact, Kennedy expressed his love for Mary Meyer. At one point, Kennedy wanted to divorce Jackie and marry Meyer.[143] Mary Meyer was killed in 1964 near her Washington, DC home. Her murder has never been solved. Cord Meyer, before his death, blamed the murder of Mary on the "same sons of bitches that killed Kennedy."[144] After Cord Meyer learned that Mary was Kennedy's mistress, he became scorned and vulnerable, and LBJ exploited this vulnerability. Cord Meyer, ironically, was out of town the day Mary was killed. Her death was a rub-out, not an alleged rape gone awry. She was shot twice at very close range—once in the back and once in the back of the head. The accused assassin, a black man, was

acquitted for lack of evidence.

I am not implicating Cord Meyer in the murder of his wife—I am implicating the CIA and military intelligence, which sought to eliminate Mary Meyer for whatever secrets JFK may have told her and for whatever information she may have garnered since his death, just like the famous columnist, journalist, and American game show panelist, Dorothy Kilgallen.[viii]

Cord Meyer's role in the assassination was as a strategist. He would design a campaign of false information and narratives that would form the basis for the WC's findings and conclusions. Some information would also be leaked to the media. These narratives included Oswald's trip to Mexico, so as to implicate Cuba in the assassination; Oswald's low-level jobs, in order to portray him as having a disgruntled, angered mentality because of his dishonorable discharge from the Marines; his ordering the rifle; his purported defection to Russia, to show his lack of loyalty to the United States; his feigned mission as the sole member of the Fair Play for Cuba Committee, to further demonstrate his loyalty to communism.

I also believe Cord Meyer, along with James Jesus Angleton, orchestrated disinformation campaigns by CIA assets and co-conspirators. For example, within an hour of Oswald's arrest on November 22, 1963, the leaders of the group, the DRE in Miami, an anti-Castro student activist group funded by the CIA, went public with their documentation of Oswald's involvement in support of Castro, providing the press information that would help shape the image just being formed by millions of Americans about the person who stood accused of killing the president.[145] Also within an hour of Oswald's arrest, Captain Westbrook knew all the discrete details of Oswald's background before anyone else learned of them, including the media and Captain Fritz, Oswald's interrogator from the Dallas Police Department. This is precisely the type of theater and created reality the CIA was known for, and Cord Meyer was among the best at it.

In short, I believe Cord Meyer was an essential behind-the-scenes planner of the assassination and used his acute disinformation skills and extensive contacts in foreign and domestic media to feed a perpetual fountain of disinformation.

Cord Meyer died in 2001 at the age of 80.

James Jesus Angleton: Here is another interesting man. Angleton started his spy career with the OSS. Then he became one of the founders of the CIA with a specialty in counterintelligence. This is what he told the Church Committee in response to interrogatories: "It is inconceivable that a secret intelligence arm of the government has to comply with all the overt orders of the government." This is precisely the type of thinking that allowed the CIA to become arrogant, rogue, irresponsible, and harmful. This type of thinking was shared among many senior CIA officials of the time.

Angleton was also known as "Orchid Man" for his patience in growing and cultivating orchids. He even wrote about them in horticulture magazines. He said that the most deceptive orchids are the ones that survive. He also was a "mind warrior," wanting to end his life in the woods, like an Apache, but he died in a hospital. Just before dying, he leaned his torso straight up, began chanting for a few seconds, and then lay back down and died of cancer from his years of chain smoking.

Angleton remained one of the most elusive senior intelligence operatives in our history by design. He oversaw counterintelligence and the 1964 defection of Yuri Nosenko, a KGB defector that knew Oswald very well. Angleton had an internal file on Oswald that had been tightly controlled inside his counterintelligence operation. He had a general 201 (military personnel) file on Oswald that appeared to have fake information in it. With it, Oswald himself could be linked to both the Soviets and Cuba.[146]

Angleton's view concerning any questions from Congress or the public through Freedom of Information Act requests were to delay everything and if you must say something, say it is classified.[147] Angleton created a wall of secrecy in an elaborate wilderness of mirrors that hid the operation for decades and that had been constructed in a way that created its own confusion when anyone attempted to unravel the truth.[148] This is again an example of the created reality at the hands of the CIA.

Interestingly, on the night Cord Meyer's wife, Mary, was killed,[149] Angleton was inside her house searching for Mary's diary. No one knew he was there and no one ever claimed to have called him. He was discovered by Mary's brother-in-law, who stated that he found Angleton burglarizing the place. Angleton destroyed the diary. I suspect the diary would have led to the real killers, and those real killers were CIA or miliary intelligence or both.

<u>William Harvey</u>: William King Harvey is yet another interesting character. He was overweight and an alcoholic. He was known to hate Ivy Leaguers, which meant he likely hated the Kennedys. He was considered by many as ultra-conservative. He broke an FBI policy of being available on a two-hour off-duty call due to sleeping off heavy drinking at a party the night before. He refused the resulting demotion and reassignment to Indianapolis, Indiana, preferring to resign. He joined the CIA shortly thereafter. William Harvey, according to many that knew him, harbored rancor and hate toward everyone that opposed him. In the CIA, he went out of his way to undermine the FBI's authority, especially in international matters. He flourished in the CIA and, after a successful mission in West Berlin, Harvey was tasked with a project to organize "executive actions" (a euphemism for the assassination of foreign political leaders) under the codename ZR/RIFLE. This operation would be kept secret and even denied by the CIA for years.

To eliminate Fidel Castro, Harvey decided he needed to employ the resources of the American Mafia, who had by this time been a trusted and reliable resource for the CIA. He drew on the connections of businessman and CIA asset Robert Maheu, who had cultivated relationships with Sam Giancana, Santo Trafficante Jr., John Roselli, and other figures. Finding Maheu's operation too convoluted, Harvey cut everyone but John Roselli out, and began running the operations against Castro himself on or about November 15, 1961.[150] It is well documented and conceded by the CIA that Harvey gave poison pills to Roselli on April 21, 1962.[151] Roselli was then to give these pills to Anthony "Tony" Varona, which would give them to an asset who worked at a restaurant that Castro frequented in Cuba.

Harvey was also involved in Operation Mongoose, a CIA operation run from Miami, Florida that had made various attempts to undermine or overthrow the Cuban Revolution. At the height of the Cuban Missile Crisis in October 1962, Harvey sent ten intelligence operatives into Cuba to gather intelligence and prepare for an invasion Harvey thought inevitable.

Bobby Kennedy, now overseeing CIA and military operations, as well as the Department of Justice, learned of the continued assassination attempts while his brother was trying to broker a deal and maintain peaceful relations with Russia that included leaving Cuba alone. Accordingly, Harvey was demoted and sent to Rome, Italy by Bobby Kennedy because RFK found out that Harvey was the mastermind behind CIA assassinations in the form of ZR-Rifle and continued to engage in sabotage and assassination attempts against Castro even after JFK ordered the CIA to stop working with the Mafia and to cease all sabotage and assassination attempts against Cuba. In short, Harvey engaged in unauthorized operations. This is another example of how rogue the CIA had become. Many claim Harvey then harbored even more hatred for the Kennedys, and this hatred resulted in the assassination.

Harvey died from a heart attack in Indianapolis on June 9, 1976 at the age of 60.

David Sanchez Morales: David Sanchez Morales was of Cuban-Mexican decent and joined the CIA in 1951. It is alleged that he was involved in Executive Action, a series of projects designed to kill foreign leaders deemed unfriendly to the United States. Morales reportedly was involved in Operation PBSuccess, the CIA covert operation that overthrew the democratically elected President of Guatemala, Jacobo Arbenz Guzmán.

<u>Key Government Figures</u>:

<u>Lyndon Baines Johnson</u>: Lyndon Baines Johnson or LBJ became the 36th president following Kennedy's death in Dallas.[152] Using his mastery of the legislative process, Johnson was able to pass much of Kennedy's stalled legislation, including the Civil Rights Act. As president, Johnson proved to be far more liberal than Kennedy, passing the Civil Rights Act, the Voting Rights Act, and "Great Society" legislation designed to expand opportunities for poor and minority populations. He appointed NAACP counselor Thurgood Marshall to the Supreme Court, making him the first black Justice.

Johnson was also deeply embedded in *quid-pro-quo* relationships with men from the Texas oil industry, industries involved with military contracts, such as Bell Helicopter, and construction businesses for the Army Corps of Engineers, including Brown & Root. In fact, thanks to Johnson, Brown & Root became an industrial colossus, which returned many favors to Johnson.[153] Brown & Root became a subsidiary of Halliburton Company, the American multinational corporation responsible for most of the world's hydraulic fracturing operations. Johnson was a 37-year government employee, but he was a multi-millionaire by 1964. Johnson also deepened the nation's involvement in Vietnam, which proved to be his undoing. Johnson famously declined to run for reelection in 1968.[154] In doing so, he may have paved the way for Nixon's election in 1968.

Congressman Albert Thomas winks at LBJ. The significance of the wink is unknown, but unusual during a national tragedy. Johnson was allegedly prepared for the ceremony with a pre-printed copy of the oath of office in his jacket pocket.

LBJ ordered the assassination of Kennedy and, as noted in Chapter 4 above, LBJ has also been implicated in several murders and numerous criminal schemes. Congress was investigating Johnson's criminal activities and he was extremely close to being indicted until Kennedy was killed, and that is when all investigations against him came to a screeching halt.

One of the most obvious signs of Johnson's foreknowledge of Kennedy's assassination is a wide-angle photo from Ike Altgens, which shows Johnson ducking into the floorboard of his limousine *before* the first shot was fired. According to the men who were escorting his car ... he started ducking down in the car a good 30 or 40 seconds before the first shots were fired.[155]

In December 1966, FBI Director J Edgar Hoover forwarded a memo to the White House that described the reaction of Soviet and Communist Party officials to Kennedy's assassination. The memo stated that Communist officials believed there was a well-organized "ultraright" conspiracy behind the assassination and indicated that the KGB was in possession of data purporting to indicate President Johnson was responsible for the assassination.[156]

This is a wide-angle close-up of the Altgens photo before it was cropped out and sent to national and international publication. It is a picture of the vice-presidential limousine, with Senator Ralph Yarborough and Lady Bird Johnson clearly visible in the back seat. Where is LBJ? He is hiding behind the seat and on the floorboard *before* the shots fired.

Johnson died of a heart attack in 1973 at age 64. He suffered from depression years before and seemed to have been burdened by his actions. He made several confessions to a psychiatrist that made him feel slightly better, but these confessions are protected by doctor-patient privilege.

<u>FBI Director J Edgar Hoover</u>: – at all relevant times, J Edgar Hoover was Director of the FBI and a close friend of LBJ. Hoover's role in the Big Event was pivotal. He and many senior FBI officials, particularly those in Washington DC, tampered, altered, and destroyed evidence. LBJ immediately assigned the FBI to investigate Kennedy's murder, and by doing so, stopped local investigations and usurped authority from state officials over a state crime at the time. Once authority had been given to the FBI, the tampering and intentional destruction of evidence began. The FBI never established a chain of possession for the magic bullet, Oswald's rifle, the two bullet fragments found in the limousine, and Oswald's revolver. nor did they test Oswald's revolver, among other things. The FBI also "lost" evidence, such as the microfilm that contained the order form and proof of payment of the alleged rifle Oswald ordered from Klein's Sporting Goods, the large bone fragment recovered the day after the assassination because it would have been evidence of a shot from the front, and all of the briefing summaries and reports made by Oswald to the FBI because the FBI did not want any association with Oswald.

Under oath before the WC, Hoover unequivocally stated that the FBI did nothing wrong in assessing Oswald's threat to national security and that it had no reason to inform the Secret Service of Oswald's danger to President Kennedy when Kennedy visited Dallas, yet privately, Hoover disciplined over seventeen FBI agents for their handling of Oswald, including Special Agent James Hosty, who tried to reopen Oswald's file several times. Hosty was ultimately transferred to the FBI Kansas City office until his retirement.

<u>Secret Service Director James J. Rowley</u>: Rowley was a close friend to LBJ and Hoover, his former boss. More relevantly, Rowley, along with other senior Secret Service men, came to dislike and distrust Kennedy because of his numerous sexual escapades that the Secret Service was forced to cover up and because Kennedy entrusted classified and arguably national security information to several of his paramours, such as Marilyn Monroe, Judith Campbell Exner, Mary Meyer, and others. These women did not have a security clearance. For purposes of brevity, here is a list of all the key actions that Rowley and other senior Secret Service men undertook in this assassination:

- Ordered the motorcade route, including the sharp turns that forced the limousine to slow down in Dealey Plaza;[157]
- Ordered Secret Service Agent Kellerman to take JFK's body out of Texas before it could be autopsied by Texas officials;
- Ordered other agents to clean the presidential limousine and have it flown back to Washington immediately, essentially destroying and removing the "crime scene" from the scene of the crime;
- Subsequently ordered the Secret Service to have the limousine flown to Detroit and then Cincinnati to have it thoroughly cleaned and repaired;
- Switched airplanes. This would ensure Jackie's presence and assure the nation of the continuity of government, that LBJ's firm hand was on the rudder and the world was safe;
- Insisted on holding the plane for Jackie to arrive with the body of JFK, thus ensuring that Jackie would unwittingly assist Kellerman in absconding with JFK's body. The larger objective was to ensure that the autopsy was conducted under the control of designated military men (it

would not be unreasonable to suspect that they had been chosen well in advance, for aptitudes—or vulnerabilities—other than their forensic pathology skills or experience, which were practically nonexistent);

- Took over JFK's quarters on Air Force One, immediately making the necessary calls from his desk telephone, knowing they would not be recorded until the plane was airborne (and subsequently causing many of those that were recorded to be erased or lost);

- Had LBJ sworn in before leaving Dallas. To set this up, he would first need to call Bobby Kennedy to put the question to him, not so much for his permission but to be able to say later that he did so and that Bobby agreed with it. (Bobby Kennedy told Johnson he did not need to be sworn in.);

- Lied to Kenneth O'Donnell and others about having been told that he should be sworn in, as quickly as possible, by RFK;

- Made the call, personally, to get Judge Sarah Hughes to Love Field for the swearing-in ceremony;

- Ensured that the presidential photographer was on hand to record the event for posterity (even though he accidentally made a photograph of Johnson exchanging winks with Congressman Thomas, a photograph which survived despite the disappearance of the negative for that particular photograph).

<u>**Key Associates of LBJ**</u>:

<u>Malcolm Everett Wallace</u>: He is commonly referred to as Mac Wallace. He was LBJ's hitman. He was an economist, and most of his adult employment had been through Johnson's efforts, including work at the Department of Agriculture and later for Ling, a defense contractor – a job requiring a security clearance which he landed despite having a murder conviction thanks to LBJ's help. As noted in Chapter 4, Mac Wallace was involved in several murders to protect Johnson's criminal schemes.

Mac Wallace's fingerprint was discovered on a box from the sniper's nest. On the day of the assassination, he was identified as a dark-skinned man, possibly Latino, with a tan jacket and horn-framed glasses. He was seen from the sixth floor of the depository as well as fleeing from the depository.

Wallace spoke Spanish, had dark olive skin, black hair, and was often confused as being Cuban or Mexican. He was fit, being a high school and college football player, but in later years became paunchy due to his alcoholism. He wore glasses, which can be seen in the few pictures of him. At the time of the assassination, Wallace wore horn-rimmed glasses and was seen by several people that day in Dealey Plaza.

What is most damaging and convincing about Wallace's involvement in the JFK assassination is that his preserved fingerprint was finally identified in 1998 on a box used to support the rifle in the sniper's nest.

On January 7, 1971, Malcolm Wallace was killed while driving to Pittsburg, Texas. He appeared to have fallen asleep. After leaving the road, he crashed his car. Wallace died of massive head injuries. He was 50 years old.

Billie Sol Estes: Billie Sol Estes, like Johnson's political son, Bobby Baker, was prosecuted by Robert F. Kennedy's Department of Justice because he wanted to ensure Johnson would not be part of the presidential ticket in 1964. RFK's DOJ had had its eyes set on Lyndon Johnson. In 1962, after information came to light that Estes had paid off four Agriculture officials for grain storage contracts, President Kennedy ordered the Justice Department and the FBI to open investigations into Estes' activities and determine if the Secretary of Agriculture had also been "compromised" (he was not). Congress conducted hearings on Estes' business dealings, including some that led to Vice President Johnson. In 1963, Estes was tried and convicted on charges related to the fraudulent ammonia tank mortgages on both federal and state charges and was sentenced to 24 years in prison. Shortly after his release, and after the death of Johnson and his close allies, Billie Sole Estes began to talk about what he knew about Johnson's numerous killings, including the order he gave to kill JFK.

Billie Sol Estes died in his home in DeCordova, Texas on May 14, 2013, at the age of 88.

<u>Edward A. Clark</u>: – Ed Clark was Johnson's personal attorney and fixer. Ed Clark paid bribes, collected illegal contributions, laundered money, and arranged murders with Mac Wallace.

Because he was the attorney-fixer, his involvement is unknown for a very good reason. He used, exploited, and abused the veil of attorney-client privilege to keep his communications protected. He stayed in the shadows, just as he wanted.

Ed Clark had a reputation for obtaining results without leaving any fingerprints. He mastered the use of telephone calls, private, off-the-record meetings, and the attorney-client privilege. He got things done. If you were Governor Jimmy Allred in 1935 and you needed someone to massage a few recalcitrant anti-New Deal state legislators, you called on your chief political adviser, Ed Clark.[158] If you owned a chain of stores and needed to get the Office of Price Administration off your back in 1943, you contacted attorney Ed Clark, who would then use his influence to see that a crony was hired in the OPA's Austin branch. And if you were Lyndon Johnson and you needed any number of things—money from Brown & Root, votes in Duval County, an endorsement from an East Texas newspaper—then Ed Clark was the man to call. From the 1930s through the 1970s, no one in Texas sustained power the way Edward

Clark did. His influence on the lives of Texans was and still is enormous: He spearheaded social policy reforms under the Allred administration, orchestrated the taming of the Texas frontier by Brown & Root, and groomed Lyndon Johnson for the White House.

Ed Clark is mentioned slightly more in Chapters 13 and 14. He was the power broker behind the scenes, just the way he liked it.

Ed Clark died in 1992 at the age of 86.

<u>Bobby Baker</u>: Robert Gene Baker, or Bobby Baker, was an American political adviser to Lyndon B. Johnson and an organizer for the Democratic Party. He became the Senate's Secretary to the Majority Leader.

LBJ often referred to Baker as his son. Baker became extremely powerful, as he knew all sorts of intimate details about members of the Senate, including their sexual proclivities and preferences. Johnson exploited Baker's knowledge to gain an advantage over their vulnerabilities. This knowledge became the reason Johnson was "the Master of the Senate."

Baker died on November 12, 2017, at the age of 89.

<u>Clifton C. Carter</u>: – Cliff Carter first became involved in politics in 1937 when he was a volunteer worker in the Lyndon B. Johnson election campaign. Carter was used to smear political rivals such as Ralph Yarborough. During the Second World War, Carter joined the 36th Infantry Division and served under Captain Edward Clark, Johnson's future fixer. Ed Clark and Cliff Carter became lifelong friends and very loyal to LBJ.

Carter was rewarded by being appointed as U.S. Marshall for the Southern District in 1949. He was confirmed by the Senate in July

1949 and served for five years until 1954. He had no law enforcement experience prior to his appointment.

In January 1957, Carter became head of Johnson's statewide political organization. According to Texas Senator Ralph Yarborough, Carter was Johnson's bagman: "He (Carter) was a very sharp operator, Lyndon could trust him to pick up the money and keep his mouth shut." Carter played an important role in collecting money from Washington lobbyists for Johnson's election campaigns. He also dealt with members of the Suite 8F Group such as George Brown and Herman Brown, of Brown & Root, Jesse H. Jones (Reconstruction Finance Corporation), Gus Wortham (American General Insurance Company) and James Abercrombie (Cameron Iron Works).

In his book, *Lyndon B. Johnson: Master of the Senate*, the historian, Robert A. Caro, claims that cash was collected by Carter, Bobby Baker, Ed Clark, or Walter Jenkins in Texas and then brought to

Johnson in Washington. Caro quotes Clark as saying that Johnson always wanted contributions given outside the office.

Cliff Carter's role in the assassination was multi-layered. He was part of the initial planning of the assassination. He was also allegedly locked in the second-floor offices of the Depository with a perfect view of the assassination and communicated with other kill zone teams. He then went to Parkland Hospital to collect Governor Connally's clothes and had them dry-cleaned. Finally, Carter made a series of calls to Dallas District Attorney Henry Wade, Dallas Police Chief Curry, Captain Fritz, and Texas' Attorney General to inform them that the FBI would be taking over the investigation, that Oswald was the sole suspect, and that any discussions of a conspiracy must cease because it may implicate an international crisis.

Cliff Carter died at age 53 in 1971.

Other Key Assassination Figures:

The remaining key figures are summarized here. Either people with inside information have mentioned them or there is more corroborating evidence concerning their activities and involvements. Those with inside information claim there were about twenty-two assassins and backup assassins and spotters. The backups would be thrown a gun to take it apart and hide it. The backups also played another important role: If the actual shooter was arrested, with gunshot residue, he would not have a gun on him. If the backup shooter was arrested with a gun on him, he would not have any gunshot residue on his hands or face. Others involved included drivers and people that planted evidence, such as the medium-sized jacket found in a parking lot that was tied to Oswald and the wallet that was found at the Tippit murder scene that included Oswald's identification as well as the identification of Oswald's alleged alias, Alek J. Hidell.

Finally, there were co-conspirators dressed as Dallas Police officers at the rear of the TSBD. Two unidentified officers were seen by witnesses at the time of the shooting. These officers were there to safely escort the sixth-floor shooters to their cars. For example, Ruth Anne Martinez and Loy Factor entered one respective car and drove to the Greyhound bus terminal.[159]

David Ferrie: David William Ferrie, or Dave Ferrie, is probably the most interesting and unique characters in this assassination. Later in his life, he suffered from alopecia areata, a skin condition that results in hair loss, usually in patches. David Ferrie was thus easily recognizable and distinguishable from others as he wore a homemade auburn-colored wig and glued-on eye lashes. In his early life, he was a devout Catholic and joined a seminary but left after being declared "emotionally unstable." He then earned his pilot's license and became a masterful pilot, being able to land planes where there were no landing strips. His job as a high school teacher and pilot ended because of his attraction to young boys.

By the late 1950s and early 1960s, Ferrie became more involved with anti-Castro groups and joined right-wing Cuban exile groups. He started doing covert sabotage missions to Cuba to assist in Castro's overthrow. Ferrie also became good friends with Guy Bannister, a former Chicago FBI Special Agent-in-Charge and later a private investigator. Also, an unconfirmed Border Patrol report from February 1962 alleges that Ferrie was the pilot who flew Carlos Marcello back into the United States from Guatemala after he had been deported in April 1961. Finally, Dave Ferrie worked with Dr. Alton Ochsner and Dr. Mary Sherman in a CIA secret project to kill Castro. This involved creating the means to ensure Castro developed cancer.

Dave Ferrie's alleged role in the assassination was to fly Lee Harvey Oswald from Houston to Mexico after the assassination. Oswald was supposed to be driven to Redbird Airport wearing a police officer's uniform and then board a plane that would take him from Dallas to Houston. In Houston, he would meet up with Dave Ferrie and he would be flown to Mexico. Oswald would then be killed in Mexico, if he made it that far, where there would be significantly less police presence.

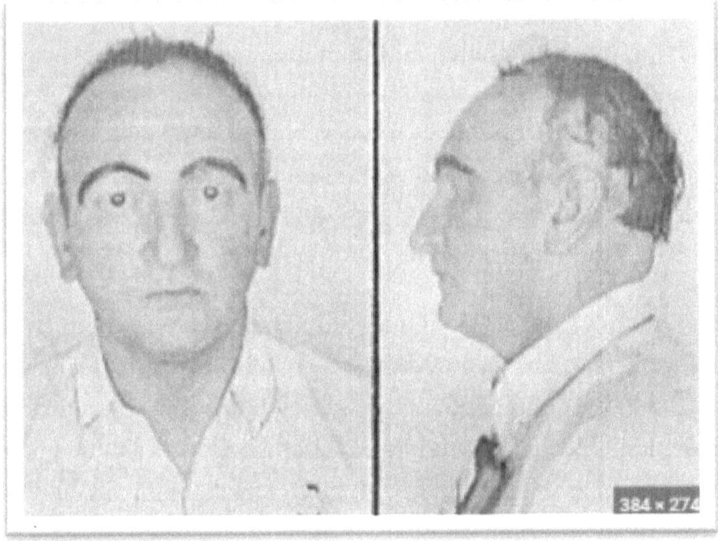

Dave Ferrie and two other people made a marathon run from New Orleans to Dallas, driving through torrential rain and thunderstorms.[160] This 400-mile trek was made on the night of the assassination, and Ferrie arrived at an isolated ice-rink in Houston at 3:15am Saturday morning. Ferrie later told New Orleans District Attorney, Jim Garrison, that the purpose of the trip was to learn about the ice-skating business, but when Ferrie arrived at the ice-skating rink, he never asked the manager any questions about the business but instead spent most of his time nervously on the phone. His task of flying Oswald to Mexico was unnecessary because Oswald was by then in police custody.

Dave Ferrie died of a cerebral hemorrhage on February 22, 1967. He was 48 years old. Many claim his death was a murder or suicide, but the official cause of death was determined to be natural, and I believe it was natural. The toxicology report showed no organic or inorganic substances in Ferrie's body.[161] He had a congenital intracranial aneurysm that ruptured, and he had complained of severe headaches before dying. His death, while untimely, was not suspicious.

<u>Frank Anthony Sturgis</u>: also known as Frank Angelo Firoini.[162] I believe Frank Sturgis had looser lips than the many CIA operatives he worked with and would have eventually told everything he knew about the JFK assassination if he had been pressed harder.

Sturgis served in the Marines and the Naval Reserves. Ultimately, Sturgis went to Cuba and became Castro's Minister for Games of Chance, meaning Frank Sturgis oversaw gambling activities in Castro's Cuba. He then started working for the CIA as an informant. Sturgis also became involved in running guns to Cuba, along with mobster Santo Trafficante, and not surprisingly, was arrested for illegal possession of arms but released without charge. In his work as Cuba's Minister for Games of Chance, Sturgis met Lewis McWillie, Trafficante's man in Cuba, and the manager of the Tropicana Casino who, by his own testimony, was a known acquaintance of Jack Ruby. Castro shut down all gambling operations in 1960, and that is when Sturgis fled Cuba because allegations were rampant that Sturgis was a CIA spy.

Frank Sturgis was also a Watergate burglar. He admitted under oath before the House Select Committee on Assassinations that he had been asked to conduct a domestic assassination in the United States by CIA Agent Bernard Barker, another Watergate burglar.[163] He also stated that the CIA provided him funds to maintain and fly his plane, and those funds came from E. Howard Hunt. He also claimed that the CIA paid him to conduct over one hundred covert missions into Cuba and that he had been paid $5,000 per mission.

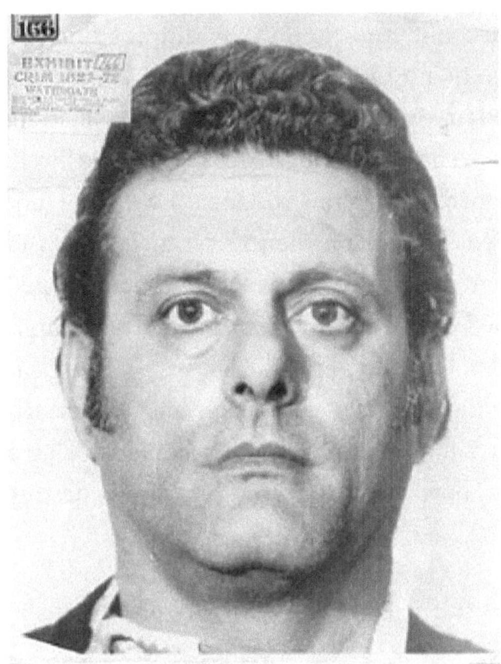

In 1977, Marita Lorenz, Castro's former girlfriend, told Paul Meskil of the New York Daily News that she met Lee Harvey Oswald in the fall of 1963 at an Operation 40 safe house in the Little Havana section of Miami.[164] According to Lorenz, she met him again before the Kennedy assassination in 1963 in the house of Orlando Bosch, with Frank Sturgis, Pedro Luis Díaz Lanz, and two other Cubans present. She said that the men studied Dallas street maps and that she suspected they were planning on raiding an arsenal. Lorenz stated that she joined the men traveling to Dallas in two cars and carrying "rifles and scopes" but flew back to Miami the day after they arrived because she did not want to be involved. Lorenz also stated that E. Howard Hunt showed up in Dallas to pay people off in envelopes stuffed with cash. Finally, Lorenz claims that after the assassination, Sturgis told her that he had had been involved in the John F. Kennedy assassination.

Sturgis denied Lorenz's account, and the HSCA did not find her credible. I do. I find little or no motive for Lorenz to lie. Others testified to seeing E. Howard Hunt on the day of the assassination, and Sturgis himself is on record as stating that he was paid by E. Howard Hunt for his numerous missions to Cuba. I believe Hunt was in Dallas precisely to pay key co-conspirators for their work and to ensure the Big Event went as planned. Hunt, of course, implicated Sturgis during his deathbed confession. Others have placed Sturgis on the grassy knoll as a shooter dressed in a business suit. Sturgis is later seen in the Dallas police precinct with a suit and fedora hat. Finally, gun running was a common thing with the people associated with Sturgis, either to support Castro's Revolution or to destroy Coastro's new Communist Cuba.

Frank Sturgis died in 1993 at the age of 68.

General Edward Geary Lansdale: General Lansdale was a United States Air Force officer until retiring in 1963 as a major general before continuing his work with the Central Intelligence Agency (CIA). Lansdale was a pioneer in clandestine operations and psychological warfare. In the early 1950s, Lansdale played a significant role in suppressing the Huk insurgency in the Philippines. In 1954, he moved to Saigon and started the Saigon Military Mission, a covert intelligence operation created to sow dissension in North Vietnam. Lansdale believed the United States could win guerrilla wars by studying the enemy's psychology, an approach that won the approval of the presidential administrations of both Kennedy and Johnson.

Interestingly, Lansdale argued against the overthrow of then South Vietnamese President Ngo Dinh Diem. He told Robert McNamara that: "There's a constitution in place... Please don't destroy that when you're trying to change the government. Remember there's a vice president (Nguyen Ngoc Tho) who's been elected and is now holding office. If anything happens to the president, he should replace him. Try to keep something sustained." In 2003, it was revealed that President Kennedy and top U.S. officials sought the November 1, 1963, coup against Diem apparently without considering the physical consequences for Diem personally. He was murdered the

following day.[165]

It was Lansdale's opposition to any coup or plot against South Vietnam that got him removed from office. The pressure to remove Lansdale came from General Curtis LeMay, General Victor Krulak and other senior members of the military. As a result, it was decided to abolish his post as assistant to the Secretary of Defense. He was awarded the Distinguished Service Medal for his counter-insurgency work and became consultant to the Food for Peace program.

This picture captures the three tramps, walking toward the camera, and General Landsdale, walking away from the camera with the arrow pointing to him. The first "tramp" is Charles Harrelson followed by Richard Montoya (a.k.a. Charles Rogers). The last tramp is Chauncey M. Holt and he can be barely seen here because Montoya is in front of him.

General Lansdale was unequivocally identified by James Files and Fletcher Prouty in Dealey Plaza on the day of the assassination. Files refers to Lansdale as the groundskeeper, verifying everyone's position in the kill zones, and is captured in the photo above along with the three tramps that were arrested and later released. Those three tramps were Chauncy Marvin Holt, Charles Rogers, and Charles Harrelson (Woody Harrelson's father).

Bernard L. Barker: Barker is another Watergate burglar. He was born in Havana, Cuba, on March 17, 1917. His father's family originally came from Russia. At a young age, Barker became involved in politics. He was involved in the Bay of Pigs invasion. He was on the grassy knoll pretending to be a Secret Service Agent and thwarting eyewitnesses and Dallas police officers that came to see where the shots came from. He was positively identified by Sheriff Deputy Seymour Weitzman years after the assassination.

Ruth Paine: Ruth Paine "babysat"[ix] Marina Oswald and played a key role as a witness before the WC in supporting the narrative that Oswald was the lone gunman and had carried his rifle to the depository on the morning of the assassination in a long bag.

Ruth Paine's most damaging role was ordering and picking up the rifle that was used to implicate Oswald, and her contributing role was to provide evidence and testimony of Oswald's guilt, all at the behest of the CIA. I remain hopeful that Ruth Paine's will unburden herself and that her deathbed confession will shed more light on the truth.

George H.W. Bush: George H.W. Bush is listed under "other" assassination figures because I have been unable to confirm whether he worked for the CIA as an operative (*i.e.,* a full-time employee of the CIA with an official cover), which is possible, or worked for a CIA-front company that he owned, Zapata Oil, as a CIA asset. George H.W. Bush was unequivocally part of the CIA in 1963, either as an agent or operative or even possibly as a supervisor. He was also unequivocally involved with the training of Cuban exiles for sabotage and assassination attempts against Castro. In fact, the Bay of Pigs internal operation name was Operation Zapata, which is the name of Bush's oil-drilling companies. He was unequivocally in Dallas on the day of the assassination. He later, of course, became the CIA Director under President Ford. Many assert he was in Dealey Plaza, and some even assert that his role was to supervise Charles Nicoletti, James Braden, and John Roselli in the Dal-Tex building.

In the picture above, a man resembling George H.W. Bush is seen leaning against the wall of the Texas School Book Depository as it appeared in 1963. George H.W. Bush claims that he could not remember where he was on this unforgettable day. Draw your own conclusion as to what, if any, his involvement may have been.. but keep in mind that several other senior CIA members were seen in and around Dealey Plaza that day. Were some there as spectators, or did they have a hand in the assassination?

James Braden: James Braden, or Eugene Hale Brading, had along criminal history of over 35 arrests. On November 21, 1963, Braden arrived in Dallas with a man named Morgan Brown. They stayed in Suite 301 of the Cabana Motel. Later that day, Braden visited the offices of Texas oil billionaire H. L. Hunt. It is believed that Jack Ruby was in those offices at the same time as Braden. He was actually arrested on the day of the assassination by the Dallas Sheriff's office because he was a stranger acting suspiciously in the secure Dal-Tex building. He was later released. Braden returned to his room at the

Cabana Motel. It was later established that Jack Ruby visited the

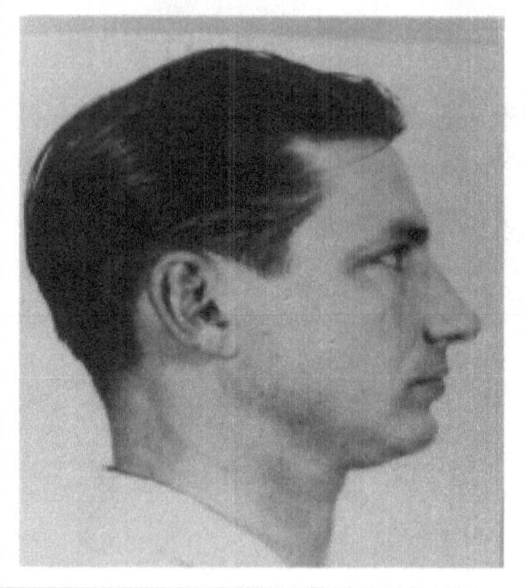

James (Jim) Braden or Eugene Hale Brading allegedly broke into the second floor of the Dal-Tex building and allowed Charles Nicoletti and John Roselli to enter so they may shoot at the President.

motel around midnight.

Braden was also allegedly present in Los Angeles during the assassination of Robert Kennedy.

Captain W.R. Westbrook: Westbrook plays a larger role in this murder-conspiracy than most people imagine. He was a member of the ultra-right conservative group, "Fans of Walker," an offshoot of the John Birch Society. Both of these groups held hatred for Kennedy. At the time of Kennedy's assassination, Westbrook was in charge of personnel of the Dallas Police Department. He effectively knew every officer, but his movements after the assassination are unusual, especially for someone in charge of personnel. He was not in charge or robbery or homicide, but he nevertheless appeared at the right moment when he searched the bus Oswald was on, Tippit was killed, and when Oswald was arrested at the Texas Theater.

His role here was to kill Oswald when he found him on a city bus brandishing a revolver, but Oswald deboarded the bus before Westbrook arrived. Westbrook was also given a wallet by an unknown person at the Tippit crime scene. This wallet would link Oswald to the alias Alek J. Hidell, which was allegedly used to order the rifle and revolver purchased through the mail. Westbrook failed to call in the identities of the names inside the wallet over his radio so that other officers could be informed as Oswald was not arrested yet, failed to write a report finding the wallet, and failed to turn the wallet over to the Identification Bureau, the Homicide Department, or anyone else at DPD headquarters. No one knows what happened to the wallet. Finally, Westbrook also retrieved the wrong-sized jacket (medium) that was used by Oswald's double when he killed Tippit. An unknown person shouted "Look! There's a jacket under the car." The person who "found" the wallet and the person who pointed out the jacket were never identified even though this case dealt with the murder of a fellow officer, which arguably should have been of greater urgency to the Dallas Police Department than JFK's assassination at that point in time.

Only minutes after Captain Fritz started interrogating Oswald, another officer began to write an incident report explaining how Oswald sustained injuries at the Texas Theater. Captain Westbrook came in a few minutes later and informed the officer that the suspect had admitted to being a communist; had previously been in the Marine Corps; had a dishonorable discharge; had been to Russia; and had some trouble with the police in New Orleans for passing out pro-Castro literature.[166] No one, including Captain Fritz, knew this information, as it was not in the public domain.

Interestingly, in 1966, Westbrook took early retirement from the Dallas Police Department and went to South Vietnam, where he worked for the Secret Police, which at the time was controlled by the CIA.[167]

<u>Reserve Sergeant Kenneth H. Croy</u>: On the day of the assassination, Croy approached fellow officers at the TSBD and allegedly asked if they need help. He said they told him no. The President of the United States had just been shot, and the Dallas Police Department had called in all reserve officers for this event, yet Croy was allegedly told he was not needed at the scene of the crime. He then said he was having lunch with his estranged wife.

After allegedly being told his services were not needed, he was the very first officer to arrive after Tippit's shooting and either found a wallet or was given a wallet by an eyewitness. If he was given a wallet by an eyewitness, Sgt. Croy never obtained this eyewitness' name. If he found it, he planted it. In that fortuitously discovered wallet were Oswald's identification and a Select Service card with the name of Oswald's alleged alias, Alek J. Hidell. A fellow officer had just been killed. A wallet was found at the scene with two identifications. What happened next, or rather what did *not* happen next defies the most basic investigative intuition and protocol. No one called in the names or description of the identifications on the police radio to alert other officers that were undoubtedly on a manhunt for Tippit's killer. The wallet was held for at least half an hour.

Sergeant Croy was allegedly one of two officers that boarded the bus Oswald sat in for two blocks and searched all the passengers. Again, this was the only bus searched after the assassination.

<u>Certain TSBD Employees</u>:

Some assert that certain TSBD depository employees also played a role in the conspiracy. Roy Truly, a former FBI agent, may have known that Oswald was an intelligence plant. Oswald's supervisor,

Bill Shelley,[168] allegedly told Oswald to go home and then reported him missing. Billy Nolan and Bill Shelley were seen by Officer Baker on the first floor just after the last shots, and one of them was standing near the electrical panel. That is when the lights went out and the freight elevators stopped working, so Truly and Baker took the northwest wooden stairs. The exact whereabouts of Billy Lovelady Nolan and Bill Shelley just after the shooting are conflicting and controverted even by their own testimonies.[169]

<u>Embittered Cuban Exiles</u>:

After the Bay of Pigs Invasion, many CIA-trained Cuban exiles were angry at JFK because he did not approve the use of air support, and the invasion was a massive failure and embarrassment. Despite JFK's apology to the brave Cuban exiles that attempted to retake their island, many held rancor, bitterness, and hatred toward Kennedy even though Kennedy, in reality, was probably their strongest ally in defeating Castro's Cuba. In Chapter 8, I will discuss the top-secret Cuban Palace coup scheduled for December 1, 1963. For now, I mention Cuban exiles that have long been suspected of being involved in the JFK assassination.

Their involvement can vary from pretending to be Dallas police officers (*e.g.,* two unidentified Dallas police officer were seen at the rear of the TSBD immediately after the shooting, probably to assist the sixth-floor assassins in escaping), to delivering guns (*e.g.,* Marita Lorenz claims several of these men, who had travelled from Miami to Dallas before the assassination, were in a hotel with numerous guns and ammunition and had gone over the plan to kill JFK), to planting evidence (*e.g.,* a wallet and jacket that were tied to Oswald and were used to connect him to the Tippit murder and the Mannlicher Carcano rifle were allegedly given to or identified by unknown persons), and driving (*e.g.,* the driver of the Nash Rambler was described as Latin-looking, and he drove Mac Wallace, Frank Sturgis, among others, away from the crime scene).

<u>Antonio Veciana</u>: Antonio Veciana was a Cuban accountant opposed to Fidel Castro. He established the assassination and sabotage group known as Alpha-66 after Castro gained power. This group would be funded almost entirely by the CIA. Many people forget that the majority of Cubans that fled Cuba after Castro took over were not wealthy, yet they were generous towards groups like

Alpha 66. Alpha 66, however, did not have a public donation campaign. Once private funding dried up, such groups were rendered largely impotent. The CIA, however, paid handsomely, and this relationship, as with many other anti-Castro groups, became a relationship dependent on the CIA's generosity. The CIA's budget at this time was secret, and the CIA had developed an expertise of hiding sources of money like any other professional money launderer. So, the CIA paid these anti-Castro groups even when the Kennedy brothers asked them to cease all sabotage and assassination attempts, particularly during the tense and sensitive negotiations during the Cuban Missile Crisis and shortly thereafter.

Sabotage attempts consisted of destroying Soviet ships near Cuba. Other efforts included arming Cuban anti-Castro fighters in Cuba with illegally shipped guns.

Orlando Bosch Avila: Bosch was a member of Operation 40 and, according to Marita Lorenz, was seen with Frank Sturgis in Dallas when Kennedy was assassinated. Bosch is suspected of being the man in the blue shirt with the officer's cap with his hand raised and his hand in a fist signaling the President's limousine to slow down.

<u>Eladio del Valle</u>: Del Valle moved to Florida where he was active in the Free Cuba Committee, another anti-Castro group. He also worked for Santo Trafficante and, with his friend, David Ferrie, was involved in fire-bombing sugar fields in Cuba.

During his investigation into the assassination of John F. Kennedy case, Jim Garrison wanted to interview Eladio del Valle to obtain information against Clay Shaw, however, he was unable to find him.

Eladio del Valle was murdered on February 22, 1967. Police reported that he had been tortured and then shot in the heart at point-blank range, and his skull split open with an axe. His murder has never been solved. Eladio del Valle's government files are still classified and held back from the public.

<u>Rafael "Chi Chi" Quintero</u>: Quintero established the Movement for the Recovery of the Revolution (MRR Party). Quintero was allegedly a member of Operation 40. One member, Frank Sturgis, claimed that "this assassination group would, upon orders naturally, assassinate either members of the military or the political parties of the foreign country that you were going to infiltrate, and if necessary, some of your own members who were suspected of being foreign agents. We were concentrating strictly in Cuba at that particular time."

Quintero is alleged to have been a sharpshooter with Charles Nicoletti in the Dal-Tex building.

<u>Nestor Tony Izquierdo</u>: Nestor 'Tony' Izquierdo was born in the Matanzas Province in Cuba in 1936. He was the son of Camilo Izquierdo and Josefina Diaz and a devoted Roman Catholic. As a young man, Nestor worked with his father in a construction business.

In 1959, Manuel Artime emerged as a leading anti-Communist. He worked closely with the Catholic University Association (CUA). Later that year he moved to the Manzanillo region where he joined up with Carlos Prio and Tony Varona. Along with Huber Matos, they planned a counter-revolution. Izquierdo joined Artime's Rural Commandos. In 1960, Izquierdo left Cuba and entered the United States via Mexico. Along with Manuel Artime, Tony Varona, Rafael Quintero, Aureliano Arango and Jose Cardona, he established the Movement for the Recovery of the Revolution (MRR Party).

It is believed that Nestor Izquierdo was involved in the assassination of John F. Kennedy. Independently of each other, James Richards and Gerry Hemming have claimed that Izquierdo was involved with the events in Dealey Plaza, specifically, as a spotter in the Dal-Tex building.

Guillermo Novo: Guillermo Novo was born in Cuba. An opponent of Fidel Castro, Novo moved to the United States where he associated with figures such as Orlando Bosch and Luis Posada. While living in America, Novo did a variety of jobs including doorman and used car salesman.

According to Marita Lorenz, Novo became involved with Operation 40, a CIA assassination squad. Lorenz pointed out that a few days before the assassination of John F. Kennedy, a group including Novo, Orlando Bosch, Frank Sturgis, Ignacio Novo, and Pedro Diaz Lanz, traveled to Dallas. She also claimed that he was at a motel in Dallas when Kennedy's murder was planned.

Pedro Luis Díaz Lanz: By April 1960, Diaz Lanz was recruited by the CIA and became a member of Operation 40. On May 27, 1960, the Miami Herald published a list of names of pilots who were placed on a U.S. Government 'blacklist,' thereby prohibiting them from flying to Cuba; on that list was Pedro Luis Díaz Lanz.

Government records establish Díaz-Lanz's numerous covert sabotage trips to Cuba. He is mentioned in numerous circles of being involved in the JFK assassination, but the role he may have played is unknown.

Díaz Lanz committed suicide by a gunshot wound to the chest in 2008 at the age of 81 after years of poverty and depression.

<u>Herminio Díaz Garcia</u>: Díaz Garcia was born in Cuba in 1923. He was a member of the Cuban Restaurant Workers Union and worked as a cashier at the Hotel Habana-Rivera. Later he became involved in illegal activities and eventually became a bodyguard for Santos Trafficante when Trafficante had significant gambling connections in Cuba. Díaz Garcia killed Pipi Hernandez in 1948 at the Cuban Consulate in Mexico. In 1957, he was involved with an assassination attempt against President Jose Figures of Costa Rica.

Díaz Garcia moved to the United States in July 1963, where he worked for Tony Varona. Some researchers believe that Díaz Garcia was one of the gunmen who killed John F. Kennedy.

In December 1963, Díaz Garcia was involved in an unsuccessful attempt to assassinate Fidel Castro. He was also involved in providing weapons to anti-Castro groups. Díaz Garcia was killed on a mission at Monte Barreto in the Miramar district of Cuba on May 29, 1966. Herminio Díaz Garcia is suspected of being a Dealey Plaza shooter disguised as a floor installer.

<u>Emilio Santana Galindo</u>: Galindo worked as a CIA asset from December 1960 until October 1963 in the JMWAVE operation. He worked as a guide for an infiltration team. On the day of JFK's assassination, he worked with Herminio Díaz Garcia disguised as a floor installer in the TSBD.

Chapter 6: Key Mafia Figures

In reading extensively about the JFK assassination, I have found many names mentioned as to who was likely responsible for planning the murder, for committing the murder, and for covering it up, and an even more exhaustive list of people possibly involved in smaller roles. It is a daunting task to sort out what people said and what weight to give their statements. Additionally, because of compartmentalization, some people were unwitting and unknowing in their participation, such as the doctors and medical staff that conducted the first unofficial autopsy to make it appear, rather unconvincingly, that JFK had been shot from the rear and the rear only. Even those responsible for actively participating in the assassination may not have known the names of the others also actively involved, as is often the case with any conspiracy. In that regard, I have consolidated and summarized the most critical and important players in this conspiracy, which serves two purposes. First, it provides an overview of the essential actors involved so that you can get quickly up to speed about them. Much about what these characters did or how they died have faded away into the ether, so this chapter may refresh your memory in that regard. Second, it highlights how dangerous it was to have been associated with this conspiracy or to have known about it. For example, Sam Giancana was killed by someone he knew because he let him in his house. Mafia murder contracts are often given to people that know their victims because it allows them to get close to the victim for a successful job. In fact, Jack Ruby knew Lee Harvey Oswald and was able to get close to him for that one fatal shot. Likewise, Charles Nicoletti was shot in the back of his head as he sat in the driver's seat of his car by someone he knew, someone he trusted enough to sit behind him in his own car.

Finally, these were real people. My summaries of them are not in any way fantastical, exaggerated, or embellished. They really existed and, I submit, did the things I say they did, which is nothing less than shocking. For purposes of simplicity, here are key figures in the assassination, as well as others that deserve honorable mention with photos and a short caption.

Did the CIA Manipulate the Mafia or did the Mafia Manipulate the CIA?

Below are the more notorious Mafia figures involved in this conspiracy. Included in this group, first and foremost, is Jack Ruby. While Ruby was considered a low-level Mafia figure, he was the lynchpin to other more dangerous and notorious Mafia leaders, such as Santo Trafficante Jr., John Roselli, and Carlos Marcello. Also included as a key Mafia figure is James Files. Files's book is called *"Primary Target: JFK—How the CIA Used the Chicago Mob to Kill the President."* In his book, *"Ultimate Sacrifice,"* Lamar Waldron concluded that it was the mob's infiltration of the CIA's operations relating to Cuba (*e.g.,* sabotage efforts, assassination attempts, disinformation campaigns, etc.) that led to JFK's death. According to Waldron, what the Mafia learned from the CIA as it related to Cuba, they applied in Dealey Plaza, and because JFK and Bobby Kennedy insisted that the CIA discontinue working with the Mafia, there had to be a cover up when JFK was killed. So, what is true: that the Mafia infiltrated and manipulated the CIA or, as James Files claims, the CIA manipulated the Mafia? While Sam Giancana said the Mafia and the CIA were two sides of the same coin, the CIA had the larger hand in the assassination and subsequent cover up.

Chauncey Holt, a notorious criminal that worked for Meyer Lansky, the mob's accountant, stated that the relationship between the Mafia and the CIA was incestuous. I assert, it was LBJ that first expressed the desire to kill Kennedy, but he left the details – the who, what, where, and why – to others.

Jack Ruby: Jacob Leon Rubenstein or Jack Ruby started his "career" with the Chicago Outfit before moving to Dallas. He was an aggressive promoter with very little business sense. He poorly managed "the Carousel Club," a burlesque strip joint, with many of his dancers and employees stealing from him. Practically speaking, however, the Carousel Club was owned by Carlos Marcello, the New Orleans Godfather (see below). Ruby was also known to appear at accident and crime scenes throughout Dallas. He also frequented the Dallas police precinct and several newspaper outlets, where he would give out free club passes to police and newspapermen. Ruby would bring donuts and coffee to the Dallas precinct and would walk around the building as if he owned it. He was in the perfect position to recruit corrupt Dallas Police Officers in this conspiracy.

Jack Ruby's CIA/Mafia missions were numerous and prolific, yet the WC concluded that it could find no ties between the Mafia and Ruby. Ruby was sent on several missions to Cuba even after it was illegal for US citizens to visit the island, in order to assist with the release of Santo Trafficante (see below) from a Cuban prison. Ruby also delivered guns and surplus Jeeps to Castro and helped Jimmy Hoffa finalize a deal to sell Castro planes.[170]

Ruby was also heavily in debt. He owed the IRS about $40,000 in back taxes and owed his Mafia associates about $25,000 because of his poor management of the Carousel Club, and as he was stealing from Carlos Marcello directly, Ruby needed money desperately. His debt would be about $391,000 to the IRS and $244,000 to the Mafia in today's money.

Early in the week of the assassination, Ruby informed his tax attorney, who was negotiating a reduced settlement with the IRS, that he would soon have the money from associates.

On the day of the assassination, Ruby was seen at Dealey Plaza before and during the assassination.

Ruby was also seen at the Texas Theater by theater patron, George J. Applin. Applin, one of only two theater patrons questioned by the Warren Commission, told the Commission he was watching the movie when the lights came on and a policeman with a rifle or shotgun began moving down his aisle.[171] Applin said he was sitting in the downstairs middle aisle about six rows from the back when the commotion began. He moved down the aisle to ask what was going on, when a policeman (apparently McDonald) passed him moving toward the rear. Applin then witnessed Oswald's arrest. At the close of his Warren Commission testimony, Applin said: "But, there is one thing puzzling me . . . and I don't even know if it has any bearing on the case, but there was one guy sitting in the back row right where I was standing at, and I said to him, I said, 'Buddy, you'd better move. There is a gun.' And he says—just sat there. He was back like this. Just like this. Just watching. . . . I don't think he could have seen the show. Just sitting there like this, just looking at me." Applin told House Select Committee on Assassinations attorney, Joseph Ball, twice he didn't know the man, but in 1979, he told a news reporter that two days later, following the Oswald slaying, he recognized the man as Jack Ruby.[172] Applin told the Dallas Morning News: "At the time the Warren Commission had me down there at the Post Office in Dallas to get my statement, I was afraid to give it. I gave everything up to the point of what I gave the police there in town. . . . I'm a pretty nervous guy anyway because I'll tell you what: After I saw that magazine where all those people they said were connected with some of this had come up dead, it just kind of made me keep a low profile. . . . [Jack] Ruby was sitting down, just watching them. And, when Oswald pulled the gun and snapped it at [McDonald's] head and missed and the darn thing wouldn't fire, that's when I tapped him on the shoulder and told him he had better move because those guns were waving around. He just turned around and looked at me. Then he turned around and started watching them."

Jack Ruby was also seen around 1:30pm at Parkland Hospital while President Kennedy and Governor Connally received treatment for their injuries.[173]

Two days after President Kennedy's assassination, Ruby killed Lee Harvey Oswald in front of numerous national and international news networks and Dallas police officers. The news media were there to capture the transfer of Lee Harvey Oswald from the Dallas Police precinct to a more secure location. Upon seeing Ruby kill Oswald, Richard Nixon recognized Ruby as a Johnson associate.

The psychologist that interviewed Ruby while he was in custody noted Ruby's very unusual behavior and stated that Ruby was more worried about the government finding out about what he did in Cuba than he was about the murder of Oswald. Why? Because what he did in Cuba was directly tied to the Mafia, and if the Mafia was clearly implicated in this conspiracy, it would then have to silence Ruby.

James Files: James Files is also a former Chicago "Outfit" hitman and military intelligence operative. He worked under Sam Giancana and Tony Accardo. According to Files, he drove trucks, managed a front restaurant business, loan-sharked, hijacked semi-trucks, sold stolen cars, and was a contract murderer, earner, enforcer and soldier for the Chicago outfit.[174] Yet, despite these ominous and risky jobs, Files said the work he did for the CIA was even darker.[175] He has confessed to being the grassy knoll shooter that made the fatal shot that entered just above Kennedy's right temple. He also implicated Charles Nicoletti and Johnny Roselli as being shooters from the Dal-Tex building, the building adjacent to the depository. Files claims he was the *only* shooter on the grassy knoll. I am not convinced Files was the *only* shooter on the grassy knoll as he claims. Why? Because he received instructions from the Mafia and because of the use of compartmentalization by both the Mafia and the CIA. Compartmentalization meant he only knew what he needed to know and he would not have access to information beyond his need to know. The purpose of compartmentalization is to avoid having a co-conspirator having knowledge of who and what other co-conspirators were doing, thus making it more difficult to difficult to prosecute as a conspiracy and, in the case of the CIA, allowing the asset to complete his or her tasks without any additional worries about other aspects of the operation.

According to James Files, this photo was taken by Lee Harvey Oswald on November 22, 1963, in James Files' motel room. James Files claims that he and Oswald spent a few days in Dallas together doing reconnaissance for "The Big Event."

James Files in 1994 while in prison serving a 50-year sentence for the murders of two policemen. At this time, Files confesses to being the grassy knoll shooter.

<u>Charles Nicoletti</u>: "Chuckie" or Charles Nicoletti was another Chicago Outfit member. He became a well-regarded contract killer. He also worked with the CIA in plots to overthrow the Castro government. According to James Files, Nicoletti was also part of the abort team and part of the mafia hit team to assassinate Kennedy on November 22, 1963.

On March 29, 1977, Nicoletti had been shot three times in the back of the head as he sat in his car. He was scheduled to appear before the House Select Committee on Assassinations.

John Roselli: John Roselli was a Chicago mobster also known as "Handsome Johnny." Roselli helped organize control of Hollywood and Las Vegas by the Chicago outfit. His birth name was Filippo Sacco. For many years, Roselli worked as a CIA operative assisting in numerous covert operations, including the training of Cuban exiles for the Bay of Pigs invasion, assassination attempts of Fidel Castro, and sabotage against the Castro regime. John Roselli was so pivotal and prolific in CIA-led operations that he was given his own cover: "Colonel John Rawlston." He was part of the Mafia hit team in Dealey Plaza on November 22, 1963, and also part of an abort team. Roselli claims he was hiding in an overflow drain on Elm Street when he fired at President Kennedy.[176] James Files, however, claims Roselli and Charles Nicoletti were in the Dal-Tex building adjacent to the Texas School Book Depository.

In 1975, Roselli testified three times for the Church Committee, one of numerous Congressional committees investigating government misconduct in intelligence and assassination attempts. Roselli was asked what he knew about any conspiracy to kill President Kennedy. He was due to appear for a fourth session, with the JFK assassination as the main topic, when he went missing on July 28, 1976. Two days prior to his disappearance, he had dinner with Santo Trafficante in Ft. Lauderdale.

The FBI investigated the disappearance, and on August 9, 1976, Roselli's decomposing body, which was cut in half, was found in a 55-gallon drum near the waters off of Miami. He died of asphyxiation, and many suspect he was killed by underworld figures. Roselli's car was found in the parking lot of Miami International Airport. Many suspect Trafficante ordered the hit on Roselli.

<u>Sam Giancana</u>: Sam "Momo" or "Mooney" Giancana was the boss of the Chicago Outfit from about 1957 to 1966. Joe Kennedy, President Kennedy's father, who was also involved with organized crime from his days as a bootlegger during Prohibition, asked Giancana and his Mafia team to assist his son win the 1960 Presidential campaign with dubious votes, and Giancana happily complied. President Kennedy won the presidency in 1960 by the narrowest of margins and with great help from the Chicago Outfit as well as Mafia leaders from other parts of the county. Like other members of the American Mafia, Giancana was also involved with CIA operations. He hoped that his help getting President Kennedy into the White House with fraudulent votes and his help with CIA operations against the Castro government would result in the Department of Justice giving him and his outfit a pass on his illegal activities. He was wrong.

Giancana and President Kennedy also shared a girlfriend by the name of Judith Exner Campbell and counted on her and others, like Frank Sinatra, to be messengers of sensitive information between the President and the underworld. These messengers also transported money disguised as campaign contributions and sensitive documents concerning attempts to assassinate Fidel Castro. FBI Director Hoover was aware of the sexual relationship between Campbell and

JFK, but Hoover kept quiet about it because the wiretaps and surveillance against the Mafia and Judith Campbell were illegal.[177] Despite Giancana's assistance to Kennedy and his administration, the Department of Justice zealously investigated and surveilled Giancana and his organization. The heat from the Department of Justice was so intense that Giancana fled to Mexico for six years. Giancana ultimately was deported from Mexico to the United States in   1974.

In June 1975, Giancana's house was being surveilled 24-hours a day by the FBI, the CIA, and the Oak Park Police Department. According to Giancana's daughter, their cars were there for several months. Whenever they took breaks, only one car would leave while the others stayed in place. On the night of June 19, 1975, however, all surveillance vehicles left for about 15 minutes. It was just enough time for a gunman to enter Giancana's home and shoot him seven times in the back of the head with a silenced .22 caliber gun. The bullets ripped through Giancana's throat and mouth. Many believe the hit was ordered because Giancana was about to speak to US Senate Select Committee members – a classic *Cosa Nostra* symbolic killing for squealing.[178] Giancana was scheduled to appear to give testimony about CIA and Mafia collusion before the Committee.

Many suspect Roselli killed him and that Trafficante ordered the hit. The gun, found nearby, was traced to a gun dealer in Miami, Fl.[179]

Most relevant to the JFK assassination, Johnny Roselli claims that Sam Giancana told him that the plot to kill Kennedy was planned by him, Sam Giancana, with Trafficante and Marcello. Additionally, John Roselli, Charles Nicoletti, and James Files were all part of the Chicago Outfit and were involved in the assassination based on order from Sam Giancana. They were all there in Dealey Plaza that day.

Jimmy Hoffa: James Riddle Hoffa was a labor union leader. He was president of the International Brotherhood of Teamsters and was largely responsible for the growth of union membership throughout his career. He was also heavily associated with organized crime. Hoffa used organized crime to encourage union membership through the use of violence, extortion, and sabotage and to dissuade other unions from taking power and influence from his union. Hoffa's access to hundreds of millions of dollars in union funds was used to provide illegal loans to organized crime, which were used by organized crime mostly for the construction of Las Vegas casinos and hotels. Following his re-election as Teamster Union president in 1961, Hoffa worked to expand the union. In 1964, he succeeded in bringing virtually all over-the-road truck drivers in North America under a single National Master Freight Agreement, which may have been his biggest achievement in a lifetime of union activity.[180] Organized crime helped Hoffa expand his power and influence. Hoffa, in short, was an extremely powerful man with easy access to   hundreds   of   millions   of   dollars.

Hoffa's role in the assassination of Kennedy came in the form of money to pay off the assassins and conspirators that ultimately were active in Dealey Plaza on November 22, 1963. Hoffa, like so many other members of organized crime, hated RFK because of RFK's war on organized crime. Hoffa was ultimately convicted of fraud and bribery and began serving his 13-year sentence in 1967. Before entering prison, Hoffa named Frank Fitzsimmons as acting or caretaker president of the Teamsters. While in prison, Hoffa resigned as union president. In 1971, President Nixon commuted Hoffa's sentence to time served. Nixon's pardon was conditioned on Hoffa not engaging in union activities until 1980.

Once released, Hoffa expected Fitzsimmons to relinquish his duties and return Hoffa to union president. Fitzsimmons refused. Hoffa threatened to inform authorities of the millions of dollars in illegal loans he made to his mobster friends. On July 30, 1975, Hoffa disappeared. His disappearance is attributed directly to organized crime. Here again, the people responsible for Hoffa's disappearance knew Hoffa personally – a classic organized crime *modus operandi*. Most states presume the death of missing persons after seven years and allow a death certificate to be issued after such time. Hoffa was declared legally dead in 1982. The FBI continues to have an open investigation concerning Hoffa's disappearance. Many suspect Anthony Provenzano or "Tony Pro," an American mobster who was a powerful caporegime in the Genovese crime family, ordered Hoffa's hit in order to prevent Hoffa from speaking to authorities about the loans he made to the Mafia. A caporegime, or "capo," is a senior member of an organized crime family with his own crew of enforcers or soldiers.

Carlos Marcello: Born Calogero Minacore, Marcello was, at all relevant times, the Godfather of the New Orleans crime syndicate that included parts of Texas and Alabama. He was born in Tunisia to Sicilian parents. His notoriety as one of the toughest crime bosses became apparent early on. In 1951, the United States Senate committee on organized crime called him one of the worst criminals in the country. On March 24, 1959, Marcello appeared before the United States Senate's McClellan Committee investigating organized crime. Serving as Chief Counsel to the committee was Robert F. Kennedy, whose his brother, Senator John F. Kennedy, was a member of the committee. In response to committee questioning, Marcello invoked the Fifth Amendment and refused to answer any questions relating to his background, activities, and associates. The Fifth Amendment, among other things, protects criminal defendants from having to testify if they might incriminate themselves through their testimony. From then on, Marcello became an avowed enemy of the Kennedys. Incidentally, Marcello refused to contribute to the Kennedy's campaign, even after being asked to do so by Bobby Kennedy. Instead, Marcello, along with Santo Trafficante, contributed $500,000 to Nixon's 1960 presidential campaign, or the equivalent of $4,940,000 in today's money. The huge political contribution was made in order to cease the prosecution of Teamster's President Jimmy Hoffa assuming Nixon won the presidency. Hoffa's union provided access to over a billion dollars' worth of loans to organized crime. The Godfather's business enterprises   also   amounted   to   billions   of   dollars.

When Bobby Kennedy became Attorney General for JFK's administration, he had the Justice Department's Immigration and Naturalization Service deport Marcello to the jungles of Guatemala, where he almost lost his life. Marcello returned to the United States and challenged his deportation order. He also vowed revenge on the Kennedy's and concluded that the best way to get rid of Bobby Kennedy was to eliminate his brother, JFK. In 1985, while Marcello was in prison serving out a sentence for his conviction for violation of racketeering laws, the FBI initiated Operation CAMTEX (the CA is for Carlos, the M is for Marcello, and TEX stood for the prison where he was being held in custody, or Texarkana, Texas). CAMTEX used a prison inmate/informant to gain the trust of Marcello in order to find out more about his crimes and his role in the JFK assassination. The operation was a success. Marcello admitted not only to killing Kennedy, but also to knowing Lee Harvey Oswald and Jack Ruby. Marcello confessed: "Yeah, I had the son of a bitch killed. I'm glad I did. I'm sorry I couldn't have done it myself!"

Two items of importance and relevance. First, many well-regarded assassination researchers conclude that Carlos Marcello, along with other underworld figures, such as John Roselli and Santo Trafficante, were primarily responsible for JFK's death. While I agree that organized crime played an important role in the assassination, I do not believe they formed the decision to kill Kennedy. Once Lyndon Johnson made the decision to kill Kennedy, Johnson's fixer, Ed Clark, along with Johnson's hitman, Mac Wallace, and a small group of CIA officers that also worked with organized crime, Cuban exiles, and retired military—people that were trusted by the CIA, were brought in to complete this task, which took over two years of planning.

These Mafia figures, former military and Cuban exiles had a history of working with the CIA on covert operations, not just in Cuba, but all over the world. They knew how to keep secrets, and they also had sufficient motive for wanting Kennedy dead. Marcello, Trafficante, Giancana and Giancana's men, namely, Roselli, Nicoletti, and James Files, were happily on board with any plan to eliminate Kennedy. The retired military men were motivated mostly by money. The Cuban exiles were motived by money and the lack of American air support during the Bay of Pigs invasion.

Second, Mafia leaders such as Trafficante (see below) and others harbored hatred for Bobby Kennedy's relentless pursuit of their illegal activities. As Attorney General, Bobby Kennedy forced J. Edgar Hoover, a friend of the Mafia, to investigate and prosecute Mafia leaders across the nation. For them, Bobby Kennedy was the target of their hate but, as mentioned above, Carlos Marcello convinced them that the best way to get rid of Bobby was to go after his brother, JFK. These Mafia leaders had mixed emotions and misgivings about killing JFK but ultimately agreed. But Trafficante, once again during a deathbed confession, said he believed a mistake had been made, and he blamed it on Marcello. "Carlos fucked up. We shouldn't have killed Giovanni. We should have killed Bobby." "Giovanni" is Italian for John and was apparently the Mafia's code name for John Kennedy.[181]

<u>Santo Trafficante Jr.</u>: This man was among the most powerful Mafia bosses in the United States. He headed the Trafficante crime family and controlled organized criminal operations in Florida and Cuba, which had previously been consolidated from several rival gangs by his father, Santo Trafficante Sr.

Chapter 7: I Led Three Lives

Ozzie, Lee, Oswaldskovich, and Bugs, because he would imitate Bugs Bunny while stationed in Atsugi Japan—all refer to Lee Harvey Oswald, to whom this chapter is devoted. I refer to him throughout this book as Oswald, and occasionally "young Oswald" when I write about his childhood days. One of the most confusing, enigmatic characters in this assassination plot is Lee Harvey Oswald. If he could be understood, more light could be shed on this tragic event, and so this chapter is dedicated to this key enigmatic figure. First, here is a quote from Marina Oswald: "Lee was such a mystery to me. He was a lousy husband, a lousy father, a lousy person. First, he told me he had no mother, that she had died. Then one day, his mother showed up. I could never figure him out. I was not and am not the enigma. Lee was the enigma."[182] If Oswald was an enigma and mystery to Marina, he will likely be an enigma to us. Nevertheless, an attempt to understand him must be made to shed light on this monumental crime.

To its credit, the WC tried to understand him, but the best they muster when describing Oswald's motives to kill the president was:

> Oswald was profoundly alienated from the world in which he lived. His life was characterized by isolation, frustration, and failure. He had very few, if any, close relationships with other people and he appeared to have great difficulty in finding a meaningful place in the world. He was never satisfied with anything.[183]

I agree that Oswald was an isolated person, even alienated, but I disagree that his isolation led to aggression, particularly toward Kennedy or what Kennedy represented.[184] I also disagree his relatively young life was characterized by failure. I do agree Oswald may have been frustrated because of his IQ of 118, well above average,[185] coupled with hearing loss and undiagnosed dyslexia. I am sure he felt few people could understand or relate to him, especially people around his age. He appeared to walk to the beat of his own drum, and this may have made him peculiar and an outcast, especially as a child. Young Oswald was an avid reader and had very little in common with children his own age. He would rather associate with his older brothers if he could than with children his own age.

Oswald is remembered by those who knew him in New Orleans as a quiet, solitary boy who made few friends.[186] He was briefly a member of the Civil Air Patrol and considered joining an organization of high school students interested in astronomy. He occasionally played pool or darts with his only friend, Ed Voebel. Around age 15, he began reading Communist literature he found at the public library. Except in his relations with his mother, he was not unusually argumentative or belligerent, but he seems not to have avoided fights if they arose; and they did come fairly frequently, perhaps in part because of his aloofness from his fellows and the traces of a northern accent in his speech.[187]

According to Oswald's older brother, Robert, "[a]ll of us had our dreams and fantasies, but Lee's always lingered a little longer. The center of Lee's fantasy world shifted from radio to television when Mother bought a television set in 1948. When it was new, all of us spent far too much time watching variety shows, dramas, and old movies. Lee, particularly, was fascinated. One of his favorite programs was "I Led Three Lives." In the early 1950's, Lee watched that show every week without fail. When I left home to join the Marines, he was still watching the reruns."[188]

The series "I led Three Lives," was loosely based on the life of Herbert Philbrick, a Boston advertising executive who infiltrated the U.S. Communist Party on behalf of the FBI in the 1940s and wrote a bestselling book on the topic, *I Led Three Lives: Citizen, 'Communist,' Counterspy* (1952). The part of Philbrick was played by Richard Carlson. The "three lives" in the title are Philbrick's outward life as a white-collar worker, his secret life as a Communist agent, and his even more secret life as an FBI operative helping to foil Communist plots. "I Led Three Lives" was a companion piece to a similar radio show called "I was a Communist for the FBI" – also a favorite of Lee Harvey Oswald's.

These very patriotic shows were Oswald's favorites, and it would be no surprise because Oswald spent a lot of time by himself from very early on in his life. Oswald was born on October 18, 1939, in New Orleans, Louisiana, to Marguerite and Robert Oswald Sr., who died of a heart attack two months prior to Oswald's birth.[189] Marguerite sent Oswald to live with his two older brothers in an orphanage called the Bethlehem Children's Home on December 26, 1942.[190] Oswald was only three years and two months old. It was a relatively happy time. His older brothers would take Oswald with them from the orphanage on the outskirts of town into New Orleans, where they would spend the afternoon with their mother. Robert in particular regarded Oswald as his "kid brother" and "stayed pretty close to him." In 1944, when Oswald was five, Marguerite finally found a businessman willing and able to support her family: Edwin A. Ekdahl. Ekdahl, trained as an electrical engineer, earned a comfortable living for his family. Marguerite withdrew Oswald from the orphanage and moved to Dallas to be with Ekdahl, whom she married in 1945. The two older boys were then enrolled at the Chamberlain-Hunt Military Academy in Mississippi, and Marguerite, little Oswald, and Ekdahl settled in Benbrook, Texas, a comfortable suburb of Fort Worth, where they rented a spacious stone house set on a large plot of land.[191]

Oswald's time in the children's home was not traumatic, at least not as traumatic as being placed in Youth House as an adolescent because of his truancy. Oswald spent time with his brothers, who protected him and treated him with care. While I am surmising, I can only imagine that Oswald, at the tender ages of five and six, had admiration toward his brothers, and that admiration must have included their stints in a military academy, then later the actual military.

Marguerite divorced Ekdahl when she caught him cheating with another woman.[192] When that happened, she pulled the older boys out of the military academy and they lived in a small house in Fort Worth. It was a return to poverty. With the divorce settlement, Marguerite bought a home but urged the older boys to go into the military to ease her financial burdens. Again, the military played an important role for young, impressionable, Oswald – it became a way out of poverty for his older brothers, and perhaps when he was of age, for him as well. One could never say Oswald's life was free of adversities. By the time he was ten, and in the fifth grade, he had attended six different public schools. In this regard, Oswald probably concluded that his own life did not mean much; that few people cared for him but, if he created his own alternative life, he could be someone of importance, someone of meaning.

In August 1952, when Oswald was twelve years old, and with both older brothers enlisted in the military, Marguerite drove to New York with Oswald. When they arrived in New York City, carrying much luggage and their TV set, Marguerite and Lee moved in with Oswald's brother, John Pic, who was then stationed in the Coast Guard on Ellis Island, and his wife and baby. John took a leave of absence to get reacquainted with his youngest brother and introduced him to the Museum of Natural History, the Staten Island ferry and other New York landmarks, which fascinated young Oswald. Over time, the living arrangement became problematic because Marguerite did not seem to want to find a job and Oswald began showing disruptive behavior, so Marguerite and Oswald went to live in a small apartment in the Bronx. Oswald was absent from school more than half the time. With his mother working long shifts, the young Oswald was often left to fend for himself, spending time at the library while developing the habit of playing hooky from his eighth-grade classes.[193] He was eventually picked up and placed in a detention hall, where his social worker described him as emotionally detached, giving off "the feeling of a kid nobody gave a darn about."

Eventually, Oswald was placed in a Youth House from April 16 to May 7, 1953, during which time he was examined by its Chief Psychiatrist, Dr. Renatus Hartogs, and interviewed and observed by other members of the Youth House staff. Contrary to reports that appeared after the assassination, the psychiatric examination did not indicate that Lee Oswald was a potential assassin, potentially dangerous, that "his outlook on life had strongly paranoid overtones," or that he should be institutionalized.[194] According to the psychological report:

> Lee is a youngster with superior mental endowments, functioning presently in the bright-normal range of mental efficiency. His abstract thinking capacity and his vocabulary are well-developed. No retardation in school subjects could be found despite truancy.[195] This 13-year-old, well-built boy has superior mental resources and functions only slightly below his capacity level in spite of chronic truancy from school which brought him into Youth House.

Dr. Renatus Hartogs described the thirteen-year-old Oswald as a "tense, withdrawn, and evasive boy, who dislikes intensely talking about himself and his feelings. Lee *has to be diagnosed* as "personality pattern disturbance with schizoid features and passive-aggressive tendencies. *Lee has to be seen* as an emotionally quite disturbed youngster who suffers under the impact of really existing emotional isolation and deprivation, lack of affection, absence of family life and rejection by a self-involved and conflicted mother."[196] Notice that because of a lack of a clear psychological disorder, Hartogs almost seems forced to conclude that Oswald "has to be seen as x," almost as if it were a last resort and in the absence of any substantive mental disorder. Then Hartogs adds that Oswald's affliction is largely the result of his mother's emotional and physical abandonment of little Oswald. This assessment is probably accurate and, if anything, demonstrates that many of Oswald's problems at that time were a direct result of his mother's neglect.

Additionally, Mrs. Evelyn D. Siegel, a social worker who interviewed both Oswald and his mother while Oswald was confined in the Youth House, reported that Oswald "confided that the worst thing about Youth House was the fact that he had to be with other boys all the time, was disturbed about disrobing in front of them, taking showers with them, etc."[197] Dr. Hartogs ultimately recommended that Oswald be placed on probation with a requirement that he seek help from a child guidance clinic, and that his mother be urged to contact a family agency for help; he recommended that Oswald *not be placed in an institution unless treatment during probation was unsuccessful.*[198]

In short, the doctor concluded that institutionalizing Oswald should be a last resort given the absence of a substantive, identifiable mental disorder. The presiding judge overseeing Oswald's truancy ordered parole and a referral to the Community Service Society, which declined to take his case because of its already full case load and the intensive treatment that Oswald was likely to require. The social worker then made a referral to the Salvation Army, which also declined the referral due to lack of resources. Oswald attended school regularly for the remaining year and graduated from the seventh grade.

Oswald's male role models were largely his two older half-brothers, both of whom went into the military. While others claim that Oswald's role model was his uncle, Charles (Dutch) Murret, a bookkeeper for Carlos Marcello, there is little evidence to support that Oswald and his uncle were close beyond obligatory family ties. His uncle testified before the WC. When asked how Oswald was as a child when he came to visit him for a few weeks, this is what he had to say:

Well, I'll tell you; I didn't take that much interest in him. I couldn't tell you anything about that because I didn't pay attention to all that. I do think he was a loud kid, you know what I mean; he was always raising his voice when he wanted something from his mother, I know that, but I think a lot of times he was just the opposite. He liked to read, and he stuck by himself pretty much in the apartment the way I understand it...

By the time Oswald was a teenager, he was convinced about his future. Aside from his stint in the Civil Air Patrol, Oswald tried to join the Marines at age 16 by lying about his age. The Marines caught the obvious fraud.[199] Ultimately, he joined when he was 17. If he were a sincere Communist, why would he want to join these two military-type agencies? Lee Harvey Oswald was sincere about one thing: being part of U.S. government intelligence in order to build a persona that was different from his true self. The idea of building this alter-ego was a result of his fascination with spy shows he heard on the radio, saw on television, and read about as a child. This persona also had to lie and manipulate because lying and manipulation were necessary parts of intelligence work.

If you look at Lee Harvey Oswald's young adult life and his accomplishments, you will come to the conclusion that this was a man heavily interested in government secrets and government intelligence, and his quiet, introverted nature lent itself perfectly to the life he chose – a life of secrets. He was a G-man all the way. You will also find scant evidence of any sincere animosity toward American society and, most importantly, toward President John F. Kennedy. He and Marina kept a copy of *Time* Magazine featuring John F. Kennedy as its "Man of the Year" prominently displayed in their home.[200] According to Marina, when asked what Oswald thought of Kennedy by famous WC critic, Cyril Wecht, "she was clear that he loved America's young leader and had been pleased that he was elected over Richard Nixon." In August 1963, when news broadcasts announced that the president and First Lady had lost their two-day-old son to lung disease, Marina felt bad, but Oswald shed tears."[201] "Lee liked Kennedy," according to Priscilla McMillan, a friend of Oswald's wife and the author of *Marina & Lee*. "He liked him in civil rights. He disliked him for the Bay of Pigs invasion of Cuba. ... But insofar as he spoke about Kennedy, it was to praise him."

Oswald knew by the time he was 11 or 12 years old that he would enter the military and try to defend this country against Communism, and his reason for doing so was largely based on the shows "I Led Three Lives" and "I was a Communist for the FBI." Toward the end of ninth grade, Oswald stated in a personal history that his future desire was to join the military; he left an alternative option as "undecided."[202] The military was his only goal.

Oswald's passion for intelligence work was also inspired by the work Oswald's half-brother, John Pic, did in the Coast Guard's Port Security Unit, which worked hand-in-glove with the FBI and the Office of Naval Intelligence to identify subversives in the maritime industry.[203] This type of job fascinated Oswald. When Pic expressed interest in joining the U.S. Air Force, it spurred Oswald's interest in the Civil Air Patrol and then the military. The Air Force, however, would not grant an exemption for Oswald's hearing impairment, but the Marines would grant an exemption under some circumstances.[204] Unfortunately, this fascination for the military, particularly intelligence work, also would be a catalyst for Oswald's death, as you will see later.

In summary, here is my assessment of Oswald based on my research and experience: He was undoubtedly emotionally stunted and reluctant to share intimate details of his life. He was fascinated, one might even say obsessed, with leading a life that was different from his own, partly or largely because he felt his own life did not matter so much. The life of a spy or infiltrator of some sort was his obsession and compulsion, and this meant having to follow the orders of his superiors, which would prove difficult for Oswald, but also to lie, which was easy for Oswald. Oswald lied when he did not have to. Leading a double life does not mean he was a pathological liar. I assert that he lied mainly to gain acceptance and trust or to avoid discussing personal issues, as opposed to compulsive lying, which is consistent with pathological liars. But in researching Oswald from the time he was in the Marines until his death, there were times when Oswald lied inexplicably.

As far as his ability to kill, I find none, except perhaps feigning to be an assassin, as he probably did with the JFK assassination in order to infiltrate and report on assassination attempts as an FBI informant and intelligence asset. While I believe the constant moving and switching schools and the discomfort he suffered in the Youth House from having to disrobe in front of other boys had a negative impact on his ability to express his feelings, I see very little in the form of major pre-adolescent abnormal behavior, such as bed-wetting, fire-starting, or animal cruelty. He was, to me, emotionally aloof, extremely bright, and introverted. He wanted his alter-ego to have attention, possibly fame and notoriety, and much of his attention went to developing this alter-ego.

Chapter 8: Fingerprints of Intelligence and the Cuba Problem

The Warren Commission and many other oversight Congressional and investigative bodies wondered whether Oswald had ties to the intelligence community, particularly because of his work with the U-2 spy plane and his defection to Russia. These investigative bodies, such as the Warren Commission, were denied access to pertinent information about Oswald's ties to intelligence until the House Select Committee on Investigations began pressing the issue in earnest.

By all indications from credible sources, Oswald had "fingerprints of [U.S.] intelligence."[205] From the time he was in the Marines until the time he was killed, Oswald was an intelligence asset. An intelligence asset means he worked for an intelligence agency, and those agencies may include the Office of Naval Intelligence (ONI), the CIA, the FBI, and evenly, possibly, the newly formed Defense Intelligence Agency or DIA, which was created in 1961 under President Kennedy. As an asset, Oswald was not considered an employee of these agencies, but instead a contractor. Contractors would be paid for ad-hoc jobs, such as delivering sensitive documents, or they may be paid for long-term projects, such as infiltrating a double-agent, or in the case of Oswald, infiltrating Presidential assassination plots.

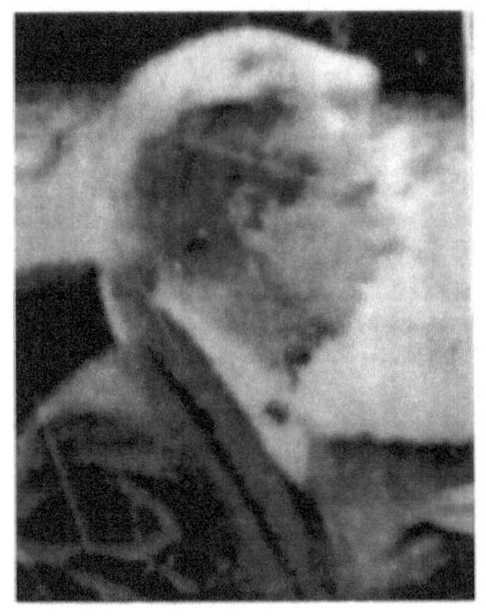

According to the Cuban Consulate in Mexico City, the person on the left represented himself to be Lee Harvey Oswald. According to the CIA, the person on the right represented himself to be Lee Harvey Oswald at the Russian embassy, which was under 24-hour surveillance by the CIA. When the CIA was questioned about why the person in the photo was clearly not Lee Harvey Oswald, the CIA purported that their cameras did not work when the real Lee Harvey Oswald visited the Russian embassy. Parenthetically, the man on the left is Ralph Geb, Mac Wallace's best friend in high school.

During the 1950s and even up until recently, the management of intelligence has been very difficult. Prior to the creation of the DIA, the three military departments, the Army, the Navy, and the Air Force, each submitted separate reports to the Joint Chiefs of States, making intelligence gathering redundant, expensive, and uncoordinated.[206] According to Lamar Waldron, Oswald was first and foremost an ONI asset upon his return from Russia, but because the ONI had very limited resources within the United States, it asked the CIA to watch over Oswald. The CIA agreed.

From being a CIA asset, Oswald infiltrated the Mafia, namely Carlos Marcello and his agents, Guy Bannister, and David Ferrie. He was also later introduced to Clay Shaw or Clay Bertrand,[x] a wealthy New Orleans businessman. Oswald first learned of plots to kill Kennedy through this New Orleans group. He was also introduced to Mac Wallace.

Oswald was also a paid informant for the FBI. He was paid $200 per month as an FBI informant, which is the equivalent of $1,938 per month in today's money. Part of the theater and puppet mastery includes Edgar Hoover's lie to the WC. Commission panel member Gerald Ford, future President of the United States, asked Hoover to confirm that Oswald was never an FBI informant. Hoover lied and stated "[t]hat is correct. I couldn't make it more emphatic." He added that, "as director, he and his top associates would know and approve of anyone working as a Bureau informant."[207] More puppet mastery.

Oswald also had a 201 file, which is a military file. This file contains information about Oswald's defection and alleged time in Mexico City visiting the Russian embassy. The WC asked to see any military files on Oswald but was told none existed. The House Select Committee on Assassinations learned these files did in fact exist and they requested them. The military told them that the files had been routinely destroyed.

Oswald's 201 files were later released in 1995.[208] This file was "sheep-dipped" numerous times. Sheep dipping is an intelligence / espionage term that is actually derived from sheep dipping. Sheep dipping means exactly what it suggests. Sheep are dipped into a chemical bath to rid them of parasites and ticks. In espionage, it is used to cleanse and eliminate the prior history of assets in order to prepare them for a new mission to ensure that their background is clean and thus cannot be compromised by the enemy.

Oswald had a propensity to account for every dollar he earned, including the money he gave to Marina. By all objective lenses, he lived meagerly and so did Marina. Oswald's big pay day, or so he thought, was completing his task relating to JFK's trip to Dallas, for which he was expecting a large cash payout and a peaceful existence in Mexico. Others had different plans for Oswald.

Mafia or CIA? And The Cuba Problem:

It is of vital importance to keep one thing in mind, as noted by Sam Giancana: the Mafia and the CIA were two different sides of the same coin. This was especially true from the late 1950s and up to the late 1960s. What does this mean? It means it is extremely difficult to tell whether the Mafia was working at the behest of the CIA or pursuing their own interests, or both. For example, James Files, Chauncey Holt, Chuck Nicoletti, Sam Giancana, John Roselli, Santo Trafficante, Carlos Marcello, Charles Harrelson (Woody Harrelson's father), and many more all worked for the CIA off and on, and of course, their work was covert and classified, but all of these men were also mobsters, gangsters, and involved in criminal enterprises. Determining whether they worked for the CIA in planning JFK's assassination has been difficult to do. The lines between the Mafia and the CIA are opaque.

Additionally, one very important note to keep in mind in the context of this assassination and its timing is the problem of Cuba. Lamar Waldron, through his research and interviews with people involved at the time, was able to discover a highly classified plan to invade Cuba on December 1, 1963, only a few days after JFK's assassination.[209] Many of the mob figures you are reading about in this book were involved in planning for that operation. The plan was called C-Day, and the operation was called AMWORLD by the CIA. It involved a general of Castro's army killing Castro in his palace, thus a palace coup. The General, Juan Almeida Bosque, was slated to be paid $500,000 for his efforts in killing Castro or the equivalent of $4,782,000 in today's money.[210] Kennedy would then support Almeida's administration as the new leader of Cuba.

Because of the payment of such a large sum, the CIA was brought into this plan because of its subject matter expertise in using foreign bank accounts and "hiding" the sources of money. The CIA was also brought in to watch over General Almeida's brother, which was being watched by the CIA in a foreign country as collateral for General Almeida's work.

The Cuba problem was a major concern for Kennedy and significant resources were dedicated to addressing it. In fact, the bulk of the intelligence budget was dedicated to Cuba sabotage, harassment, and assassination attempts that ran through the largest CIA covert office after Langley. That office was in Miami and the general umbrella was known as Operation JMWAVE (named so because it was on a campus known as Wave Station). It had at least 500 CIA workers and many more in the form of assets from Cuban exiles and other trusted assets. While the C-Day plan was substantive in the number of resources and military power, it was highly classified and remained so even after the fall of the Soviet Union because Kennedy did not want to dishonor his promise with Khrushchev of leaving Cuba alone after the Cuban Missile Crisis. Keeping the plan secret also perpetuated Kennedy's legacy as a peace president. This plan, if discovered, might have been a catalyst for World War Three. Why is C-Plan important? Partly because it had been planned for years and it is how the mob largely learned all about CIA operations and techniques.

JFK also ordered training of Cuban exiles but insisted that the training had to be done oversees. But that was not all. The planning also included US air attacks and air cover *a la* Pearl Harbor, thus the name of the plan became C-Day.[211] The plan also included using 71,000 soldiers and 35,000 Marines on the ground in Cuba and another 29,000 soldiers in support positions.[212] Major units involved would include two Army airborne divisions, an infantry brigade, an armored combat command, a naval amphibious attack force and 17 Air Force tactical fighter squadrons and 53 troop carrier or transport squadrons.[213] Bobby Kennedy oversaw this plan even though he was the Attorney General. In fact, Bobby Kennedy oversaw *all* covert intelligence operations, or at least, the ones he was told about, including Operation Mongoose, the terrorist plans against Cuba. The plan also included trained assassins and sharpshooters that would enter Cuba. This was no small operation and it was Kennedy's top priority to topple Castro even after the Cuban Missile Crisis and the disastrous Bay of Pigs Invasion.

The most damning aspect of this massive and costly operation is that it came after a promise to leave Cuba alone. Russian premier Nikita Khrushchev brought an end to the Cuban Missile Crisis, which was largely perceived in America as a victory over communist expansionism.[214] In reality, it was a *quid pro quo* deal in which Russia withdrew its missiles from Cuba in return for America's removing its missiles from Turkey *plus pledging not to support any further Cuban invasions.*[215]

Please keep in mind that US efforts to harass and topple Castro were extensive and also involved many of the same Mafia and Cuban exile figures already mentioned above. Examples of such efforts include poison pills, cigars embedded with botulinum toxin, exploding devices, disseminating LSD from a plane ostensibly with the hope that some key Cuban figures would commit suicide, interrupting Castro's radio speeches, disinformation campaigns, and most notably, application of Executive Action or Operation ZR-RIFLE, the CIA's assassination operation headed by William Harvey.[216]

Inasmuch as C-Day was slated for December 1, 1963, why did the CIA try to make Oswald look like a Cuban agent or try to implicate Cuba? I believe that setting Oswald up to be perceived as a Cuban agent was additional insurance to make sure C-Day went forward. As noted in other parts of this book, Johnson gave the order to kill Kennedy to his attorney, Ed Clark, and left the details of the planning to Mac Wallace. Johnson was only informed of what his responsibilities were once Kennedy was killed (*e.g.,* remove his body from Dallas, order the FBI to investigate and have exclusive jurisdiction, conduct a surgery to ensure bullet trajectories appeared to come from behind, establish a commission to investigate, etc.).

In planning the assassination, Mac Wallace recruited some CIA agents as well as other hitmen. Those CIA agents, in turn, recruited well-known operatives, such as the Mafia and Cuban exiles. The CIA, not the Mafia, had the means and manner to implicate Oswald as being a Cuban operative and create the fable that Oswald went to Mexico City with the purpose of going to Cuba. What the CIA did not bank on was Johnson's refusal to implicate a foreign power in Kennedy's assassination. In fact, just days after the assassination, Johnson effectively shut down any indications that Cuba or Russia were involved in Kennedy's assassination because he did not want his new presidency to be remembered for starting WWIII. Put simply, the CIA never mentioned and certainly did not obtain Johnson's approval of its plan to tie Oswald to Cuba.

Chapter 9: An Oswald Double?

As stated by the father of criminal forensics, the fictional character Sherlock Holmes, "when you have eliminated the impossible, whatever remains, however improbable, must be the truth." The notion of an Oswald double certainly sounds improbable. To be honest, the use of a double was the stuff highly conspiratorial people believed, including the use of mind-altering techniques, such as hypnosis.[xi] I did not believe in the use of an Oswald double until I started looking closely at certain events in this murder-conspiracy.

Three important events, in fact, were left unresolved and, to me, underscored the clever use of a double. First, there were reports from six witnesses that saw Oswald running from the north end or rear of the TSBD annex, across the grassy knoll, and entering a double-parked green or light-grey Nash Rambler station wagon with a chrome luggage rack. On the other hand, Oswald was seen by several witnesses walking away from the TSBD heading east, catching a bus, then a taxi and being dropped off near his rooming house in Oak Cliff. Second, Oswald's movements and whereabouts after leaving his rooming house in Oak Cliff casted serious doubts that he could have killed Tippit. It seemed logistically and physically impossible that Oswald had enough time to walk from his rooming house to the scene of the Tippit murder, which is what the WC asserted, and then walk to the Texas Theater when there was only a span of about five minutes between the last time the rooming housekeeper, Earlene Roberts, saw him, at around 1:03pm, and a patron in the movie theater, Jack Davis, saw him, at around 1:07pm. A walk timed by a WC investigator found it would have taken Oswald almost 18 minutes to get to the Tippit crime scene. Yet the eyewitness description of Tippit's shooter described a person that was similar to Oswald, but older, about 30 pounds heavier, and "stocky." Third, numerous credible witnesses saw Oswald on several occasions before the assassination, for example: in a furniture store with his wife, Marina, and daughter, June; four separate sightings at a local rifle range; sightings of Jack Ruby and Oswald together; a sighting by a prominent Cuban dissident, Silvia Odio, who testified to seeing a "Leon" Oswald and two other men in her Dallas apartment before the assassination; a sighting at a grocery store, and numerous sightings at a barbershop in Irving, Texas that was near Ruth Paine's home. Despite the abundance of sightings of Oswald from credible and numerous sources, the WC shockingly dismissed all allegations of any Oswald sightings and credited both Earlene Roberts, the housekeeper at Oswald's rooming house, and Ruth Paine. Ruth Paine and Earlene Roberts testified and accounted for Oswald's whereabouts, stating that he was at his rooming house when he was not working at the TSBD or with Ruth Paine on certain weekends. Finally, Dallas police officers swarmed the Texas Theater and arrested Oswald on the first-floor rear of the theater, yet another police document states that Oswald was arrested on the second-floor balcony of the theater.

The WC discredited any Oswald sightings prior to the assassination, including the numerous sightings of him at a firing range, and credited Ruth Paine because she had to be a credible witness in order to nail Oswald as the sole killer of JFK and Tippit. In other words, the WC chose to believe Ruth Paine over substantial, credible, probative evidence that Oswald was seen firing his rifle in order to prepare to make the spectacular shots from the TSBD. Incredibly, the WC preferred to conclude that Oswald never practiced with his 1940 rifle and that otherwise credible witnesses were wrong in order to rely on Ruth Paine's testimony instead. How's that for results-oriented decision making? If the WC Report were a trial court decision, it would have been reversed on appeal for this fact alone.

These incidents bring to the surface the prospect that there was an Oswald double. I was reluctant to write about this issue but felt compelled to do so because of these disparate and contrary sightings of Oswald, which were corroborated by several credible people. My training is in the law, thus the simpler the story made to a jury, the more likely they will grasp all the issues and make a favorable finding. Evidence of an Oswald double really mucks up the water and is simply an uncommon concept in criminal schemes. Plus, I am disinclined to give any credibility to wild, unsubstantiated, uncorroborated conspiracy theories. It is simply not in my nature or training.

But then I had to remind myself that we are talking about a highly orchestrated murder-conspiracy by an agency that excels in deception if nothing else, especially during this time frame. The use of disguises by the CIA is well known, masterful, and beyond compare.[217] The CIA of recent years and during the Cold War has used artists to develop the highest quality silicone-based disguises that look and feel like human skin. The CIA also used these disguises to create twins that could distract enemies that were tracking important assets so that "the twin" could throw off these enemies. It is no stretch of the imagination to conclude that the use of a double, especially in 1963, was a well-established deception technique in espionage even though it may not have been known by the public at that time. There simply is no other way to reconcile all of these sightings of different Oswalds other than to conclude there was an Oswald lookalike.

As I noted before, there is no shortage of information in this multi-faceted murder-conspiracy. The WC, with its budget of $10 million dollars, came to one conclusion after sorting through mountains of information: Oswald was the lone assassin.

As for an Oswald double, I credit the thorough book of John Armstrong, *Harvey and Lee—How the CIA Framed Oswald* (Quasar Ltd, 2003) as a pivotal piece that fills in and explains these disparate and conflicting occurrences. Armstrong also has an excellent website called *Harvey and Lee,* available at: https://harveyandlee.net/index.html. Armstrong's book and website are both excellent bodies of work that encompass a level of granularity all investigative authors should strive to emulate.

According to Armstrong, the two identities were merged to make one person, and this operation was called "Oswald Project." Jim Wilcott was a CIA finance officer in the 1950s. He testified before the 1978 House Select Committee on Assassinations of his knowledge of the funding of the Oswald Project. Wilcott's testimony was the first to indicate that Oswald was specially recruited by the CIA with the express purpose of a double agent assignment in the U.S.S.R. But the HSCA failed to follow through in   investigating   Oswald's   ties   to   intelligence.[218]

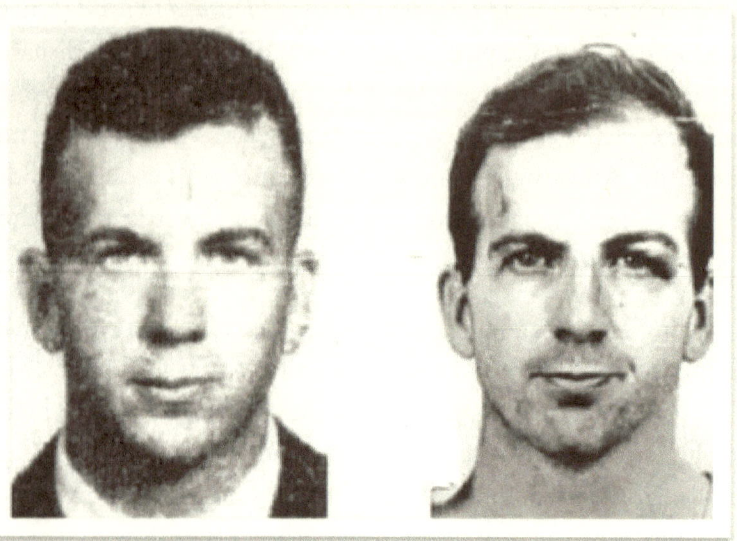

The person on the left is the Oswald double. The person on the right is Lee Harvey Oswald, the patsy. While the resemblance is uncanny, there are subtle differences in hairlines, lips, ears, nose, neck thicknesses, and chins.

The goal of this top-secret project was the planting of a Russian-speaking spy in the Soviet Union at the height of the Cold War. In light of this evidence, the lives of two boys were conflated into the single "legend" of Oswald as a truant, a high school dropout, a Marxist sympathizer, and an embittered Marine for having been court martialed twice (both court martials were a result of Oswald shooting himself with a contraband Derringer and shooting at others he believed to be enemies and both led to convictions).

When Marina first met Oswald at the Palace of Culture in Minsk, she was introduced to him as Alik. Alik seemed instantly drawn to her.[219] They danced, and when they spoke, she noticed he spoke Russian with a slight accent. At first she thought he was from one of the Baltic parts of the Soviet Union—Estonia, Latvia or

Lithuania—but then found to her surprise that he was an American named Lee Harvey Oswald living in Minsk. The WC narratives would have us believe that Oswald acquired an almost perfect command of the Russian language with only a slight Baltic accent by reading language books. The Russian language is still considered one of the most difficult languages to learn.

In January 1960, five months after Harvey Oswald "defected" to the Soviet Union, FBI Director J. Edgar Hoover wrote a memo stating that someone else was using Lee Harvey Oswald's birth certificate.[220] On January 20, 1961, while Oswald was supposed to be in Russia, a Lee Oswald appeared at the Bolton Ford Dealership in New Orleans to purchase ten trucks for Cuba on behalf of former FBI agent Guy Banister and Gerald Tujague's Friends of Democratic Cuba (Oswald had worked for Tujague in 1955-56). On March 31, 1961, a memo was sent from the passport office to John White, an official at the consular section of the State Department, reiterating the concern about two Oswalds originally expressed by Hoover months earlier. In the fall of 1961, while Oswald was still allegedly in Russia, Police Officer Charles Noto arrested Lee Oswald and Celso Hernandez on Breakwater Road on the Lakefront in New Orleans. In April 1962, while Oswald was still supposedly in Russia, Lee Oswald visited the Texas Employment Commission in Fort Worth and filled out form E-40a, Aptitude Profile Test (APT) B-1002 and the Occupational Aptitude Pattern test (WC Volume XIX, p. 491). There is no doubt that Hoover knew about one Lee Harvey Oswald in the United States while another Lee Harvey Oswald was in the Soviet Union as early as January 30, 1960.[221]

One of the young men had a great facility with the Russian language and would be sent to the Soviet Union in the guise of Lee Harvey Oswald, the son of Marguerite Oswald and Robert E. Lee Oswald.

According to Armstrong and others, this legend was carefully crafted for years in the period leading up to the Oswald defection in 1959.

For purposes of this chapter and clarity, I will describe the Oswald double as the "Oswald double" and the Oswald the world saw on live television as simply "Oswald."

Oswald and his double are not related by blood, but an initial side-by-side photo of them shows an uncanny resemblance. Only upon a careful inspection of their respective photos do you begin to see subtle differences.

Oswald

- Foreign born of possibly Hungarian parents;

- Brought to the US after WWII;
- Russian speaking;
- Was not able to drive;
- Went to Russia as a defector and met and quickly married Marina;
- As an adult, was 5'8" tall and weighed 135 pounds;
- Had a complete set of teeth, albeit crooked and crammed;
- Seldom cut his hair and had a receding hairline;
- Worked full-time at the TSBD and was driven to work on 11.22.1963 from Irving to the TSBD by Buell Wesley Frazier;
- Wore a rust brown shirt with

Oswald's Double

- Born in New Orleans;
- Could not speak Russian;
- Was able to drive;
- Was within a year of Oswald's age, but generally described as being closer to 30 years old in 1963;
- Was described as husky and athletic;
- As an adult, was 5'9" tall and weighed 165 pounds;
- Received haircuts twice per month in a barbershop in Irving;
- Had a sharper hairline all around his head and a fuller head of hair;
- Had straighter teeth than Oswald, but had one prominent missing front tooth

light grey torn khaki pants while at work on 11.22.1963; He also wore a dark blue or grey jacket;

- Exited the TSBD at approximately 12:36pm from the main front door, headed east, and boarded a bus where he was tracked by at least two people;
- Ultimately, he took a cab to his rooming house, where he changed his shirt and pants to dark grey dress-like pants and a dark brown shirt;
- At around 1:04pm on 11.22.1963, Oswald is seen at a bus stop near his rooming. Busses stopping at this stop would be driving in a northbound direction, yet the Texas Theater was south of this location;
- Probably driven from his rooming house to the Texas Theater by Captain Westbrook and Reserve Seargeant Croy;
- Was arrested on the first-floor rear of the Texas Theater where he obtained a swollen upper left eyelid in a scuffle with police

- Exited the TSBD from the rear annex and ran to a double-parked Nash Rambler at 12:40pm;
- Wore a tan windbreaker jacket with dark grey pants and a white undershirt on 11.22.1963;
- Drove a Nash Rambler from a Holland Avenue safehouse to a Tidy Lady Launderette in the Oak Cliff neighborhood. He parked the Nash Rambler and walked four blocks and met up with Officer Tippit;
- Killed Officer Tippit;
- Walked .07 miles from the scene of the Tippit murder to the Texas Theater;
- Was arrested in the balcony of the Texas Theater, then taken to the rear of the theater and later released.

officers; and

- Was killed by Jack Ruby in the
  basement of the Dallas police
  precinct two days after
  Kennedy's assassination.

Lee Harvey Oswald weighed 135 pounds and was 5'8" tall. He had just turned twenty-four years old at the time of the assassination. The Oswald double was more athletic, and many eyewitnesses put his age at 30, his weight at 165 pounds, and his height at 5'9" or 5'10." Oswald could not drive; whereas his double could. Oswald was not a sharpshooter; the double was. Oswald had thinning, unkempt hair; the double kept his hair short and allegedly received a haircut every two weeks.

James Files Sutton claims that he arrived in the greater Dallas area days before the assassination and Lee Harvey Oswald appeared at his motel room door.[222] Sutton says that David Atlee Phillips sent Oswald to his motel room because no one but Philipps knew where he was. Oswald's purpose in meeting with Sutton was to show James Files around Dallas. He did reconnaissance with Oswald from Love Field to the Trade Mart two or three times a day for three days in a row. On the day before the assassination, Oswald took Sutton to a field where Sutton practiced with his special weapon and Oswald collected the shell casings for him. This is how Sutton claims that Oswald acquired gunshot residue on his hand when the Dallas police department conducted a paraffin test.[223] The only problem with Sutton's story is that Lee Harvey Oswald was at work each day at the TSBD. This leaves only three logical explanations: 1) Sutton was being escorted by Oswald's double; 2) Oswald's employment records were altered; or 3) Sutton is lying. All three possibilities have merit.

First, as to the work records being altered: During this time, it was not unusual for the CIA to place assets with private employers in order to support a cover. The employer, generally an ally of American intelligence, would agree to place ghost employees at their location, but the actual pay for the employee came from the CIA or the agency responsible for the asset (ONI, DIA, FBI, etc.). In fact, many claim that the Reily Foods company in New Orleans, Oswald's employer from May 10 to June 19, 1963, had several "ghost" positions that Judyth Vary Baker, Lee Harvey Oswald, and others allegedly occupied. Reily was a very conservative business.[224] William Reily was a charter member of The Information Council of The Americas, INCA, a well-funded anti-Castro, anti-Communist group that produced "Truth Tapes" for distribution throughout Latin and South America. Reily Foods required background checks and credit reports on all employees and customers. A divorce or low credit score might bar a candidate from employment. Yet Oswald, a high school dropout, twice court martialed in the Marine Corps, a defector to the Soviet Union, repatriated to the US with his Russian wife and young daughter, recently fired from his last two jobs in Texas, and living on unemployment checks, was hired by Reily, and hired by one William Monaghan, VP at Reily, ex-FBI agent and future head of the Metropolitan Crime Commission in New Orleans. Many suspect that the TSBD was a similar type of employer. While I agree that the owner of the TSBD was conservative and an ally of oil tycoon H. L. Hunt and Clint Murchison, two notorious foes of Kennedy and his policies, I do not believe that work records were altered or that Oswald's position was a ghost position for an intelligence agency for the following reasons.

First, the TSBD did not conduct background checks on its employees. Entry level TSBD employees were largely hired off the street. Second, the TSBD historically hired temporary employees during the end of summer because this was a busy time for the sale of new school textbooks, and the TSBD sold books to schools in several states, not just the greater Dallas area. Third, Oswald was a paid informant of the FBI and possibly received additional money from an intelligence agency. It is more likely that Oswald was told to find a job when he returned to Dallas, whereas he was "placed" in Reily Foods because he was fairly new to the city and was meant to befriend other Reily employees that would lead him to the likes of Guy Bannister, Dave Ferrie, Clay Shaw, and Carlos Marcello. It was part of the manipulation of Oswald.

As for the possibility that Sutton is lying, well, I will let you draw your own conclusions about that. Many aspects of his book are revealing, and others are hard to believe. But if I give him the benefit of the doubt, then the greatest possibility is that Sutton did recon with Oswald's double for several days before the assassination, and not with the real Lee Harvey Oswald. In other words, Sutton unwittingly spent time with Oswald's double and not the real Oswald.

I believe that the person seen running into a Nash Rambler, the person that killed Tippit, the person seen numerous times driving and at firing ranges, and the person that was arrested in the balcony of the Texas Theater and later released was Oswald's double.[225]

Chapter 10: The Tippit Murder

This chapter flushes out the many conflicting and confusing events and reports concerning the killing of Officer Jefferson Davis (or J.D.) Tippit. Before I attempt to sort those reports out, here is an interesting fact. The WC did not focus much attention on the actual murder of J.D. Tippit because the evidence was extremely dubious. In fact, both the WC and the HSCA knew that the bullets retrieved from Tippit's body could not be linked to the revolver found on Oswald. Regardless, the WC concluded that Oswald *must have killed Tippit* because an obviously incriminating wallet was left near the crime scene. Witnesses did not definitively tie Oswald to the murder until they were coerced. Nevertheless, the WC concluded that the murder of Tippit was effectively the Rosetta Stone of the JFK assassination because the obviously planted wallet contained a fake selective service card of Oswald's photo, though in the name Alek James Hidell. Hidell is the name Oswald allegedly used to order the Mannlicher-Carcano rifle, so the wallet itself was, for the WC, pivotal in tying Oswald to the JFK assassination through the purchase of the rifle. Just more evidence of theater and created reality.

The remainder of this chapter explores: Tippit's whereabouts and his unusual behavior just before his murder; when Tippit may have been murdered, in order to better explain whether it was possible for Oswald to have killed Tippit; Oswald's whereabouts, in order to determine the likelihood of him being physically able to kill Tippit; the bullets that were retrieved from Tippit's body versus the bullets that were found on Oswald when he was arrested in the Texas

Theater; and finally, who I believe killed Tippit and why.

1-Oswald's Rooming House;
2-Tippit's Murder;

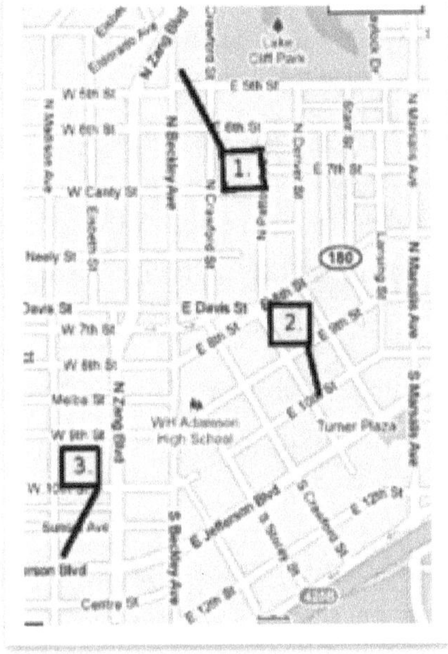

<u>Tippit's Whereabouts from 12:40pm until his death</u>:

Tippit's whereabouts on the early afternoon of the murder have been a source of peculiarity, but luckily, not much controversy.

From 12:40pm to 12:50pm, Tippit was seen at the GLOCO, or Good Luck Oil Company, gas station located at 1502 N. Zang Blvd. Cecil McWatter's bus was scheduled to arrive at the corner of Zang and Marsalis in just a few minutes. Oswald was supposed to be on it. Tippit was watching the cars from the Houston Street Viaduct and had a clear view of all the cars coming into Oak Cliff. Five witnesses saw Tippit at the gas station.

At 12:45pm, Tippit received instructions from the dispatcher to move into the central Oak Cliff area.[226] Officer R. C. Nelson (unit 87) received the same message.

McWatter's bus crossed the Houston Street viaduct at 12:50pm, without Oswald, and turned south on Marsalis without stopping. When the bus failed to stop at the corner, Tippit knew there was a problem, and his actions demonstrates desperation, confusion, and frustration. Tippit left the GLOCO gas station at 12:50pm.

The police radio dispatcher called Tippit at 12:54, and asked "You are in the Oak Cliff area, are you not?" Tippit responded that he was at Lancaster Avenue and Eighth Street. The dispatcher ordered him, "You will be at large for any emergency that comes in." Tippit replied, "10-4." The intersection of Lancaster and Eighth Street is about half a mile from the site of the eventual shooting at Tenth and Patton. Desperately and futilely, Tippit followed McWatter's bus stop-by-stop to see if Oswald exited. He did not. Tippit's frustration increased at each stop when Oswald was not seen.

At 1:02pm or 1:03pm, Tippit hurriedly ran into the Top Ten Records store. Tippit asked store employee, Louis Cortinas, whether he could use the phone. Tippit said nothing during the call, which led Cortinas to believe that his call was not completed. After hanging up the telephone, Tippit hurried out of the store, got into his car, drove north across Jefferson Blvd, and was last seen driving north on Bishop Street. The dispatcher called Tippit at 1:03pm, but Tippit did not answer because he was inside the record store.

At about 1:04pm to 1:06 pm, insurance salesman James A. Andrews was driving west on Tenth Street (8-9 blocks west of Tenth and Patton), a couple of blocks from the Top Ten Record Store. A police car following Andrews suddenly passed him and forced his car to the curb. The officer jumped out of the patrol car, motioned for Andrews to stay put, and then ran back to Andrews' car. The officer looked in the front and back seat of the car and then, without saying a word, returned to his patrol car and drove off. Andrews looked at the officer's nameplate, which read "Tippit," and was perplexed by his actions. He recalled that Tippit seemed to be very upset, agitated, and acting wild. After returning to his police car, Tippit turned the car around and began driving east on Tenth Street toward Patton. At that point, Tippit had about two minutes to live.

<u>When Was Tippit Killed</u>?

While Tippit's movements are largely not in dispute, his time of death is. Several witnesses put the time of Tippit's killing at 1:06pm,[227] but there is controversy over the timing, and most watches and clocks were analog and not precisely synchronized back in 1963. The WC, in order to make it *barely* physically possible for Oswald to have been on the scene, delayed the killing of Tippit to 1:15pm. As you will see, substantial evidence supports Tippit's murder between 1:06pm and 1:10pm.

The location of Tippit's murder in relation to Oswald's rooming house is about 8 or 9 tenths of a mile.[228] There is no way Oswald could have made the trek on foot from his rooming house to the scene of the murder in four, possibly five, minutes. At 1:04pm, Helen Markham left the laundromat, which was located on the first floor of the apartment house where she resided.[229] Two and a half minutes later, she was standing on the corner of Tenth and Patton watching as Tippit pulled over to the curb. In her original statement, Helen Markham placed the time of the shooting at 1:06 pm. Helen Markham was on a routine schedule. She took this bus, which ran every ten minutes, on a regular basis to go to work. The bus was slated to arrive at 1:12pm. It could not have been the 1:02pm or the 1:22pm bus based on the scant evidence to support this time.

T. F. Bowley, the man who called the police dispatcher with Tippit's car radio, was never called to testify before the WC.[230] Bowley heard shots, saw Tippit's body lying next to his squad car, and looked at his watch—it was 1:10 p.m.[231]

Ambulance driver Jasper Clayton Butler said it was less than four minutes from the time he received the call from the company dispatch office to the time Tippit was pronounced dead at the Methodist Hospital on North Beckley. The time of death listed on the authorization for Tippit's autopsy was 1:15pm. If accurate, the time of the Tippit shooting was approximately 1:11pm.

I conclude that Tippit was killed between 1:06pm and 1:10pm based on reports of the above individuals. Although Helen Markham's credibility has been called into question because she undoubtedly went into hysterics *upon* seeing Tippit killed, her typical work routine and schedule corroborate a time of about

1:06pm to 1:10pm so that she could catch the 1:12pm bus and arrive on time for work.

As you will see below, Oswald was seen on the first floor of the Texas Theater at or around 1:07pm, making it logistically impossible for Oswald to have killed Tippit. Additional evidence supports Oswald's innocence in Tippit's murder.

<u>Oswald's Whereabouts After Exiting the Cab and Before Entering the Texas Theater</u>:

According to cab driver Whaley's log, Oswald paid 95 cents for the cab fare, and he was dropped off two blocks from his rooming house at approximately 12:53pm. Oswald requested to be dropped off two blocks from his rooming house because he was at that point now suspicious that this operation had taken a turn for the worse and that he was being set up. Oswald's gut told him something was wrong, but even if there had been, he must have felt stuck and trapped. His gut also told him that he could not trust Tippit. Oswald felt that getting to the Texas Theater would render him safe. And he would   be   proven   wrong.

At least five witnesses saw Oswald wearing this jacket, including Wesley Frazier's sister, some fellow TSBD co-workers, the bus driver, and the taxicab driver. Apparently, Oswald ditched this jacket after exiting the taxicab and before entering his rooming house in Oak Cliff.

The housekeeper, Earlene Roberts,[xii] distinctly remembered Oswald entering the rooming house at 1:00pm because he was in a hurry, "all but running," and he was usually not in a hurry.[232] She had just been told that the President had been shot, and she was trying to adjust the picture on the television. Roberts' testimony is a bit unclear because she said she had been watching *As The World Turns,* which started at 12:30pm and had been interrupted by the news of shots being fired upon the President, yet she also stated that she was told by someone else in the rooming house that the President had been shot.[233] Nevertheless, her recollections thereafter seem clearer and more coherent. Oswald apparently ditched the *grey jacket* he was wearing when he left the TSBD and while he was on the bus and in the taxi because Roberts testified that he came into the house without a jacket and left wearing a light-colored jacket.

While in his room, Oswald removed his grey pants and his long-sleeved button-down reddish brown, tweed-like shirt, and put them in the lower drawer of his dresser. He put on a long-sleeved, dark brown shirt over his dirty white T-shirt, dark grey pants, and a lightweight coat that Earlene Roberts distinctly remembered he zipped up as he left the rooming house. Earlene Roberts said she did not see a gun and never saw Oswald with a gun on him or in his room. Earlene Roberts, before the WC, had a difficult time identifying the jacket allegedly found in a parking lot as belonging to Oswald. The WC asked her leading questions, and she ultimately identified the jacket.

After Tippit's murder, Captain Westbrook retrieved a tan jacket underneath a car in a parking lot. The jacket retrieved was a size medium with a dry-cleaning tag that could not be identified as having come from any Dallas-area dry cleaners.[234] Marina identified this jacket as belonging to her husband, but as I assert above, Marina was a coerced witness whose potential deportation from the United States was used to unduly influence her. Other witnesses failed to identify the jacket. Captain Westbrook said someone pointed out this jacket to him and he retrieved it. This "someone" was never identified. Please note that another "someone" gave or pointed out to Reserve Sergeant Croy a wallet with Oswald's identification and alias. In the murder of a police officer, neither Sergeant Croy nor Captain Westbrook identified this someone. I assert that they planted the evidence: Westbrook planting the jacket and Croy planting the wallet. Alternatively, the wallet and jacket were planted by co-conspirators. Both items of evidence would later be used by the WC in its ultimate finding that Oswald killed Tippit.

While Oswald was in his room, a Dallas police patrol car drove in front of 1026 N. Beckley. Earlene Roberts saw the car and told the WC, "right direct in front of that door, there was a police car, stopped and honked ... just glanced out and saw the number ... think it was 106, it seems to me like it was 106." Roberts later corrected herself and said the police car was number 107. The police car may have been numbered 201 and not 107. She said there were two uniformed policemen in a black unmarked car, not a squad car, and the driver honked the horn twice. She then watched the patrol car and told the WC, "they just eased on down the way—it was the third house off of Zangs and they just went on around the corner that way." Again, I assert that the two officers in the police car were Captain Westbrook and Sergeant Croy.

Oswald was seen standing at the bus stop on Zang Boulevard near his rooming house. Within three or four minutes, Oswald was seen inside the Texas Theater by movie patron Jack Davis.[235] Davis remembered the time as being 1:07pm because when Oswald arrived, the credits were scrolling for the first movie. Davis distinctly recalled Oswald's odd behavior because Oswald sat next to him even though there were only about twenty-five patrons in the theater, yet there were about 900 seats, so there were plenty of empty seats.[236] Then Oswald moved and sat next to someone else, and then moved again and sat next to a third patron.

A walk timed by a WC investigator found it would have taken Oswald almost 18 minutes to get to the Tippit crime scene. That would make his arrival at the scene near 1:24pm. I believe Oswald was instead driven to the Texas Theater because it would have been impossible for him to have walked the almost one-mile distance within such a short time span. There is no evidence he took a taxi or   a   bus.

This is the jacket that was recovered by Captain Westbrook about half a block away from the Tippit murder scene. For purposes of clarity, the color is tan, not grey or white. It was in a size medium. Oswald wore small. Earlene Roberts had a difficult time identifying this jacket until she was asked a leading question by the WC. This is the jacket worn by Oswald's double when he killed Tippit.

The Bullets Relating to the Tippit Murder:

Tippit was killed by three bullets in his chest and one bullet in his right temple. One bullet apparently missed him, although several witnesses heard only four shots being fired in sequence; not five.

Dr. Liguori, the emergency room surgeon the attended Tippit, stated that: one bullet was in the left chest, the bullet being deflected by a brass button of the uniform worn by Officer Tippit; another bullet being found only about one inch under the surface; and the third wound in the upper abdomen.[237] Four bullets in all were removed from Tippit's body.[238]

The revolver recovered from Oswald was a Smith & Wesson .38 special.[239] When Oswald was arrested, he had five live .38 Western Special bullets in his left front pocket.[240] Four cartridge cases were found in the shrubbery on the corner of Tenth and Patton by several witnesses.[241] Two cartridge cases were from Western Cartridge Company and another two were from Remington-Peters. An additional four bullets were in the revolver—two were Western and two were Remington. Many have questioned the oddity of having bullets from different manufacturers as bullets are generally sold in sets from the same manufacturer. Many have also questioned the oddity of dumping shell cartridges near the scene of a crime. Additionally, two officers first on the scene reported that, because of the location and marks on the bullet casings, it appeared that Tippit was shot by an automatic .38 pistol, and not a revolver, which was what Oswald had.[242]

Oswald reportedly was carrying five live Winchester-Western pistol bullets in his pocket in addition to the fully loaded revolver, which apparently was never tested to determine if it had been fired recently.[243] There is a very good reason why it was not tested immediately, as explained in Chapter 18. Even the FBI's resources failed to prove that the slugs recovered from Tippit's body had been fired from Oswald's gun, nevertheless, the WC concluded that the revolver recovered from Oswald was the one used to kill Tippit "to the exclusion of all other weapons."

In short, if Oswald is believed to have been Tippit's shooter and to have retrieved the revolver and bullets from his rooming house, he would have had to have six bullets in the revolver and an additional eight bullets in his pocket. He would have had to shoot Tippit four times, then reload four bullets back into the revolver en route from the murder scene and the Texas Theater, leaving five bullets in his pocket.

The shell casings found near the scene of the crime were, in fact, linked by the FBI to Oswald's revolver, but the bullets from Tippit's body were not. What does this mean? What it means is that Oswald did not shoot Tippit, and someone planted those shell casings to implicate Oswald.

There was a six-day delay by Dallas police in submitting the cartridges found at the crime scene to the FBI. The cartridges, belatedly submitted to the FBI, did not bear the initials of Officer Poe, who had marked them with his initials when he found them.[244] This was a classic "chain of custody" error.

Who Killed Tippit?

The first police officer to arrive at the scene of Tippit's murder was Reserve Sergeant Kenneth H. Croy.[245] Croy was driving west on Colorado Boulevard. When he reached Zang and heard the call that a police officer had been shot, Croy drove a half mile south and arrived at the scene as Tippit's body was being loaded into an ambulance. A civilian, who has never been identified, approached Croy and handed him a wallet, which Croy later gave to Sergeant Calvin Owens. Shortly thereafter, Officer Roy Walker arrived. More officers arrived shortly after Walker.

Warren Reynolds, a witness to the shooting, gave Officer Walker a description of the gunman, which he broadcast on the police radio at 1:22pm: "We have a description on this suspect over here on Jefferson, last seen about 300 block of East Jefferson. He's a white male, *about 30, 5' 8,"* black hair, slender, *wearing a white jacket, white shirt* and dark slacks."[246] Again, Oswald was wearing a reddish-brown shirt. This brown shirt can be seen in the arrest photo of Oswald in front of the Texas Theater.

An unknown civilian, who has never been identified, approached Sergeant Owens and Sergeant Hill and told the officers the gunman had thrown down his jacket in the parking lot across the street from the Dudley Hughes Funeral Home. Officers then went to that location.

Several credible witnesses, ironically not called by the WC, reported seeing two individuals near Tippit just before he was killed. One of those credible witnesses was Acquilla Clemons, who was interviewed by long-time WC critic Mark Lane. Clemons described one of the individuals as short and stocky and was the actual shooter. She described the other as tall and thin, in dark khaki trousers and a white shirt. Please note that the pants were of dark khaki material, not khaki as in the color beige. The short, stocky man waived his pistol at the other tall, thin man, as if to waive him off. The tall, thin man then entered an older, grey Ford and drove off quickly.

Jack Tatum, driving his red Ford Galaxie, heard three shots as he entered the intersection of Tenth and Patton. He stopped his car, turned around to look back, and saw the man in the white jacket standing by the front of the squad car. Tatum recalled that Helen Markham, standing on the curb to his right at the northwest corner of Tenth and Patton, fell to her knees and covered her head after the shots. (As I noted above, she became hysterical *upon* seeing Tippit being murdered, but her timing of events appears logical).

After shooting Tippit three times, the shooter hurried to the back of Tippit's car but then stopped.[247] He likely knew that if Tippit survived the shooting, his knowledge of events could expose the conspiracy. He turned, walked around the rear of the car, past the driver's side door and stood over Tippit. Jack Tatum watched as the man in the white jacket carefully took aim and deliberately fired a fourth shot into Tippit's head.

A fourth shot was fired from a different angle and struck Tippit in the head. The HSCA noted in their final report, "This action, which is often encountered in gangland murders and commonly described as a *coup de grace,* is more indicative of an execution than an act of defense intended to allow escape or prevent apprehension."

Tippit's presence in the vicinity of Tenth and Patton suggests that he may have been stationed in that area for the specific purpose of intercepting Oswald and killing him. All other Dallas police units, with the exception of Officer Nelson, as noted above, were advised to proceed downtown to the vicinity of Elm and Houston after the assassination. Officer Tippit failed to notify the dispatcher of his intention to question a suspect, failed to notify the dispatcher of his intention to leave his vehicle, and failed to notify the dispatcher of his location.[248]

After Tippit emerged from his police car and stepped around to the driver's side door, Domingo Benavides saw him reach for his gun as Tippit walked toward the front of the car. Tippit's gun was later found unholstered and near his right hand by ambulance attendants Jasper Clayton Butler, Jr., Ted Callaway, and T.R. Bowley.

Author Anthony Summers quotes HSCA counsel Andy Purdy as suggesting "that Officer Tippit, by himself or with others, was involved in a conspiracy to silence Oswald. When the attempt to kill Oswald by Tippit failed, then Jack Ruby was a fallback."[249] Several others claim Jack Ruby was the short, stocky person that killed Tippit. Others claim it was Officer Roscoe White. I disagree with both assertions.

Officer Tippit was likely killed by men that he knew, neither of whom was Lee Harvey Oswald.

Oswald's wallet was also found at the scene of the crime. Some say Oswald slipped his wallet through the vent window into Tippit's car (the window was rolled up). Others say the wallet was on the ground near Tippit's car. Regardless, I would like to highlight the ridiculousness of the thought that someone, who just walked away from shooting the President, would leave his wallet behind, either by intentionally turning it over to the police officer he kills seconds later, or by dropping it after killing a police officer. Additionally, who would hand over his entire wallet to a police officer? It belies logic *and* stupidity, and Oswald was not stupid. The wallet was an intentional plant by Reserve Sergeant Kenneth Croy, who arrived at the scene as the ambulance pulled up, around 1:17pm. Croy alleged a witness turned the wallet over to him, but his statements defy credibility. Croy never called in the names in the wallet (Oswald and Alek Hidell) over the radio, and the wallet was held for at least thirty minutes without any official police action. Croy did not take down the name of the person who allegedly gave him the wallet. Remember, a Dallas Police Officer had just been killed, and for many of them, the killing of a fellow Dallas police officer was likely even more important than the killing of the President. Famous New Orleans District Attorney, Jim Garrison, expressed the belief that Oswald was supposed to be shot by police officers after they learned that Oswald had killed one of their own.

Many assert that the Tippit murder had nothing to do with Oswald or the JFK assassination at all. I disagree. Tippit's behavior just before being killed tells me he was hunting Oswald down in the Oak Cliff neighborhood.

Others assert that it was a Mafia style killing because Tippit failed to kill Oswald as Tippit promised in exchange for money. This theory has some meat inasmuch as Tippit was in a desperate financial situation with two mortgages and only a meager Dallas Police Department salary and income from smaller side jobs as security or bouncer.

Finally, as James Files asserts, Tippit was killed by Chicago mob man and CIA contract killer, Gary Eugene Marlow, also known as the Raven. Marlow was contracted to kill Oswald, not Tippit. Tippit spotted Marlow and they knew each other from the Bay of Pigs operation.[250] Because Tippit recognized him, he approached Marlow without having his gun drawn. Marlow, as the story goes, could not have a "tie-back" to him because no one was supposed to know he was in Dallas that day, so he shot Tippit on the spot.[251] Files made this conclusion because Gary Marlow came to his motel room the day after the assassination where Marlow stated to Files that "he had to burn a cop" and asked if Files would take his gun to a mob-related gun expert for modification/sanitation. Files declined to accept the gun and told Marlow to get rid of the gun himself.

The problem here is that there were credible reports that two people were involved in the Tippit shooting. The bigger problem with Files's version, of course, is why Marlow, a professional contract-killer, would dump shell casings at the scene of what can only be described as a spontaneous, unplanned murder.

So, what was Tippit's role here and who killed him? Domingo Benavides, another credible witness whose life took a turn for the worse after this tragic incident, was the closest person to the scene of the murder, and he was quite observant. Benavides ducked down on the seat of his truck during the shooting. Moments after the last shot was fired, he carefully peered over the dash of his truck and watched Oswald leave the scene. Benavides observed Oswald from as close as twenty feet and remembered that *he was wearing a light beige jacket and dark pants* (emphasis added). He said, "The back of his head seemed like his hairline sort of went square instead of tapering off. His hair didn't taper off, it kind of went down and squared off." Oswald was known by several people, including the people he worked with, to keep his hair in an unkempt manner and was reluctant to get a haircut. The Oswald double, however, received bi-monthly haircuts and had a much sharper hairline than Oswald's. In fact, he received haircuts in a barbershop in nearby Irving, Texas.[252] Additionally, while Acquilla Clemons, a humble, uneducated, credible witness, described the shooter as being stocky, many interpret the word stockiness with fat, and this is where Jack Ruby and Roscoe White are surmised to be the killers. I interpret stockiness, at least in the way Acquilla Clemons uses the term, as huskiness and athleticism. Oswald's double was about the same height as Oswald, but he had about 30 pounds more muscle on him than Oswald did. So, when Clemons described someone as short and stocky, she really meant athletic or strong. Finally, the description of khaki pants meant khaki material, usually a blend of cotton and wool, not khaki the beige color. Both Oswald and the double were wearing dark pants, except Oswald's double wore dark pants of khaki material.

The Oswald double theory also explains Sylvia Duran's sighting of someone she came to know as "Leon Oswald" in her Dallas apartment before the assassination. Her account was dismissed by the WC because they believed Oswald was in Mexico City during this time.

Finally, the Dallas Police Department removed "smudged fingerprints" from the right passenger window and "fairly good prints" from the right front fender of Tippit's patrol car.[253] Both sets of fingerprints were turned over to the identification bureau and are now located at the Dallas Municipal Archives and Records Center in Dallas. Neither set of prints was examined by the WC. A researcher later compared Oswald's fingerprints with those retrieved from Tippit's car and concluded that they were not the same.

Accordingly, I conclude that Tippit was killed by Oswald's double. As to why he was killed and what Tippit's role was in hunting down Oswald, as Jim Garrison surmised, Tippit was killed to further underscore Oswald's dangerousness in the hopes that he would be found and killed by Dallas Police Officers as a cop killer. I assert that Tippit was supposed to kill Oswald as he exited the bus at the first stop past the Houston Street viaduct as a fleeing assassin of the President. When Tippit "lost" Oswald because he was not on the bus as he was supposed to be, things went awry. When Oswald's double saw Tippit, Tippit likely informed him that he lost the real Oswald. I believe it is more likely than not that Oswald's double followed the original plan to kill Tippit, unbeknownst to Tippit of course, in order to set up Oswald as a cop killer.

Later in the theater, Oswald, knowing something was up and thinking on his feet, yelled "I am not resisting" with about twenty-five witnesses, thus averting a deadly encounter.

Chapter 11: The General Walker Incident

On the night of April 10, 1963, someone shot at the house of General Edwin Walker as he sat in his study doing his taxes. The bullet missed his head by inches. General Walker was the only witness to this incident. The WC pinned this shooting on Lee Harvey Oswald and only Oswald to demonstrate Oswald's violent propensity. They did so based primarily on the testimony of his wife, Marina, who said that Oswald came home late that night, nervous and excited, and confessed to her that he had attempted to kill General Walker.[254] After that night, Marina told the WC that she told her husband he should flee to New Orleans.[255] Please note the nuance here. Marina, probably under duress from the WC, told Oswald to flee to New Orleans, but Oswald was not one to follow Marina's orders or suggestions of any substance. Moreover, it was Oswald's intelligence-related mission that led him to New Orleans, not Marina's suggestion to flee. This is an example of how the WC manipulated and fine-tuned the "facts" to fit a narrative. Oswald's rifle could not be linked by the FBI to the bullet fragment recovered from Walker's home.[256]

In reality, the shooting was probably not an assassination attempt. While it is true that Oswald's statements to Marina and George de Mohrenschildt certainly made it appear that Oswald wanted to kill Walker because he likened him to Adolf Hitler, it was a publicity stunt to restart Walker's fledgling notoriety as an extremist and bring him back to the national stage.[257] General Edwin Walker was an outspoken critic of Kennedy and Democrats in general, often making unbecoming remarks of his leadership, such as calling Eleanor Roosevelt and Harry Truman "pink." He was admonished by his supervisors several times. President Kennedy wanted to avoid firing him and drawing more media attention to him, so he offered him a post in Hawaii. Walker turned it down and resigned.

The shooting incident at Walker's home received regional and national publicity, as it was reported as an assassination attempt that was avoided because Walker, 54 years old at the time, bent down at exactly the right moment and avoided a head shot.[258] It was a dramatic story indeed, but more relevant, the shooting of Walker's home was a way to test Oswald's inclination to be manipulated and to follow the orders of the people that were directing him. It was not an assassination attempt, but rather an orchestrated publicity stunt and a way to test Oswald's mettle.[259] It worked.

The bullet recovered in the assassination attempt on General Walker does not match either the magic bullet or two fragments recovered from President Kennedy's limousine.[260] The WC's linking of Oswald to the Walker assassination attempt is seriously weakened. Contemporary news stories of the April 10 incident quote Dallas police as saying the recovered bullet was "identified as a .30-06," not a 6.5-millimeter Mannlicher-Carcano.[261] A .30-06 (pronounced thirty-aught-six) rifle was Mac Wallace's favorite and he was extremely proficient in its use.

Even if Oswald were responsible for the Walker shooting, there is evidence that he did not act alone. Walter Kirk Coleman, who in 1963 was a fourteen-year-old neighbor to Walker, told police he heard the shot and, peeking over a fence, saw some men speeding down the alley in a light green or light blue Ford, either a 1959 or 1960 model. Coleman also said he saw another car, a 1958 black Chevrolet with white down the side, in a church parking lot adjacent to Walker's house. The car door was open and a man was bending over the backseat as though he was placing something on the floor of the car. At the time of the WC, Coleman was not called to testify and in fact told Walker that authorities had ordered him not to discuss the incident. Just prior to the Walker shooting, two of the general's aides saw suspicious activity around his home. Walker aide Robert Surrey said that on April 6 he saw two men prowling around the house, peeking in windows. Surrey said the pair were driving a 1963 dark purple or brown Ford with no license plates. And Walker aide Max Claunch told researcher Gary Shaw that a few nights before the shooting incident he noticed a "Cuban or dark-complected man in a 1957 Chevrolet" cruise around Walker's home several times.

The many problems with the official version of the Walker shooting as well as the many unfollowed leads in this area are troubling to assassination researchers. But please note four things: 1) Mac Wallace spoke Spanish and was olive-skinned—he was often confused for being Mexican or Cuban, so it was possible that Mac Wallace was the "Cuban or dark-complected man in the Chevrolet"; 2) Mac Wallace's favorite gun was a .30-06 rifle and he was an expert at using it, so killing Walker, if that was the real intent, should have been a breeze for him; 3) the WC expects us to believe that Oswald could fire three quick rounds on a moving, distant target successfully with a 23-year-old rifle, yet he could not fire one round a short distance at a stable object with success from the same rifle; and 4) Walker was supported by H. L. Hunt, the rich conservative Texas oil man, and he wanted Walker to run for governor of Texas, but Walker lost to Governor Connally. Hunt was also good friends with Johnson.

In summary, the evidence shows that Oswald did not shoot at Walker with his 1940 rifle. The evidence shows that the bullet was a

.30-06 and that this was more likely than not a publicity stunt and not an assassination attempt.

Chapter 12: The Clever Use of a Patsy and Its Reinforcement for a Great Getaway

By the time 1963 came around, the use of a patsy or a fall guy was not new. It had been done successfully many times before. In this chapter, I discuss the American Mafia's early use of a patsy that was indebted to the mob. People in debt, naturally, are vulnerable, and that vulnerability lends itself to exploitation. The successful use of a patsy significantly reinforces the *modus operandi* of criminals because it effectively allows them to escape the heat of an investigation and ultimately get away with their crimes. In this chapter, I also underscore how terribly wrong things can go when a fall guy is not used.

Below is an excerpt from *Double Cross,* a book written by Sam Giancana's brother, Chuck:

> Picking a nut case—who was also a sharpshooter and in debt up to his eyeballs—to take the fall for political assassination was as old as the Sicilian hills according to Mooney, who used the examples of Huey Long and Anton Cermak to prove his point.[262] Anton Cermak had been mayor of Chicago and a Capone rival. A real double crosser Mooney said for years, he had waged a war against Capone on behalf of another rival mobster.[263]
>
> In fact, Cermak became mayor by making a promise to fight local corruption and organized crime. After an unsuccessful attempt on the life of Capone enforcer Frank Nitty by Sir Mack henchman in 1932, Paul Ricca, Capone's assessor, turned the tables, killing Newberry. Rightfully fearing for his life, Cermak fled to Florida in December of 1932. In further retaliation, Ricky enlisted what Moody called a real patsy, a guy named Joe Zangara, to eliminate Cermak. Thirty-three-year-old Zangara had been sponsored by diamond Joe

Esposito from Sicily just five years before and was placed in Florida to work the sugar runs from Cuba. A sharpshooter in the Italian army and a heavy gambler, Zangara was deeply in debt and in real trouble with his Chicago bosses. He was given a choice: Hit Cernak or die.

On February 15, 1933, while riding in an open car with president-elect Roosevelt in Miami, Cermak was shot and Zangara was quickly apprehended by the authorities. He immediately began spouting anti-capitalist political rants, claiming he had missed his real target, FDR. But in fact, Mooney said his political rantings were a carefully devised smokescreen; Zangara had no connection to communism or fascism but was actually a registered republican.

Zangara's connections were to the Chicago syndicate, something that escaped the attention of the press and was covered up by the paid off police and investigators. Three weeks later, Cermak died. And as had been planned along, Zangara was convicted of murder and sent to the electric chair. Nice and neat, Mooney grinds. Nice and neat.[264]

Quizzed about Huey Long, Mooney told Chuck that for years the senator had worked closely with the syndicate on everything from slot machines to casinos, becoming partners with Carlos Marcello in New Orleans; Frank Costello, Lucky Luciano, and Meyer Lansky in New York.[265] But by 1935, Long had gotten out of hand and another loony assassin was located. Unlike Cermak, Long was no turncoat traitor; he simply became too greedy, demanding over $3 million a year in payoffs from his friends. He was cutting into profits ... greed killed Huey Long, Mooney insisted. It'll get you every time. Always remember, any profit is a good profit and always leave something for the other guy. That's what Long forgot.[266]

On September 8, Huey Long was in the State Capitol in Baton Rouge for a special session of the Louisiana legislature, pushing through a number of bills.[267] According to the generally accepted version of events, Dr. Carl Weiss, approached Long in a corridor and shot him at close range in the abdomen. Long's bodyguards immediately opened fired on Weiss as Huey Long ran to safety. Weiss was killed instantly, and Long was rushed to a nearby hospital, where emergency surgery failed to stop internal bleeding. Long died two days later on September

10, 1935, eleven days after his 42nd birthday.[268] The implication here is that Long was actually shot by one of his bodyguards, and not the reported assassin, Dr. Weiss. Weiss owned a .32 caliber pistol while his bodyguards owned .38s and .45 pistols—a .38 was recovered from Long's abdomen during his unsuccessful surgery. Weiss was, as Sam Giancana described to his brother, Chuck, the "loony assassin," albeit unwittingly, and the Mafia had paid off the cops to make it look like an open-and-shut case.

Does any of this sound familiar? If not, it will as we approach later chapters in this monumental crime. But for now, I would like to discuss how things can go awry for the Mafia when a patsy or fall guy is not used.

Phenix City in Alabama was on the state border between Georgia and Alabama.[269] Alabama was under the shared control of Carlos Marcello and Santo Trafficante, Jr. Across the state line was Columbus, Georgia, a well-ordered city with a large military community based on Fort Benning. Phenix City on the other side of the Chattahoochee River was virtually a 'wide open town' offering 'every conceivable vice: gambling, prostitution, bootleg whiskey, drugs... backroom abortions, and baby selling.'[270] Phenix City was Mafia heaven, but by 1954 Phenix City was out of control. The outraged citizens of Alabama demanded action. A local lawyer, Albert Patterson, ran for the post of Attorney General of Alabama on a 'Clean Up Phenix City' ticket. He won and announced that his first step would be to move against the organized crime syndicates operating in the town. Santo Trafficante's response to this threat to his criminal empire was swift and brutal. On June 18, 1954, the new Alabama State Attorney General was gunned down in a very obvious Mafia 'hit.' The Alabama National Guard moved into Phenix City and declared martial law. The military police raided the vice dens and arrested the lowlifes. The Mafia could take on and bribe politicians and businessmen, but the US Army on the warpath was out of their league. The Mafia leaders and their corrupt friends fled to safer states. But for the Mafia leaders, two lessons were clear from their 1954 experience: First, any overt Mafia hits or murders of politicians could bring the wrath and full might of the Federal authorities down around their ears; second, it followed logically that if there were to be any such future murders, then they would have to look deniable. The finger of suspicion should be pointed at a patsy, never at the Mafia. Marcello and Trafficante, the two Mafia leaders most affected by the debacle of Phenix City, begrudgingly absorbed the lesson.[271]

In summary, we have seen in the very early case of Mayor Cermak how well a patsy worked to keep the heat off the Mafia. Then in 1954, we have seen what happens when the Mafia hits another politician without the use of a patsy – a heavy-handed reaction by law enforcement that results in Mafia leaders fleeing their own territory and calling unwanted attention to their illegal businesses.

The Mafia had formed plans to assassinate political rivals in the past. When they worked, they worked fabulously. And when they failed, they failed fabulously. The Mafia, like the CIA, learned quickly from any mistakes.

Planning and setting an ambush involve at least 10 key elements for success: timely, accurate intelligence on the target and its movements; detailed descriptions of any protective arrangements; clear fields of fire; triangulation of the target; an open kill zone; close target reconnaissance; concealed firing positions; good communications; secure withdrawal and escape routes; and if it is to be a 'deniable' operation, a carefully thought-out deception and cover plan. In an ideal world, the ambush should also be rehearsed. An operation of this nature is, in fact, a highly complex affair, demanding good command and control arrangements. It is a job for professionals who cannot only shoot straight but can also follow a plan and coolly make their escape. Dealey Plaza demonstrated all these characteristics on the fateful day. Professional sharpshooters were readily available. 'Operation 40' and 'Alpha 66' were staffed by just such men and they all believed that Kennedy was a traitor to their cause. The CIA's renegade anti-Castro exiles were ideal for any deniable operation.

The next step was the target himself. JFK was a popular and populist president. Young, charismatic, with film-star looks and a beautiful wife, he liked to display himself openly to the people. This vanity offered many opportunities to shoot him from a distance. His visits to big cities and the big crowds he attracted seemed ideal. On these semi-royal processions, JFK liked to sit in an open car—an open and highly visible target to a sniper in a tall building with a well-zeroed rifle. More problematic was the target's protection. Wherever the President traveled, the FBI and the Secret Service provided a threat assessment, and the Secret Service provided 'close protection' on the presidential car operating according to strict security procedures. Fortunately for the plotters, this was not a problem. With an eye to the future, a worried LBJ had already provided the ever-busy 'Mr. Ed,' or Ed Clark, his fixer, with a copy of the Secret Service's standard operating procedures for protecting the President. LBJ had handed his personal lawyer and long-time confidant a large envelope containing the official – and highly secret – manual of 'Instructions on Presidential Security.' A patsy was needed, and a patsy that would be killed at or near the site of the assassination was even better. More about this event is included in Chapter 14 (The Order to Kill Kennedy is Given).

Chapter 13: An Incestuous Relationship Begins and Later is Given a License

So now we know the importance of using a patsy, particularly by organized crime. Now, I would like to discuss how U.S. government intelligence agencies have used the Mafia and underworld figures to successfully carry out its mission. Before I do so, I want to underscore the importance of secrecy. Intelligence agencies must work in secret. CIA agents are given a cover, *e.g.,* David Atlee Phillips was known as Maurice Bishop and E. Howard Hunt as Eduardo. The agents are authorized to use fake identification documents in their work, including the use of fake passports. Their operations, assets, spending, safehouses, techniques, disguises, and documents are almost always classified and remain classified even years after they cease using them or after they have become common knowledge.

The Mafia is also an inherently secret society. They work behind the scenes to accomplish their various goals. While some Mafia leaders become public and notorious, such as Al Capone or John "Teflon Don" Gotti, their actual business is mainly covert – they work in the shadows. The most secret aspect of organized crime is its enforcement mechanism – violence and murder. Organized crime enforces and achieves its results through the use of violence, extortion, and murder, and often that murder is by someone known to the victim so that the murderer can get close and kill successfully. Sam Giancana, Charles Nicoletti, and John Roselli were all killed by someone they knew. In that regard, the Mafia and American intelligence working together is a perfect match – both keep secrets and work in the shadows in order to achieve their goals. Sam Giancana described the work between the Mafia and CIA as "two sides of the same coin."

Chauncey M. Holt was the person responsible for delivering fifteen fake secret service credentials to ward off witnesses and Dallas police officers on the grassy knoll. He was one of the three tramps arrested shortly after the assassination. He described the relationship between the CIA and organized crime as incestuous, and so I will stick to that description.

Operation Underworld:

The first official instance of the Mafia working with American intelligence officials happened in 1942 under the name "Operation Underworld." It was born out of necessity and mutual convenience. After the attack on Pearl Harbor, German U-boats sank over 120 merchant ships along the Atlantic coast. The Navy wondered how these German boats were able to refuel and resupply so far away from their bases. The Navy believed that former rum runners from the prohibition were refueling German U-boats so that they could approach the north Atlantic coast and sink ships. The Navy needed to gather intelligence about the New York waterfront and the tightly controlled labor unions in order to identify possible refueling and resupply operations for German submarines. In a failed attempt to gather intelligence, Navy operatives in plainclothes tried to infiltrate the New York docks in order to gather intelligence, but they were met with silence because of the Mafia's tight hold on the docks. The workers refused to collaborate with the Navy. The Office of Naval Intelligence ultimately approached Meyer Lansky and other Mafia leaders to assist in gathering intelligence, and they readily agreed, with conditions of course. The Mafia would agree to assist with providing intelligence in exchange for the early release of Charles "Lucky" Luciano, who was serving a 30-to-50-year sentence for running a prostitution ring. The Mafia also wanted Luciano to be transferred to a lower-security prison. The Navy agreed on condition that Luciano be deported upon his release. The collaboration worked better than the Navy thought. Luciano's contacts provided the intelligence the Navy needed and even assisted in the Allies' 1943 amphibious invasion of Sicily by providing maps of the island's harbors, photographs of its coastline and names of trusted contacts inside the Sicilian Mafia, who also wished to see Mussolini toppled. On July 22, 1943, General Patton captured the Sicilian capital of Palermo. Nineteen days later, Allied troops entered Messina and ended the Sicilian campaign.

The Navy immediately burned all evidence of its cooperation with organized crime. On the same day as the armistice, Lucky Luciano applied for executive clemency on the grounds of his cooperation with the Navy. His request was granted, and on January 9, 1945, the aging racketeer was released and deported. And so, the incestuous relationship began.

<u>The Bay of Pigs and Licensing the Mafia and CIA Relationship</u>:

During Dwight Eisenhower's second term of office, many assert that he "checked out," spending a considerable amount of time traveling and playing golf. At the helm, was Vice-President Nixon, who was given more and more authority, including primary responsibility for the planning of the Bay of Pigs invasion. Nixon was believed by most to be the next President of the United States, and perhaps he would have but for Kennedy's request to organized crime for assistance in the form of fraudulent votes. The Mafia, in order to hedge their bets, often curried the favor of both political adversaries to ensure they always had a winner in power. Unfortunately, Kennedy did not return the Mafia any favors.

Nixon, already heavily associated with the Mafia, told the CIA to work with the Mafia on the planning of the Bay of Pigs invasion, thus effectively sanctioning the federal government's use of the mafia once again. The CIA reached out to John Roselli. While American intelligence and the American Mafia had been working together in the past, as shown above, this was a license to work together by the second highest in command of the federal government.

The Bay of Pigs was a massive failure, and to me, underscores the arrogance of the CIA in attempting to manipulate Presidents and other senior government officials, and in further trying to create situations that would force Presidents to act imprudently. President Kennedy knew about the Bay of Pigs invasion before he became President and approved of the operation. But Kennedy specifically asked the CIA whether air support would be needed beyond the air support that was already approved. The CIA told them that no air support would be needed, but they intentionally lied. They knew the President was reluctant to move forward with a plan calling for air support beyond those already approved, so the CIA instead thought it would wait until the last minute, when the CIA-supplied bombers were being shot down, to ask for more air support banking that the President would not allow the operation to fail. The CIA was wrong. The President took responsibility for the failed invasion and apologized to the trained Cuban exiles, but the damage had already been done. The experience left the President properly cynical and mistrustful toward the CIA.

Chapter 14: The Order to Kill Kennedy

By the end of summer, 1961, the tension between President Kennedy and Vice President Johnson had reached an intolerable point for LBJ. The two men were opposites in so many ways, and their differences never complemented one another. LBJ was an emotional thinker, was not well-read, used manipulation, lies, and threats to convince people, put his needs before others, had a fickle ego, and loved money. JFK, on the other hand, came from wealth, was Ivy-League educated, was strategic in his thinking, seldom raised his voice or betrayed his emotions, exuded confidence and charm, was tempered in his dealings with people, and personally grew to disdain what greed, graft, and corruption did to families and society in general.

While LBJ could not tolerate JFK, the hatred between RFK and LBJ was palpable to others in the same room as them. JFK barely tolerated LBJ, but he nevertheless often poked fun at him or gently dismissed him, whereas RFK had a harder time holding back his true feelings. RFK was the bulldog of the family and had a way of expressing his views with passion, and he despised the way LBJ would squirm, cry, suddenly alter his mood, and lie when questioned. RFK knew LBJ would not be part of the future 1964 ticket, but he knew he had to find evidence of Johnson's complicity in the Billie Sol Estes and Bobby Baker affairs with the hope that it would lead to a conviction, or at a minimum, a scandal that would force Johnson to bow out of politics and government forever. RFK also fed information to *Life* magazine in their investigation of LBJ's back-door dealings. RFK dismissively referred to LBJ as "Uncle Cornpone."[272] LBJ, in return, when someone mentioned RFK, would raise his big right hand, use his index finger, draw the side of it across his neck in a slow, slitting movement.[273] In circles of trust, LBJ would be more descriptive and simply state: "I'll cut his throat if it's the last thing I do."

As far as LBJ was concerned, the bigger worry was the scandal of Billie Sol Estes and finding a way out of it. The Department of Agriculture investigation led to another meeting with Estes in October 1961. LBJ was notified in early August 1961 that a meeting was planned. For LBJ, it was a clear warning that Estes still had serious problems.[274] The problem was not just corruption by Estes; now it was murder by Wallace. LBJ knew something had to be done. The notice also increased LBJ's suspicions about who was working against him. After all, Estes was being investigated by RFK's DOJ, and Johnson could not simply pick up the phone and ask him to drop the case—it would never happen.

LBJ felt that he had no choice. He summoned Clark, his intimate friend and fixer, to his ranch because extraordinary help was needed. The two men had to be alone. There could be no witnesses. He called upon the only man he trusted, the one he knew could do anything. Johnson asked Clark to take care of his legal problems, and there was only one way: assassinate President Kennedy. At the meeting, Johnson gave Clark the Secret Service policy manual for protection of the President, and the basic planning for the assassination began.

Clark took the manual and had his managing partner prepare a memo concerning the protection afforded a Vice-President.[275] The memo was protected by attorney-client privilege, and with it, the beginnings of a monstrous and highly orchestrated crime were planned. Because of the privilege, that memo and many more documents and confidential correspondence were created and protected, never to be disclosed and compromised.[276]

Yes, it is true, after only seven or eight months of working with JFK and RFK, LBJ had become desperate. He had also grown tired of the pet projects JFK threw at him to keep him busy and out of the way. As the master of the Senate under the Eisenhower administration, he had been more powerful than the President and had greater perks and discretion. He had also enjoyed greater access to legislation that would provide him with a handsome income through kickbacks. He had a perfect system of graft in place as senator. In LBJ's eyes, he was King before he became Vice-President, and now he had been made to feel that he was insignificant, and RFK was after him in a bad way. His tender and capricious ego was hurt. It was time to get rid of yet another obstacle in Johnson's rise to power – JFK, and with him, RFK. Aside from LBJ's relentless and unquiet ego, Billie Sol Estes' empire was crumbling, and the risk of a conviction by RFK's DOJ was too great. LBJ could not risk going down with Estes.

As an interesting side note, and to further drive the point home, I quote from the hand-written notes Jack Ruby wrote while sitting in prison for the murder of Oswald:

> *Remember the only one who had all to gain was Johnson himself.* Figure that out. Remember all points. Also about Oswald who has been a drifter all of his life, suddenly decided to go to work in the book-binding building weeks before Kennedy himself knew he was coming to Dallas...where did Oswald get the information that far in advance...*It had to be someone pretty high in Washington who had made up Kennedy's mind about the trip. All that was planned by Johnson, no one would question the president about a conspiracy.... Johnson could commit any crime he cared to because he knew he was going to be the president and have all the power he needed.*[277]

Jack Ruby's notes were predicated upon the plan to kill Kennedy being successful, but as you shall see, Kennedy would not leave Dallas alive. The order to kill JFK came around August of 1961, only seven months after Kennedy assumed the Office of the President. Ed Clark then summoned Mac Wallace, and from there a convoluted two-year plan was devised to kill

Kennedy and Senator Yarborough—two birds with one stone, so to speak. Yarborough and Kennedy were two obstacles in LBJ's path to the Presidency and LBK hated both almost equally. The fall guy would be Oswald. Mac Wallace, leading the operation, would lean heavily on the CIA. In typical CIA fashion, there would be numerous redundancies built into this plan—a back-up plan for the back-up plan. And of course, the CIA would never get its hands dirty. The CIA was a strategic planning agency. Instead, the CIA would rely heavily on trusted old friends—the Mafia, Cuban exiles, and former CIA assets with a proven track record of being able to follow orders and keep their mouths shut. The Mafia separately leaned on someone they could rely upon and who was indebted to them in Dallas. That someone had significant ties to corrupt Dallas police officers—Jack Ruby. In the end, Oswald would die, but who would kill him depended on how things played out.

Finally, the albatrosses were really circling by the time November 22, 1963 rolled around. While Kennedy's limousine approached Dealey Plaza, Don Reynolds, an associate of Bobby Baker, was testifying to a closed session of the Senate Rules Committee about LBJ's kickbacks and corruption with Bobby Baker.[278] Additionally, Life magazine, arguably the most important news source at the time, was conducting its own investigation into Johnson's back-dealing ways by the end of summer, 1963. The LBJ piece was in the final editing stages and was scheduled to break in the issue of the magazine due out the week of November 24, 1963.[279] The magazine would have made it to the newsstands on November 26th or 27th. It had been prepared in relative secrecy by a small special editorial team that was not influenced by outside sources, including the CIA. Upon Kennedy's death, the research on LBJ's corruption and all numbered copies of the nearly print-ready draft were gathered up by *Life* senior management and shredded. (The issue that was to expose LBJ instead featured the Zapruder film.) The Senate investigation also ended upon LBJ's ascension to the Presidency. Between LBJ's hatred for the Kennedys and Senator Ralph Yarborough, LBJ's greed and need to be at the top, and to a greater extent, the need for LBJ to save his reputation for criminal, Congressional, and media investigators, Kennedy had go. Once President, LBJ would ensure a thorough cover up by removing Kennedy's body from Dallas, ensuring that all bullet wounds appeared to have come initially from the rear, and that a group of LBJ's cronies would investigate the assassination with a semblance of legality and bi-partisanship and conclude that Oswald acted alone.

Cui bono? Who had the most to gain by killing JFK, knowing that *Life* magazine was about to expose LBJ's criminal business dealings, and others were testifying before Congress about LBJ's corrupt dealings with Billie Sol Estes and Bobby Baker? After the assassination, all Congressional investigations into these three men were dropped. In my view, this was the plan all along, and not just a lucky break for LBJ.

Chapter 15: Refining the Use of a Patsy

This chapter is dedicated to one more patsy. This patsy was used in Guatemala and was assigned the blame for the assassination of President Carlos Castillo Armas. The use of this patsy is illustrative of how crucial a patsy was for a successful mission, especially if that patsy died during the assassination attempt—so successful, in fact, that this strategy became a very important *modus operandi* and signature of both the Mafia and the CIA. It also shows how the Mafia evolved in its tried-and-true use of an indebted patsy, such as Guiseppe Zangara, and simply found one to be manipulated and killed.

<u>The Patsy in Guatemala, Romeo Vazquez Sanchez</u>: The parallels between President Kennedy and Guatemalan President Carlos Castillo Armas, including their respective assassinations, are uncanny. Castillo Armas was installed by the CIA and took over as President in July 1954. He was known as a humble, honest man. His honesty and humility were a problem because the many men that served under him were exactly the opposite. His honesty and humility would eventually cost him his life. Although the new strait-laced President forbade gambling, American gangsters enlisted the support of Army officers to create a luxurious gambling hall in Guatemala City.[280] The military officers all took a cut from this casino.[281] The owner of the gambling hall was named Ted Lewin and he was heavily associated with John Roselli, who by this time was heavily involved in Las Vegas gambling and the Los Angeles film industry. Roselli was also active in Guatemalan labor and governmental affairs.[282]

According to one informant, Roselli had his hands in everything in Guatemala City and other countries in Central America.[283] This includes the profitable fruit companies that exploited poor farmers. Despite Armas' position of forbidding gambling, the casino flourished. More casinos opened. While Armas ordered raids on these casinos, they were never fully stamped out, probably out of complicity from Armas' still-corrupt government. Armas simply did not have control over his officials. Armas' government had similar parallels to Kennedy's administration. Kennedy, to me, was a disruptor of cronyism and wanted to break the old boy's network that permeated Washington, but many in his administration and many in Congress liked things just the way they were. The corruption in Guatemala, fueled undoubtedly by the American Mafia, grew to the point where one party had to exert its authority, and that party was the Mafia and corrupt Guatemalan government officials. Armas did not play ball and he refused bribes. He had to go. On July 22, 1957, Armas moved to close the casinos and jailed Ted Lewin. Four days later, on July 26, 1957, Armas was assassinated.[284]

According to reports from that day, several shots rang out and Armas was killed almost immediately. Police found the assassin, a Palace Guard by the name of Romeo Vasquez Sanchez, dead on the floor nearby. A quickly issued message to the media stated that Vasquez Sanchez committed suicide with the same rifle he used to kill Armas.[285] The police portrayed Vasquez Sanchez as a lone Communist fanatic. Sound familiar? The police even produced Communist literature and propaganda found in his pocket and a suspicious diary, but few Guatemalans believed it. The more plausible explanation was that Armas went against the special relationship that had formed between the military and the Mafia.

The government described Vasquez Sanchez as a Communist fanatic who had been expelled from the Guatemalan Army six months prior to the assassination, but shockingly, he had been allowed to join the "Presidential Palace Guard."

As Lamar Waldron put it in *Ultimate Sacrifice,* both Oswald and Vasquez Sanchez were ex-military men that allegedly killed their respective presidents with a rifle, where conveniently placed Communist literature was found where they lived and were soon killed after the assassination. There would be no trial or attempt at a thorough investigation. In the case of Oswald, there would be no trial either, but there was a feigned attempt to investigate the assassination by the blue-ribbon, bipartisan panel known as the Warren Commission, which was put together to draw only one preconceived conclusion—Oswald acted alone because he was a lone nut. The death of Armas, an honest, humble Guatemalan was, by many investigative historians and journalists, perpetrated by the Mafia, who did not want to lose their casino-based interests. It is further suspected that John Roselli was behind it in some form or fashion.

There is no evidence that the CIA knew in advance of the plot to kill Armas, but David Atlee Phillips, the man responsible for putting Armas in power, copied this very same strategy in an attempt to kill Castro in Chile in 1971 and was true to the assassination template employed against the Guatemalan and American presidents.

Chapter 16: The Abort Team Plan

This chapter deals with a relatively recent phenomenon or rumor. Several people have asserted that they were part of an abort team. These people say there were teams of people working covertly to protect, not harm, the President and they believed they were called upon because numerous intelligence sources found credible threats against JFK. Still, government officials brought before numerous Congressional committees investigating the assassination or domestic intelligence activities have never discussed or divulged the existence of any abort teams designed to protect JFK.

As for the people in Dealey Plaza, it was common knowledge that many eyewitnesses, including police officers, heard a shot or shots fired from the grassy knoll. In fact, once the shooting ended, witnesses, along with Dallas police officers ran up the grassy knoll to investigate. Some reported being shunted away by men flashing Secret Service credentials or badges. Later, it was discovered that no Secret Service agents were assigned to the grassy knoll. While some Warren Commission apologists claim that many eyewitnesses may have confused Secret Service credentials with other military or other agency credentials, I find this hard to believe for several reasons. First, Chauncey Holt admitted to delivering 15 fake secret service credentials for use that day. Second, several Dallas police officers saw men flashing their credentials on the grassy knoll and I cannot find one that stated it was a military ID. Third, there is no evidence that the military was officially assigned to any part of Dealey Plaza, let alone the grassy knoll. The only known military officer was off duty and his name is James Powell of the 112th Intelligence Group.[286]

James Files claims he was part of an abort team, along with Charles Nicoletti and John Roselli. Files says he was informed that the abort team was canceled by John Roselli, but he then reminded Chuck Nicoletti that they (Files, Nicoletti, and Roselli) were there on behalf of Sam Giancana and the Chicago Outfit; therefore, the abort team could only be called off by Sam Giancana. They went forward with the assassination. Files says the abort team was designed to protect the President and intercept a would-be assassin, thus "aborting" the situation.

There is substantial support for an abort team model and the fact that several men were there to actually protect the President. For example, Robert Tosh Plumlee, a contract pilot for the CIA, along with two other men that were part of his particular surveillance team, flew into Dallas that day, and their assignment was to protect the President.[287] Plumlee said he and the rest of the surveillance team experienced extreme grief and dejection over the failure to detect the shooter or shooters in time to save Kennedy. Plumlee said he had been installed on the south knoll, about 150 yards east of the triple underpass. He said he heard between four and five gunshots. "That's when I knew the team had failed and the president was dead," Plumlee said. "It was something that if you saw it, you knew it and didn't have to wait for a hospital doctor to tell you. It was a professional, solid hit. We knew in that moment, as it happened—we knew that we had failed, also."

"The flight out of Dallas that day was a somber occasion," Plumlee said. "There was very little chatter. Nobody looked the other in the eye. There were tears and red eyes, sniffles ... minutes were hours, and hours days." Plumlee provided testimony and other information about that day's events to Congressional and law enforcement investigators. Plumlee's team was supposed to report any suspicious activity to law enforcement to prevent an attempted assassination. But many things went wrong with the wider coordination, he said, and the shots caught the team off guard. Plumlee was later discredited, probably by the CIA's disinformation unit, for having allegedly passed a bad check, but his account is specific and detailed. Recall the term *falsus in uno, falsus in omnibus* and ask whether an allegedly bounced check is to discredit a man with an unblemished record with the military and his story of being part of an abort team. I believe Plumlee, and I believe he and his fellow team members carry unnecessary guilt over Kennedy's death. Also, on the plane ride to Dallas, Plumlee identified John Roselli as one of the passengers.

Ricardo Morales Sr., through his son, also claimed to be part of a clean-up crew on the day of the assassination.[288] Morales was a sniper instructor and was training individuals in a secret CIA camp prior to the assassination. Morales went to Dallas two days before the assassination as part of a clean-up crew, but later returned saying the mission was canceled. When the family learned that Oswald was the killer, Morales Sr. told his son that he recognized the man as one of his former trainees. He noted that he did not believe Oswald could actually be the killer because his aim was not good enough during training.

Chauncey Holt explained his foreknowledge of a situation on the day of the assassination in his book, *"Self-Portrait of a Scoundrel"*[289] as follows:

I was told specifically by Phillip Twombly that there was going to be a nonviolent demonstration, an incident that was going to be laid at the door of the pro-Castro Cubans. I just assumed it was going to be serious enough to inject some life into the anti-Castro program. That it would be more than a few placards, more than those 'We hate Kennedy' placards. I would assume that they were going to take a shot at that motorcade, with no intention of hitting anyone. Maybe that's why they were going to use that Mannlicher-Carcano because they couldn't possibly hit anyone with that. ... You know that there was going to be a swell of public opinion. Hey, it would turn the screws on Castro. They would have been yelling again to invade Cuba and everything else."

Holt described his realization of the meaning of the shots as follows: "Immediately, I came to the grim realization I, at least, had been duped and I started running for the boxcar, as soon as I heard the first two shots."

Chauncey Holt stood in the parking lot between the Texas School Book Depository and boxcars during the shooting. Holt told James Fetzer that he had seen "more mercenaries and assassins in Dealey Plaza before JFK was taken out than you would at a Soldiers of Fortune convention."[290]

Holt gave a detailed description of four shots he heard. He realized that he had been set up immediately as he heard the shots and ran to one of the boxcars where he was joined by two other individuals, Richard Montoya (also known as Charles Rogers) and Charles Harrelson.[291] Holt's role in Dallas was to prepare and hand over 15 fake secret service credentials. Thus, Holt was aware of a secret plot potentially involving a non-violent shooting, however, he did not know that the real purpose of the plot was to kill President Kennedy. Holt's foreknowledge of an incident, perhaps in form of a mock shooting, led to an immediate re-evaluation of the situation once he registered the number and directions of the shots; such shots were incompatible with a mock shooting. Further, Holt's realization that a true assassination was in place led him to believe that he had been set up and to seek a hideout in a boxcar. Holt's foreknowledge contrasted with his interpretation of the shots, and this had two consequences: First, Holt understood that he might have been set up, and second, Holt sought a hideout.

Lt. J. Goode ("Randy Ely") was a member of yet another abort team operating at Dealey Plaza. Lt. Goode confirmed that he had been at Dealey Plaza with his boss, U.S. Marshall Robert I. Nash on that fateful Friday, November 22, 1963.[292] Both men were part of one of the abort teams that happened to be located at Dealey Plaza. The Dealey Plaza abort team comprised of four men—Goode, Nash, and two other men. Nash stood on the top of triple underpass while Lt. Goode was located below the underpass near the entrance to Stemmons Freeway. Lt. Goode located one of the shots as originating from the southeast side of Dealey Plaza and had noticed two shooters: one was crouched on the roof of the County Records building and the other shooter was aiming his rifle from one of the top windows of the same building. The presence of a puff of smoke signaled shooting from the top of the County Records building. Goode and Nash ran directly to the southeast corner of Dealey Plaza and later to the County Records building and even to the TSBD, where they helped in the search of the building. Marshall Nash participated in at least one interrogation of Oswald, which is evidenced in Captain Fritz's testimony to the WC. No written report pertaining to Nash's and Goode's presence at Dealey Plaza exists, and their story never made it to any official records or the Warren Commission's Report. Their behavior suggests that they understood the meaning of the shots immediately, however, being on the other side of the plot than Holt, and decided to pursue the assassins rather than to flee the scene.

The strong evidence of CIA-assigned abort teams is initially befuddling. Why would there be CIA-approved teams dedicated to aborting an assassination of the President? A simple answer is that there was overwhelming intelligence of assassination plots in several cities, such as Chicago, Tampa, Los Angeles, and Dallas. Nevertheless, that simple answer does not hold water. First, the CIA had no covert authority—all CIA covert operations had to be approved by the Joint Chiefs of Staff as Kennedy's way of curtailing the rogue CIA, especially after the Bay of Pigs fiasco. Second, the CIA's authority to conduct a domestic operation, even in 1963, did not exist. The FBI, along with the Secret Service, would have had primary authority over such an operation. Third, the existence of abort teams came primarily from individuals that were actually part of the abort team operation, such as Chauncey Holt, Robert Tosh Plumlee, and Lt. Goode. As of this writing, no government agency ever came forward and admitted that they sanctioned and cooperated in an abort team operation.

The better explanation for the creation of an abort team operation, I believe, is plausible deniability. If Congress or law enforcement speculated that the CIA were involved in the killing of President Kennedy, the CIA, in response, could submit *prima facie* evidence or superficial evidence that they actually were there to save the President's life by responding to intelligence concerning death threats against the President and could declare "we would never harm the President. In fact, we set up these teams to prevent an incident," and this would be enough to deflect any additional negative attention on the CIA from any would-be oversight committee. The abort team operation, while not authorized or approved by the Joint Chiefs of Staff or senior White House officials, would nevertheless be considered a sincere attempt to protect the President and deflect any attention away from the CIA, which is what they would have wanted. Unfortunately, the precise question of whether the CIA was involved in any way with JFK's assassination was never put to them, and the habitual lying and misleading by the CIA and other federal agencies led Congressional committee members to work only with what they had. In short, the misleading and lying by the CIA was enough to frustrate the Congressional committee to the point where it did not have enough reliable information even to ask the CIA or other intelligence agencies whether they had authorized abort teams, so the CIA never had to utilize the "abort team" defense.

Chapter 17: The Privileged Character

The Privileged Character or P.C. is the name given to Jack Ruby, according to Madeleine Brown, Lyndon Johnson's long-time lover and mother of his son.[293] Jack Ruby silenced Oswald two days after JKF's assassination in the Dallas police precinct. Ruby said the following to the Warden after his arrest: "In order to understand the assassination, you have to read the book *A Texan Looks at Lyndon*." In that early, self-published book about Johnson's deadly dealings, author J. Evetts Haley lays out the murder of John Kinser and Mac Wallace's suspended sentence for that murder after a jury trial. There was a similar plan for Ruby if he had to shoot Oswald. This is why Ruby was assigned a high-priced Mafia-lawyer from San Francisco. Ruby was promised that he would receive the best attorney money could buy, and consequently obtained the services of Melvin Belli, a prominent tort law attorney tied to the Mafia. Remember, Ruby had no money. In fact, Ruby was in significant debt to the IRS and the Mafia, so he became the Mafia's puppet. He became the equivalent of Guiseppe Zangara, the assassin of Major Cermak. Kill for us or be killed.

Now let us turn to the day of the Big Event. Arlen Fuhlendorf, a Group Manager in the Dallas Intelligence Division of the Internal Revenue Service, told the FBI that one of his IRS informants had been with Jack Ruby at the time of the shooting. The informant said that Ruby had contacted him the morning of the assassination and asked if he "would like to watch the fireworks."[294] The informant was with Ruby at the corner of the Postal Annex Building, on the south side of Dealey Plaza, at the time of the assassination.

On November 30th, FBI Agent Alan Manning interviewed Mrs. Evelyn Harris. In his summary of that interview, he wrote:

> [T]he daughter of Mrs. Lucy Lopez, a white woman married to a
> Mexican, worked at a sewing room across the street from the TSBD.
> Her daughter and some of the other girls knew Lee Harvey Oswald
> and also were acquainted with Jack Ruby. They observed Jack Ruby give
> Oswald a pistol when Oswald came out of the building.

While Dallas Police officers were searching the TSBD, Ruby telephoned his sister, Eva Grant, from the Dallas Morning News building.[295] He left the building around 1:10pm and was next seen at Parkland Hospital by Wilma Tice and Scripps-Howard news reporter Seth Kantor at 1:30pm. Parenthetically, two days later, Seth Kantor was in the basement of the Dallas Police Precinct, where he was checked twice by uniformed police men, and then a third time by a plainclothes police officer before being allowed into the basement to get a glimpse of Oswald being transferred. That should give you an idea of how tight security was when Oswald was being transferred.[296] Nevertheless, Ruby easily bypassed the heavy police security and, just at the right time, shot Oswald once, fatally injuring him.

George J. Applin, one of only two theater patrons questioned by the WC, told the Commission he was watching the movie at the Texas Theater when the lights came on and a policeman with a rifle or shotgun began moving down his aisle.[297] Applin said he was sitting in the middle aisle downstairs, about six rows from the back, when the commotion began. He had moved down the aisle to ask what was going on, when a policeman, apparently McDonald, passed him, moving toward the rear. Applin then witnessed Oswald's arrest. At the close of his Warren Commission testimony, Applin said: "But, there is one thing puzzling me . . . and I don't even know if it has any bearing on the case, but there was one guy sitting in the back row right where I was standing at, and I said to him, I said, "Buddy, you'd better move. There is a gun." And, Applin added, he "just sat there.

He was back like this. Just like this. Just watching... I don't think he could have seen the show. Just sitting there like this, just looking at me." Applin told Commission attorney Joseph Ball twice he didn't know the man, but in 1979, he told a news reporter that two days later, following the Oswald slaying, he recognized the man as Jack Ruby. Applin told the Dallas Morning News:

> At the time the Warren Commission had me down there at the Post Office in Dallas to get my statement, I was afraid to give it. I gave everything up to the point of what I gave the police there in town... I'm a pretty nervous guy anyway because I'll tell you what: After I saw that magazine where all those people they said were connected with some of this had come up dead, it just kind of made me keep a low profile... [Jack] Ruby was sitting down, just watching them. And, when Oswald pulled the gun and snapped it at McDonald's head and missed *and the darn thing wouldn't fire*, that's when I tapped him on the shoulder and told him he had better move because those guns were waving around. He just turned around and looked at me. Then he turned around and started watching them.

Notice how Applin, as well as several other theater patrons, heard Oswald's revolver snap but no gun fire was heard. Again, this is because the gun that Oswald was given had a bent firing pin and could not fire.

Ruby was also seen at Parkland Hospital at 1:30pm. Oswald was arrested by Dallas police officers at 1:51pm. I am unsure whether Ruby could have moved that quickly from Parkland Hospital to the Texas Theater, but Google Maps says this trip would take about 13 minutes today, and I am inclined to assert that Ruby's movements may have been aided by a corrupt Dallas police officer. Also, traffic was probably lighter in 1963, thus cutting the approximate 13-minute timeframe by a few additional minutes.

On the morning of Sunday, November 24, 1963, Ruby sent a money transfer through Western Union near the Dallas Police Precinct where Oswald was still being interrogated and where over 80 police officers and approximately 300 members of the media were situated. The wire transfer was time-stamped at 11:17am. Ruby entered the Dallas precinct basement. He had a press ID belonging to someone else. He stood behind Reserve Sergeant Croy.[298] At 11:21am, Lee Harvey Oswald was escorted by Detective James Leavelle. Ruby leapt past Sergeant Croy and extended his right arm and shot at Oswald, fatally wounding him.

Jack Ruby was immediately arrested. At Ruby's trial, his attorney put forward an insanity defense. As one factor to demonstrate a lack of planning concerning Oswald's murder, Jack Ruby had left his beloved dachshund, Sheba, in the car while he shot Oswald. But days before the assassination, Ruby called his brother to inquire how to ship his dog to California, where his brother lived at the time. I believe Ruby made initial plans to have someone else take care of his dog, but also knew that there would be at least three scenarios where Oswald would be killed, and Ruby secretly hoped he would not have to do this dirty task for the Mafia: 1) Plan A—on Cecil McWatter's bus, searched by Captain Westbrook and Sergeant Croy;

2) Plan B—when Tippit encountered Oswald in Oak Cliff; and 3) Plan C—in the Texas Theater, where Oswald had the revolver that had a bent firing pin and would be used to incite a shootout of a suspected cop killer and assassin of the President. When Oswald was not killed in any of these three scenarios, Ruby had to complete the task himself. He was effectively Plan D and was not happy about it.

While waiting for his second trial to begin, Ruby died of cancer on January 3, 1967, at the age of 55. Before his death, he believed that he had been poisoned.

Chapter 18: Six Unresolved Issues from November 22, 1963

This chapter fills in the gaps of several odd, and of course, controverted facts that happened on that fateful day of November 22, 1963. Some of these odd facts have almost become legendary in their own right because they have persisted largely since this murder-conspiracy occurred and these events cast serious doubt from the picture the WC tried to paint with largely coerced, planted, deficient, destroyed, and fabricated evidence and testimonies. Other odd facts may be new to you. I refer to these differing facts as "legends."

This chapter answers or resolves some lingering issues from that day. I call them the six legends from November 22, 1963, and I explain why they permeate and came to exist:

1. Oswald's exact whereabouts at the time of the shooting of the President;
2. Whether there was only one shooter from the TSBD;
3. Why there were initial reports of a Mauser being found, then later a Mannlicher-Carcano;
4. Whether Oswald took a bus or ran to a double-parked Nash Rambler station wagon near the grassy knoll;
5. Why Oswald's revolver, which allegedly was used to kill Officer J.D. Tippit, was never tested; and
6. Why initial Dallas police reports state that Oswald was arrested on the balcony of the Texas Theater.

<u>#1: Oswald's Exact Whereabouts at the Time of the Shooting of the President</u>:

The precise location of Oswald at the time of the shooting and, to a lesser extent, his location just minutes before the shooting comprise a large source of controversy. The official version, of course, was that Oswald shot the President and was first seen by Dallas Police Officer Marrion Baker,[299] who was on a motorcycle with the motorcade, and by building manager Roy Truly on the second floor lunchroom of the depository about 75 to 90 seconds *after* the last shot rang out.[300] Oswald himself stated that he was in the first floor lunchroom when the President passed the front of the building. During Oswald's morning shift, he asked two fellow employees what the commotion was outside and was informed that the President was coming by the front of the building. He acted indifferent to this news, and I believe this was intentional. This is also why I believe he was one of the only people to stay in the lunchroom during the President's passing—he wanted to appear indifferent.

Before I explain why I believe Oswald was on the first floor when the shots rang out, I would like to dismiss the unfounded, irresponsible, and misleading assertion that Oswald was in the main doorway of the front of the depository, as some researchers have asserted.

James W. Altgens, an Associated Press photographer, took several photos near Dealey plaza. In one photo, Altgens captures the presidential limousine just as it passes the front of the Texas School Book Depository. In this famous picture, JFK had already been shot and can be seen grabbing his throat. In the background is a grainy picture of a man standing in the first-floor doorway steps of the depository looking on as the presidential limousine passed. Many claim that this person is Lee Harvey Oswald. I disagree.

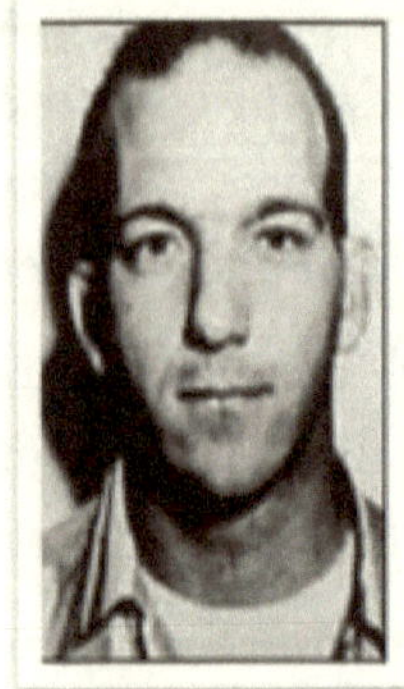

On the left is a picture of Billy N. Lovelady, a depository employee. In the center is Altgens photo and in the background, a man standing in the doorway of the Texas School Book Depository can be seen just as the presidential limousine passed. Some claim that the person in the doorway is Lee Havery Oswald. I disagree. Close examination of Lovelady's right ear, hairline, and pronounced, yet soft, rounded chin make me conclude that this is Billy Lovelady. Oswald's ears are less pronounced, his hairline is completely different, and his chin is more etched. Additionally, his affidavit to the Dallas police department confirmed his location at this time.

I believe that person is fellow depository worker Billy Nolan Lovelady. Although the resemblance is close upon initial view, other photos of Lovelady show that his hairline and right ear are identical to the photo taken by Altgens. Lovelady's affidavit also confirms his presence in the front of the building at this time.[301] In fact, I am so certain about this photo not being Oswald, that I openly challenge anyone to show me any evidence that this person is none other than Billy Nolan Lovelady. Some researchers, undoubtedly desperate to show they found unequivocal evidence of a conspiracy *vis-à-vis* an alibi for Oswald, even have gone so far as to conclude that the Altgens photo above was intentionally altered to make it look like Lovelady so that Oswald would be deprived of an otherwise solid alibi.

I do not believe the Altgens photo was altered in any meaningful and deceptive way, and the person that we see in the doorway is, in fact, Billy Nolan Lovelady and not Oswald. Researchers that "forcefully" and irresponsibly conclude that Oswald was in front of the building at the time of the shooting, and thus could not have shot the

President, ignore the simple fact that Oswald was seen on the first floor by numerous people from noon until about 12:25pm and possibly until 12:30pm. There is no need to twist evidence to their preconceived conclusions. It is a desperate and fickle attempt to exonerate Oswald. Disciplined lawyers, investigators, and objective researchers allow the evidence to lead to a conclusion, and not the other way around, which English psychologist Peter Wason would call "confirmation bias." The evidence itself indicates more likely than not that Oswald was in the first-floor domino lunchroom and then went up to a second-floor lunchroom to buy a coke just after the shooting.

The timing here is crucial. Did Oswald have enough time to shoot at the President, squirm his way out of the 48 or so boxes that created a wall surrounding the sniper's nest, hide his rifle in the fifth-floor stairwell, where it was found, and descend to the second floor where Oswald was seen calmly and not out of breath by Officer Baker and Supervisor Truly? Another magical trajectory besides the magic bullet? I doubt it.

Also, initial reports stated that Oswald had a bottle of Coke in his hands, but later versions excised this fact.[302] In fact, Marrion Baker's initial affidavit to the WC stated that Oswald had a bottle of Coke in his hands when Baker encountered him, but again, this fact was deleted. The final version of the WC went out of its way to note that when Baker encountered Oswald, he was empty handed.[303] Whether Oswald had a bottle of Coke in his hands or not is also crucial. Inserting coins, retrieving the bottle, opening the bottle, and drinking from it would have taken away precious seconds from his purported journey from the sixth floor to the second floor. Additionally, if he took the stairs down from the sixth floor, no one saw him, including Victoria Adams, who was in the stairwell at the time of, and immediately after, the shooting, but she did not see Oswald or hear anyone else in the stairwell that Oswald would have used.[304]

So now, I would like to hyper-focus on the whereabouts of Officer Marrion L. Baker to assist us in determining where Oswald really was during the shooting. Officer Baker was part of the motorcade motorcycle escort team assigned to the last press car. His original affidavit and his testimony before the WC differ in certain aspects. According to his first affidavit, he was on Houston Street and saw the President's limousine make the sharp left onto Elm.[305] As Baker approached that same corner, he heard the shots ring out and recognized them as rifle shots. Ironically, if he had been approaching that corner where the depository was, he would have had an unobstructed view of the building, as there was no building in front of the depository and he could have looked up to see any sixth-floor shooters. In fact, the WC stated that as Baker approached the building, he could see pigeons scattering in the air from their perches on the TSBD.[306] Nevertheless, he assessed that the shots came from the depository, jumped off his bike, and entered the depository where he quickly found Supervisor Truly to assist him in moving through   the   building.

AFFIDAVIT IN ANY FACT

Witness Pauline Saunders told the FBI that a police officer with a white helmet entered the building within ten seconds after the shooting.[307] Her testimony, of course, was not considered by the WC because it would have shown it to be impossible for Oswald to have been on the sixth floor at the time of the shooting. I believe this is the most accurate timetable because it dovetails with Baker's fresh-from-memory affidavit and his logical movements.

I believe it took no more than an additional 15 seconds for Baker to find Oswald on the second floor near the Coke machine. In contrast, in his later statement to the WC, Baker states that "upon hearing shots, I rode my motorcycle 180 to 200 feet, parked the motorcycle, and ran 45 feet to the Texas School Book Depository Building."[308] His first affidavit states he "jumped off his motorcycle" as he approached the corner where the depository building was, but his WC affidavit states that he parked it, suggesting he was not rushed by the surrounding events, which is highly unlikely. He also provides distances in his later WC testimony that he left out of his initial affidavit. Oddly, he also states that the WC had him go through a reenactment where his actions were timed—arriving at the recessed door (or main door) of the depository within 15 seconds after the last shot.

The WC, in order to force the notion that Oswald fired from the sixth floor and was seen calmly on the second floor when Baker arrived, concluded the time was one minute and 15 seconds to one minute and 30 seconds.[309] This is an unbelievable twisting of the facts. How did we go from ten or fifteen seconds to one minute and thirty seconds? Again, no one saw Oswald in the northwest stairwell, including people in that very same stairwell and Baker's own testimony and logical flow of events do not allow for much more than 15 seconds between the last shot and Baker's arrival at the depository. Keep in mind that the entire time from the first shot to the last shot was over seven seconds, so Baker had even additional seconds to react from the very first shot.

At around 11:40 to 11:50 am, all sixth-floor depository employees minus Oswald decided to leave a little early for lunch. Their normal lunch time was 12 noon until 12:45pm. They took the elevators down to the first floor, had their lunches in what is called the "domino room," and then dispersed to get the best views they could of the motorcade. The motorcade was slated to pass in front of the depository at 12:25pm but was running late. Oswald stayed on the sixth floor a little bit longer, but then went downstairs and was seen by three other people on the first floor at noon.

Bonnie Ray Williams, another sixth-floor employee, also came down for lunch around this time, but Williams grabbed his lunch and went back up to the sixth floor of the depository. Williams was eating his lunch, chicken and a Dr. Pepper, on the sixth floor at about noon.[310] He said it took him maybe 10 or 12 minutes to finish his lunch. He did not see anyone else on the sixth floor at this time.

Williams was on the sixth floor from 12:00pm to about 12:15pm, and then he went down one floor at around 12:20pm to join Harold (Hank) Norman and James Earl Jarman Junior.[311]

Williams, along with another employee, Danny Garcia Arce, were occasionally employed to install plywood sheets over the rotting floor of the sixth floor of the depository, where Loy Factor recalled seeing a circular table saw, which Harold (Hank) Norman also confirmed.[312]

Eddie Piper, the Depository's janitor, saw Oswald on the first floor around noon. Bill Shelley, Oswald's supervisor, also recalls seeing Oswald on the first floor near the front of the building around noon. Oswald stated that he was in the first-floor lunchroom by noon, and around 12:15pm was seen by James Earl Jarman Junior and Harold (Hank) Norman.[313] This makes sense insofar as both men came down to retrieve their lunches but went to the fifth floor to see the motorcade and finish eating their lunch. Both said they walked through the lunchroom around 12:15pm to get their sandwiches while they watched the motorcade from the fifth floor. Both said they saw someone eating lunch but could not identify Oswald as that person. They did say a person was there eating lunch. In fact, Oswald was the only one there.

Although no formal transcripts of the questioning of Oswald were made, Captain Fritz, FBI agent James Bookhout, and Secret Service Inspector Thomas Kelley kept informal notes. They all said Oswald mentioned seeing James Jarman and Harold Norman on the first floor sometime around 12:15pm. The last person to see Oswald before the first shot rang was Carolyn Arnold. She said she saw Oswald at 12:25pm in the first-floor lunchroom.

A more recent discovery of handwritten notes in 2019 show that "[Oswald] was present for work at [the Depository] on the morning of November 22, and at noon went to lunch. He went to the second floor to get Coca Cola to have with his lunch (or possibly to digest his lunch).[314]

In addition to all of this uncertainty concerning Oswald's whereabouts before and after the shooting, the WC's own star witness, Howard Brennan, who claimed he saw the sixth-floor shooter and could identify him in a line-up, was also less-than-promising.[315] Brennan claimed he saw the sniper shoot at the President from the book depository. He had excellent eyesight at the distance he witnessed the shooting, about one hundred feet. He stated to the WC he believed Oswald was the shooter. He told the police immediately after the shooting he could identify the gunman. But he did not pick Oswald as the shooter from a line up a few hours after the crime. Even though Oswald had facial wounds and bruising, and even though he was shorter, and his clothes were different from the others in the line-up. And even though he had seen Oswald on television that day, Brennan still could not identify Oswald as the shooter only a few hours after the President was killed.

Additionally, and somewhat inexplicably, although Brennan provided a description of the shooter to the police and the WC found his description to be the first broadcast of Oswald as the shooter, Brennan could not identify Oswald in a line-up.[316]

In summary, Oswald was in the first-floor lunchroom at the time of the shooting, and within seconds, went upstairs to the second floor to buy a Coke. In summary, Oswald was never in front of the building just before shots were fired and all objective evidence convincingly point to Oswald being in either of the lunchrooms at the time of the shooting.

<u>#2: Whether there was one shooter or several shooters firing from the TSBD</u>:

The WC said Oswald was the only shooter from the southeast window of the TSBD. Several witnesses saw several shooters from the sixth floor.

As far as I know, *The Men on the Sixth Floor* was the first book that named two additional male shooters on the sixth floor, as well as a female "coordinator" of these men. The female's name is Ruth Anne Martinez. She signaled when the men should start shooting and communicated via walkie-talkie with other kill teams at Dealey Plaza. The other two men, aside from Oswald, were Loy Factor, a Chickasaw Native American that was around 35 years old at the time of the assassination, and Malcolm (Mac) Wallace, a long-time associate and hitman for LBJ, who was 42 years old at the time of the assassination.

Toward the end of his life, Loy Factor admitted to being on the sixth floor and said he had a 7.65mm Mauser with a scope.[317] Factor also said Oswald had his Mannlicher-Carcano rifle and was situated at the eastern window, and Mac Wallace had a bolt-action .30-06 rifle with no scope and he was situated somewhere near the middle window.[318] Not only did Loy Factor admit to having a 7.65mm Mauser with a scope that day, he also admitted to being in the west-end of the depository.[319] Again, the west end is where Police Officer Weitzman and Deputy Sheriff Boone stated they found the Mauser.

While Factor claims he did not shoot that day, I disagree, and I support the theory, as did Glen Sample and Marc Collom, that he fired one shot and he intentionally missed the president. Factor was initially paid $2,000 before the assassination and then $8,000 on the day of the assassination.[320] When Factor relayed to Sample and Collom that he denied being involved in the shooting despite being paid $10,000 by Wallace (or about $97,000 in today's money), Sample and Collom tried to give Factor a way out by suggesting he did, in fact, fire, but he intentionally missed in order to appear to fulfill his contractual obligation, but Factor again denied shooting.[321]

Loy Factor was a very simple, humble man, literally living off the land for several weeks at a time in Oklahoma. He was injured in World War II and had a metal plate in his head. In June 1948, the Veterans Administration said he was incompetent and thus entitled to receive compensation in the amount of $60 per month.[322] Why is this relevant? As noted in the first chapter of this book, dying confessions are inherently reliable, and, more relevantly, humble people tend to downplay or diminish their involvement in crimes when they make them. I believe Loy Factor fired that day, and for this he was paid $10,000. His part in confessing to being involved in the crime of the century was merely to admit he was there as a backup shooter and that he never knew that Kennedy was going to be the target until the very end.[323]

Loy Factor fired the Mauser once, stood up, ran toward the back or north part of the building, hastily slid the Mauser across the floor, went down the steps with Ruth Ann, and was later driven to Oklahoma by Ruth Anne Martinez and Mac Wallace. This is exactly where the Mauser was found. All four of the officers reported the sixth-floor rifle to be a 7.65mm German Mauser and described the rifle in detail, noting the color of the sling and scope.

Another man was seen on the sixth floor shortly before the assassination by Richard Carr. Carr described that man as "heavy set, wearing a hat, tan sport coat and horn rim glasses." Minutes after the shooting, James Worrell saw a person described as "five foot ten and wearing some sort of coat" leave the rear of the Depository heading south on Houston Street. Carr saw the same man and recognized him as the man he had seen on the sixth floor of the TSBD. The man walked south on Houston, turned east on Commerce, and got into a Rambler station wagon parked on the corner of Commerce and Record. The Rambler was next seen in front of the Book Depository by Deputy Sheriff Roger Craig.[xiii]

#3: Why There Were Initial Reports of a Mauser Being Found, Then Later, a Mannlicher-Carcano?:

It is well known that initial reports after the shooting, Dallas Police officers stated that they found a 7.65mm German Mauser rifle with a scope and a sling. These initial reports trickled to the media. Later in the day, additional reports confirmed that it was an Italian Mannlicher-Carcano. The picture below shows several rifles and their   similarities:

To an untrained eye, it would be very easy to confuse a Mannlicher with the many other rifles shown in the picture, including the German and Austrian Mausers, except perhaps by their length. But this underscores one important fact: If many rifles with wooden stocks look the same, why would anyone positively identify it as the wrong rifle? If you have a hard time distinguishing a Honda Civic from a Toyota Corolla, and if the difference really matters, then you look closely at the vehicle's emblems or badges to be certain. It really mattered here. We are talking about the rifle that killed or seriously wounded the President of the United States and the Texas Governor. In other words, police officers that have experience working with firearms should have known to look very closely at this rifle, and to be precise when identifying it, especially before that information was reported to the media.

The first officers on the sixth floor were Sheriff Deputy Roger Dean Craig, Dallas Police Officer Seymour Weitzman, Deputy Sheriff Eugene (Gene) Boone, and Deputy Sheriff Luke E. Mooney.

Mooney was the first to arrive on the sixth floor. The relevant portion of his report states the following:

> I then took to the stairs and went to the 6th floor, and Officers Webster and Victory went up to the 7th floor. I was the only person on the 6th floor when I searched it and was reasonably sure that there was no one else on this floor as I searched it and then crisscrossed it, seeing only stacks of cartons of books. I was at that time also checking for open windows and fire escapes. I found where someone had been using a skill saw in laying some flooring in one corner of this floor and I then went to the 7th floor and was assisting in searching it out and crawled into the attic opening and decided it was too dark and came down to order flashlights. I then went on back to the 6th floor and went direct to the far corner and then discovered a cubby hole which had been constructed out of cartons which protected it from sight and found where someone had been in an area of perhaps 2 feet surrounded by cardboard cartons of books. Inside this cubby hole affair were three more boxes so arranged as to provide what appeared to be a rest for a rifle. On one of these cartons was a half-eaten piece of chicken. *The minute that I saw the expended shells on the floor, I hung my head out of the half-opened window and signaled to Sheriff Bill Decker and Captain Will Fritz who were outside the building and advised them to send up the Crime Lab Officers* at once that I had located the area from which the shots had been fired. At this time, Officers Webster, Victory, and McCurley came over to this spot and we guarded this spot until Crime Lab Officers got upstairs within a matter of a few minutes. We then turned this area over to Captain Fritz and his officers for processing. At this time, I continued to search this 6th floor along with many other officers and within a few minutes, *I heard Deputy Sheriff Eugene Boone holler out that he had found the rifle near the staircase between some rows of cartons.* We continued to search the building for a suspect.[324]

The staircase that Deputy Sheriff Mooney mentions in his report is the staircase on the northwest end of the building. Keep this in mind when I describe how the events of that day unfolded in the final chapter.

Captain Fritz' duties for that day were to work the head of the President's table in the Trade Mart.[325] At around 12:40pm, Fritz was informed that the President was involved in an accident and was at Parkland Hospital. Fritz and two other officers drove to Parkland. Once at Parkland, Chief Curry told Fritz and others to go to the Depository. Fritz and the other officers arrived at the depository at 12:58pm. When they arrived, the building was swarming with police officers, and they were on every floor. Captain Fritz and other officers made their way up by elevator floor-by-floor and verified that there were officers on each floor as they ascended. Just as Captain Fritz was getting to the sixth floor or shortly after arriving on the sixth floor, someone yelled that they found three hulls near the southeast window. The time was 1:15pm.[326] As I noted in Chapter 2, there is controversy over the number of hulls or shells that were discovered (two versus three). For now, I focus on whether a Mauser was found, when and where it was found, and when the Mannlicher-Carcano came into play.

Pictured here is the affidavit of Dallas Police Officer Seymour Weitzman. It states that shortly after the shooting, Captain Fritz arrived and ordered that the sixth floor be sealed off and searched. Officer Weitzman then said "I was working with Deputy [Sheriff Eugene] Boone in the *northwest corner of the sixth floor* when Deputy Sheriff Boone and myself spotted a rifle about the same time. *The rifle was a 7.65 Mauser bolt-action equipped with a 4/18 scope with a thick leather brownish/black sling.* The time the rifle was found was at 1:22pm" (emphasis added).[327]

AFFIDAVIT IN ANY FACT

THE STATE OF TEXAS
COUNTY OF DALLAS

This affidavit is pretty specific. It does not state that the rifle "appeared to be" or "looks like" or use some other qualifier concerning its make and model. It states that the rifle was not only a 7.65mm Mauser bolt-action, but described in detail the scope type, the color of the sling, and the time it was found. It also included something very odd – the location of the rifle. The sniper's nest was in the *southeast corner* of the building, but this rifle was found in the *northwest corner* of the sixth floor. In fact, in another report, it notes that the rifle was found five feet from the west wall and eight feet from the west stairway.[328] Even District Attorney Henry Wade, the highest law enforcement official in Dallas County and the one whose office would have prosecuted Oswald for the murder of JFK and attempted murder of Connally had Oswald survived, initially reported that the rifle found was a Mauser.[329]

Here again, we have controverted evidence. Subsequent reports clarified that the rifle that was found was an Italian Mannlicher-Carcano. If you are not sure what to believe, then consider these factors. First, the initial reports were quite specific about the Mauser, its type of scope, its sling, its location, and the time it was found. Second, the report was authored by two of the initial officers on the sixth floor, so there was little or no opportunity for tampering. Third, the reports were the freshest and most recent I could find, and because they were contemporaneous with the events they describe, they would have greater indicia of reliability and would be admissible in a court of law. In fact, police reports are generally admissible because they are regular business records that are made contemporaneously. If you are still unsure, I now turn to the excellent self-published book by Glen Sample and Mark Collom, *The Men on the Sixth Floor*, to further convince you that there was, in fact, a Mauser being used that day by a very credible witness/ participant.

As far as I now, *The Men on the Sixth Floor* was the first book that named two additional male shooters on the sixth floor, as well as a female "coordinator" of these men. The female's name is Ruth Anne Martinez. She signaled when the men should start shooting and communicated via walkie-talkie with other kill teams at Dealey Plaza. The other two men, aside from Oswald, were Loy Factor, a Chickasaw Native American who was around 35 years old at the time of the assassination, and Malcolm (Mac) Wallace, a long-time associate and hitman for LBJ, who was 42 years old at the time of the assassination.

Mannlicher-Carcano being held up for display. Note the time of day: 6:16pm.

Toward the end of his life, Loy Factor admitted to being on the sixth floor and said he had a 7.65mm Mauser with a scope.[330] Factor also said Oswald had his Mannlicher-Carcano rifle and was situated at the eastern window, and Mac Wallace had a bolt-action .30-06 rifle with no scope and was situated somewhere near the middle window.[331] Not only did Loy Factor admit to having a 7.65mm Mauser with a scope that day, he also admitted to being in the west end of the depository.[332] Again, the west end is where Police Officer Weitzman and Deputy Sheriff Boone stated they found the Mauser.

While Factor claimed he did not shoot that day, I disagree, and I support the theory, as did Glen Sample and Marc Collom, that he fired one shot, and that he intentionally missed the President. Factor was initially paid $2,000 before the assassination and then $8,000 on the day of the assassination.[333] When Factor relayed to Sample and Collom that he denied being involved in the shooting despite being paid $10,000 by Wallace (or about $97,000 in today's money), Sample and Collom tried to give Factor a way out by suggesting he did, in fact, fire but intentionally missed in order to appear to fulfill his contractual obligation. Nevertheless, Factor again denied shooting.[334]

District Attorney Henry M. Wade, in a television interview, said the rifle discovered on the sixth floor was a Mauser.[335] Then, in a subsequent search, sometime after 1:30pm, they finally found the 6.5mm Mannlicher Carcano by the fifth floor stairwell, where the Dallas Police Department actually found it; confirmed by ATF Agent Frank Ellsworth, who said it was found there during the second search of the depository, conducted after 1:30pm. Ellsworth added that he remembered talking about it with the Dallas detectives, and that they had noted the 6.5mm Mannlicher Carcano was not found on the same floor as the three spent Carcano shells.

In summary, a Mauser was, in fact, used that day by Loy Factor, and was, in fact, found first by police officers. Later, after 1:30pm, the Mannlicher Carcano was found in the fifth-floor stairwell. The Mauser went missing because it clearly would have shown a conspiracy.

Parenthetically, while Captain Fritz never shared his true story about what happened that day, he was forever troubled that President Johnson and Director Hoover claimed Oswald was the lone assassin. Everyone that knew him said he changed after that event. Fritz knew there was a conspiracy, and in an interview before his death, he said someday he might tell what he knew. He never did. Some secrets die with the person holding them dear.

Oswald said he never owned a rifle during his interrogation. The ordering and receiving of the Mannlicher-Carcano, like so many other aspects to this case, is controverted as well as confounding. The initial news reports stated that the rifle was purchased for $12.78, then $21.95, then $21.45. Some reports say it was purchased with a scope and others say it was not purchased with a scope. Was it 36" long or 40" long?

Despite the confusion, the evidence that Oswald ordered and received the rifle is dubious. Normally, it is not common to question the government's statements or assertions, but this is not a normal case. Many researchers have had to question and critically analyze everything the government has said about this case, for obvious reasons.

The WC alleged that Oswald left work at his mapping job at Jaggers-Chiles-Stovall on the morning of March 12, 1963, walked nine blocks to the post office, purchased a money order, filled out an order form and the money order and inserted them along with a coupon into an envelope and mailed it off to Kleins in Chicago. His letter was franked and postmarked by the post office at 10:30am that day.[336] The only problem is that work records show Oswald never left the Jaggers-Chiles-Stovall building and worked continuously that day from 8am until 12:15pm when he took his lunch.[337] Additionally, the post office code was not from that post office nine blocks away from Oswald's work but from a post office about three miles further west. Irving is west of Dallas.

Klein's Sporting Goods routinely scanned and microfilmed the order and form of payment of all purchases it received through the mail, a business record admissible as evidence and reliable. This is exactly how the FBI knew when the rifle was purchased and how it was paid for. Nevertheless, the WC intentionally excluded the form of payment. The original microfilm was taken from Kleins by the FBI and was never seen again once it was sent to FBI headquarters.[338] This is because the microfilm records do not show that Oswald purchased the rifle. It is more created reality, or fabrication, mainly by the FBI in Washington, DC.

An anonymous person called the Dallas local news to report that Oswald had his rifle "sighted in" on November 21 at a gun shop located at 111 or 212 Irving Boulevard, Irving, Texas. Oswald worked all day at the Depository, rode to Irving with Buell Wesley Frazier, and stayed with Marina and Ruth Paine all night.

#4: Whether Oswald Took a Bus or Ran To a Nash Rambler Station Wagon:

Did Oswald take a bus and then a taxi to Oak Cliff? Or did Oswald run from the Depository and jump into a double-parked Nash Rambler station wagon. Oswald was allegedly seen by six witnesses running from the Depository to this Nash Rambler station wagon blocking traffic near the grassy knoll. One of those credible witnesses was Roger Craig, a Deputy Sheriff at the time. Many people have questioned Craig's credibility. I do not. Those that question his credibility often point to the strong evidence that Oswald took a bus because a bus transfer was found in his shirt pocket, witnesses saw Oswald on the bus, including his former landlady, and there was a record and specific testimony by the taxi driver that drove him near his rooming house. The grandness of the problem with people that attack Craig is that he could not have known that telling what he saw that day would lead to many troubles in his life, and ultimately lead to him take his own life. I believe him. This myth is probably one of the more important ones and lends credence to the Oswald-double theory.

Craig saw a person wearing a light-colored, short-sleeved shirt, whom he later identified as Oswald, get into the station wagon and then travel under the triple overpass towards Oak Cliff. Marvin Robinson was driving his Cadillac when the Rambler station wagon in front of him abruptly stopped in front of the Book Depository. A young man walked down the grassy incline and got into the station wagon, which subsequently sped away under the triple overpass. A third witness, Roy Cooper, was behind Marvin Robinson's Cadillac. He observed a white male wave at, enter, and leave in the station wagon. A photograph, taken by Jim Murray, shows a man wearing a light-colored short-sleeved shirt headed toward the Nash Rambler station wagon in front of the Book Depository. Deputy Sheriff Roger Craig, also in the photo, is pictured looking at the man and the station wagon. The Hertz sign, on top of the Book Depository, shows the time as 12:40 PM.[339]

Finally, a Nash Rambler was an uncommon car. A Nash Rambler station wagon was even more uncommon. Light-colored Nash Rambler station wagons were owned by only two people whose names are familiar to JFK researchers.[340] A 1962 Rambler Ambassador, 4-door station wagon was owned by Clay Shaw. A 1959 or 1960 light blue or light green Nash Rambler was owned by Lawrence   Howard.

In this photo, taken at 12:40pm CST, a vague image of a person is seen entering a vague image of a Nash Rambler parked behind a city bus.

Lawrence Howard was a member of Interpen (Intercontinental Penetration Force) that was established in 1961. Interpen was a CIA cover agency that primarily made payments to assassins and saboteurs and set up training camps for them. Clay Shaw was a wealthy businessman and the only person ever prosecuted for the assassination of the President by New Orleans prosecutor Jim Garrison. I conclude that the Rambler wagon belonged to Clay Shaw based on the grill and quad headlights.

A photo of a 1962 Nash Rambler. Notice the quad headlamps. A 1959 Nash Rambler only had two headlamps. A 1960 Nash Rambler had dual headlamps in their two-door models and quad headlamps in the four-door, "Cross Country" version, but the grills are different from the photo shown above taken on Nov. 22, 1963, at 12:40pm. Accordingly, I conclude that the Nash Rambler was owned by Clay Shaw.

One important aspect concerning Clay Shaw: Jim Garrison unsuccessfully prosecuted him. Garrison's theory was that Clay Shaw was a CIA asset and, therefore, the CIA must have been involved in the assassination of President Kennedy. Shaw became a domestic contact source for the CIA one year after the CIA was created.[341] From 1948 until 1956, Shaw voluntarily provided 33 reports to the CIA concerning export and devaluation trends in Europe and Central and South America. The relationship between the CIA and

Shaw ended in 1956 for unknown reasons.[342] In that regard, Clay Shaw was probably not an asset of the CIA in any activity relating to JFK's assassination, effectively meaning that Jim Garrison's theory was flawed. Garrison had asked the CIA if Shaw was a CIA asset. The CIA denied that he was, and technically they were correct, but the CIA could have been more forthcoming about Shaw's former relationship with the CIA. While Clay Shaw may not have been involved with the CIA in an assassination attempt against Kennedy, one cannot conclude that he was *never* involved in a separate Kennedy assassination plot. It merely means that Clay Shaw acted out of his own interests and associated with others that had animosity toward Kennedy, such as Dave Ferrie, Guy Banister, and Carlos Marcello.

A   Photographer   Follows   Oswald's   Movements:

These two photos are clearly focused on the bus Oswald boarded and then unexpectedly deboarded due to heavy traffic. No explanation has ever been given as to why someone would be focused on this particular city bus at this particular time. Two officers, Captain Westbrook and Reserve Sargeant Kenneth Croy boarded that bus with the intention of killing Oswald, but Oswald had already deboarded and was on his way to take a taxi to his rooming house from the nearby Greyhound Bus Station.

Those familiar with the JFK assassination know that the innumerable coincidences in this case are suspicious and almost compel a conclusion that a conspiracy was in play even if you credit the absurd magic bullet theory as true. Well, what about a photographer on leave from the military that takes pictures of Oswald's bus, the front of the TSBD, and Oswald's arrest in front of the Texas Theater, then signs a release to the FBI for them to develop his pictures? Coincidence, or foreknowledge of Oswald's exact whereabouts after the assassination, thus a conspiracy? You already know what I think.

Stuart L. Reed was a civilian Army employee stationed in the Panama Canal Zone, but he was in Dallas on the day of the assassination. Not only was he in Dallas, but apparently, he had a job to do in Dallas. He took color photos of Oswald's movements almost immediately after the shooting of the President.[343] These photos clearly focus on the bus Oswald was predetermined to take and his arrest in front of the theater, also a predetermined location Oswald was scheduled to visit on this day. After taking pictures of the bus Oswald was on, Reed then walks to the front of the TSBD and takes a picture of it. You will note that there are four open window sets; three of them were used by the shooters. Loy Factor's window was furthest from the left with the windows wide open (west windows); Mac Wallace's window is the third from the left with only one of the two windows partially open. The window where the alleged sniper's nest was located was the one furthest to the right with one window partially open (east windows).

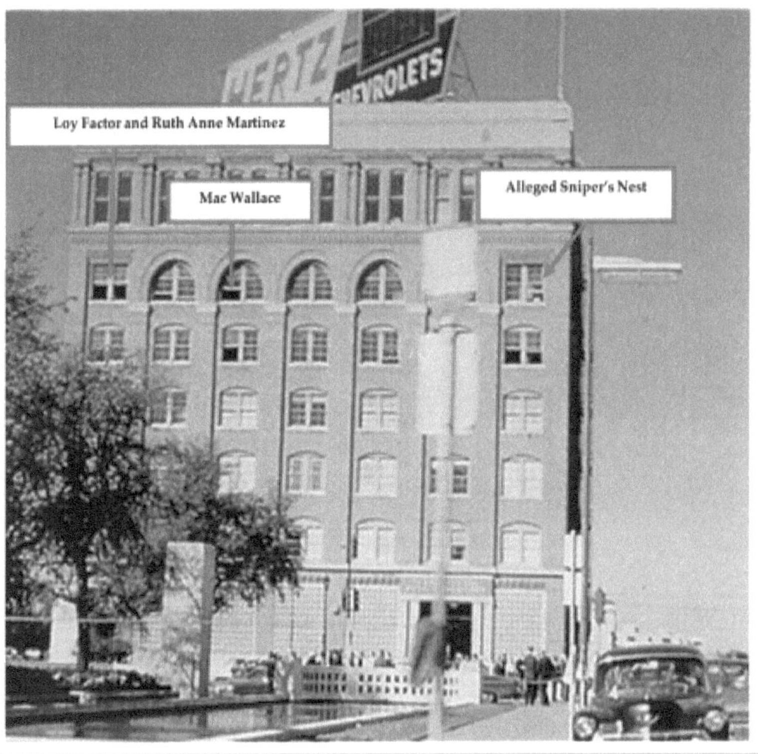

Reed then apparently was informed beforehand to go to the theater and take a picture of Oswald as he was being arrested (if Oswald were alive at this point). In this photo, Oswald can be seen with his white t-shirt mostly visible just before being placed in the police car. Then, before leaving for Panama, Reed signs a release to the FBI allowing them to develop his pictures and do whatever they deem pertinent to their investigation. Also, for unknown reasons, the witnesses of the release Reed signed on November 26, 1963 were two FBI Agents from the New Orleans office. Why New Orleans? Did Reed fly or sail out from there? Were New Orleans officers temporarily assigned to Dallas from New Orleans to assist in the investigation of Kennedy's assassination? Who knows? Reed apparently already knew that Oswald was the "patsy."

#5: Why Oswald's Revolver, Which Allegedly Was Used to Kill Officer J.D. Tippit, Was Never Tested?:

Four cartridges allegedly found at the crime scene were matched to Oswald's revolver, but not until a six-day delay by the Dallas police, during which time they had possession of the revolver. The initial list of evidence by the Dallas police did not include cartridges of any kind, arousing suspicion that Oswald's revolver had been fired after the fact to produce the cartridges. But to the embarrassment of the Dallas police and the WC, it was discovered that the cartridges submitted belatedly as evidence were probably not the cartridges actually found at the scene, because the ones that were found had been handed to Officer J. M. Poe, who later testified that he believed he had marked them with his initials, a common law-enforcement practice at the time. There were no initials of any kind on any of the four cartridges.

According to the WC, the four bullets found in Tippit's body could not be identified with Oswald's revolver. Of the four bullets, three were from one manufacturer and the fourth from another manufacturer. Bullets are generally not sold in mixed lots. There was a six-day delay by Dallas police in submitting the cartridges to the FBI, during which time they had possession of the revolver and plausibly could have fired bullets to create the cartridges. The cartridges, belatedly submitted to the FBI, did not bear the initials of Officer Poe, who had marked them with his initials when he found them.

As Oswald was being arrested, several witnesses and Dallas police officers heard a "snap" from Oswald's revolver, but no shot was fired. Oswald had plenty of bullets and he may have allegedly tried to fire at the arresting officer, but all that was heard was a snap. Why? Because Jack Ruby handed him a revolver with a bent firing pin. It could not fire, but Oswald did not know that. Ruby and the conspiracy team was hoping that Oswald would be killed at the scene as the President's assassin and later as the assassin of a fellow police officer. Because Oswald yelled "police brutality" and "I'm not resisting" in a theater, albeit a theater with only twenty-four patrons in it, Oswald's life was saved at that time. Once in police custody,

Jack Ruby role became activated and he would kill Oswald in a matter of 46 hours.

#6: Why the Dallas Police Department Made Two Arrests—With one Oswald Arrested On The Balcony of the Texas Theater; and Another Arrest of another Oswald Arrested On the First Floor of the Theater?

The President was just killed. Dallas was the epicenter for a manhunt to capture the President's killer. While the exact timing of Oswald's arrest may have been muddied by the WC in its efforts to develop a particular narrative, there was no doubt that Lee Harvey Oswald was arrested in the rear of the first floor of the theater. Yet in the Texas archives, there is a police statement declaring that Oswald was arrested in the balcony of the Texas Theater and charged with the President's murder.[344] Johnny Brewer, the employee from Hardy's show store across the street from the theater, coaxed Julia Postal, the kiosk employee at the theater, into calling the police, but Postal was   not   the   only   person   to   call   the   police.

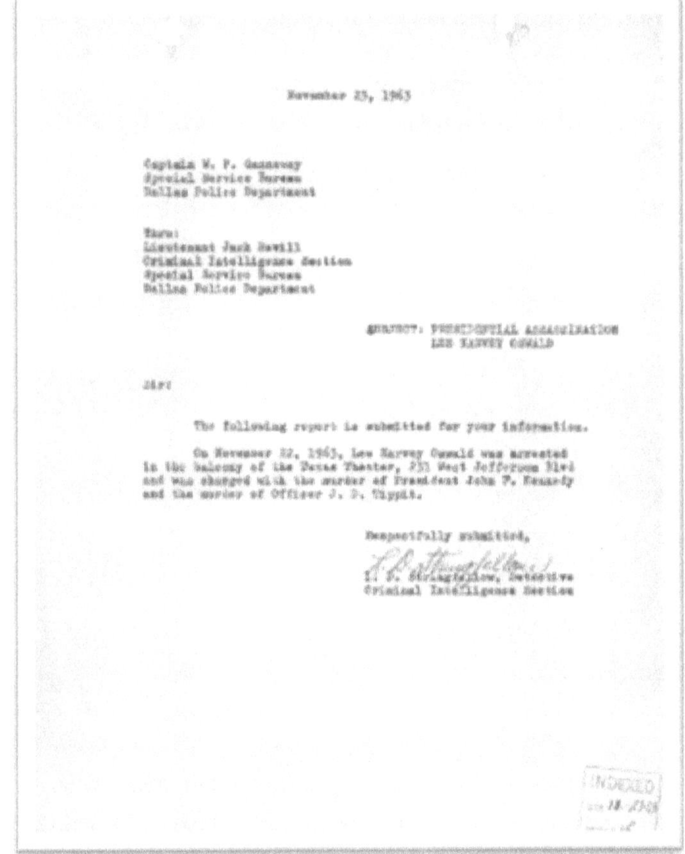

Dallas Assistant District Attorney Jim Bowie said "there were over a half-dozen anonymous phone calls made to the Dallas Police advising that a suspicious man had gone into the Texas Theater." All of these calls to police headquarters were made for the express purpose of cajoling and luring the police to the Texas Theater in search of a "suspicious man," who may have murdered Officer Tippit. After a "half-dozen" anonymous phone calls, the police dispatcher announced that a suspect had entered the Texas Theater *and was*

hiding in the balcony. Julia Postal called the police at 1:45pm about someone entering the theater without paying.[345]

At 1:46pm, the Dallas Police dispatcher broadcast the following message: "Have information a suspect just went in the Texas Theater on West Jefferson ..... *supposed to be hiding in balcony*." Once the police arrived, Julia Postal tells the police officer that the man that did not pay for a ticket was upstairs in the balcony.[346] To truth of the matter is that both Oswald and his double paid for a ticket.

Again, Jack Davis, a movie patron, saw Oswald inside the Texas Theater. Jack Davis remembered the time of 1:07pm because when Oswald arrived, the credits were rolling for the first movie. Davis distinctly recalled Oswald's odd behavior because Oswald sat next to him even though there were only about twenty-four patrons in the entire theater, yet there were about 900 seats, so there were plenty of empty seats.[347] Then Oswald moved and sat next to someone else, and then moved again and sat next to another patron.

Oswald was looking for his contact that would drive him to Redbird Airport. That contact would have matched the half-torn dollar bill he was given by Bill Shelley, his supervisor at the TSBD. Oswald was desperate to find this contact so he could safely get out of Dallas, but the contact was never found.

Between approximately 1:07pm, when Jack Davis saw Oswald, until around 1:45pm, Oswald was in the theater trying to find his contact.[348] Oswald's double entered the theater around 1:44pm and went upstairs and smoked a cigarette, still wearing the white shirt he had been seen wearing when he killed officer Tippit. As of this writing, two police statements from the Dallas Police Department show one Oswald being arrested in the balcony and another Oswald being arrested on the first floor of the theater. The

Oswald encountered in the balcony was questioned and then released.[349] In total, 16 Officers swarmed the theater and officially arrested Oswald on the first floor of the theater, but many more showed up that were responding to a report of someone not paying for a 93-cent movie ticket.

Chapter 19: The Big Event

The time has come to lay out what I conclude happened in Dallas on November 22, 1963. We have gone through a journey of peeling away and looking critically at witness statements, evidence, and facts. Now we have come to the "The Big Event" without any created reality, theater, or puppet mastery. It lays out exactly what happened that day based on the best evidence available today. President Kennedy had almost completed his fateful trip to Texas. He had one major speaking engagement scheduled after his motorcade had gone through Dealey Plaza, but he would not be leaving Dealey Plaza alive.

This chapter is largely a timeline of the key events that happened that day. I tried to be as precise and granular as I could with all relevant facts, but it may never be known exactly how many shooters and bullets were fired on or at President Kennedy or Governor Connally that day. It was an operation that intentionally created confusion and mayhem, especially in Dealey Plaza.[350] It may also never be understood what Lee Harvey Oswald knew about that day's plans. He certainly knew an attempt on Kennedy's life would be made, but did he know more than that? While I assert that Oswald did not kill Tippit or Kennedy, it seems clear that he tried to kill a police officer with a revolver not knowing the revolver had a bent firing pin as many people heard the revolver clearly "click." We may never know what Oswald knew since he had been silenced by a bullet from Jack Ruby's pistol.

In the timeline below, I place an asterisk (*) after certain times to indicate approximate times based on the best evidence and deductive reasoning. Where there is no asterisk after the time, it is largely undisputed and corroborated by several sources. I meticulously went through the number of gunshots that were fired and, whenever possible, I refer to Zapruder frames as a point of reference, as well as other relevant photos.[351] Zapruder's 8mm camera recorded at 18.3 frames per second on average, which comes to about .0546 seconds per frame. The loudest gun shots from the digitally remastered Dictabelt recording were superimposed onto the Zapruder film to further identify when the shots were fired. There are also reports that some shooters used sabots that may have slowed the velocity of the bullets to subsonic speeds, thus avoiding the boom or shockwave crash that higher-velocity bullets make. Also, there are other shots unaccounted for because they missed their target, such as the signal shot, the shot that hit the freeway sign, the shot or shots that caused damage to the limousine's windshield and rear-view mirror, and another shot that was fired from the grassy knoll and missed the limousine altogether. Finally, please also note that it is unknown whether Connally was shot by one bullet or two, but in the timeline below, I assert only one bullet wounded him. The scenario below assumes Connally was shot once by Mac Wallace's .30-06 non-bolt action rifle.

The remastered Dictabelt recording clearly indicates that four shots were fired that day but remember that some shooters used silencers, thus avoiding detection from the Dictabelt. The House Select Committee on Assassinations used the digitally remastered Dictabelt recording that was superimposed onto the Zapruder film to conclude that four shots were fired and one came from a location other than the TSBD, probably from the grassy knoll. This, in turn, formed the basis for the HSCA's ultimate conclusion that President Kennedy had been killed by a conspiracy, but the HSCA could not come to a firm conclusion as to who the conspirators were.

Please note that a Congressional body, the HSCA, effectively disagreed with and arguably rescinded the Warren Commission's findings and conclusions. Recall that the WC was merely an Executive-branch body created by Presidential Order. The HSCA disagreed with the WC in two important ways: 1) there were at least four shots fired that day; and 2) that one shot came from a location other than the TSBD. What weight is given to the HSCA conclusions? To me, the HSCA is entitled to more persuasive weight than the Warren Commission because one the members of the WC were appointed by LBJ, whereas the members of the HSCA were elected by the American people. I also merely underscore that those that believe in the WC's findings have to reconcile the HSCA's findings.

One important fact to note here as well. Roderick A. MacKenzie III wrote a book called *"The Men that Don't Fit In."*[352] In it, he claims to have run a safehouse located on Holland Avenue, where Jack Ruby, Ruth Anne Martinez, Loy Factor, Mac Wallace, Oswald and / or Oswald's double, and others met to go over plans for this assassination. More importantly, MacKenzie claims that Mac Wallace became drunk one night after the assassination, as he often did, and spilled all the details of the assassination to him, including naming the numerous shooters in Dealey Plaza, as well as the people that were located in locked offices of the second floor front of the TSBD.[353] These offices provided a clear view of the assassination scene and were a central communications center for the conspirators. In other words, the second-floor executive offices were converted into a command center that day. Those allegedly in the command center were Cliff Carter, Carlos Marcello, Jack Ruby, George Reese, and possibly, Sam Giancana.

While I cannot confirm the presence of any of these men in the command center, there is evidence that the offices were locked and that the people inside the offices did not open their doors even when people knocked on them.[354] Additionally, the TSBD was owned by David Harrold Byrd and friends of Clint Murchison, Haroldson L. Hunt and Sid Richardson, and was part of the Big Oil group in Dallas. Byrd was also a part of the Suite 8F group of businessmen that supported Johnson. Byrd would have been the one to authorize any personnel and actions needed to support an operation such as this. The notion of a command center, especially in this location, is logical, probable, and supported by some evidence. Recall that this was a secret operation that could not fail. Johnson was about to be exposed and his corrupt empire was about to fall. Time was against him. The President had to be killed in Dallas.

And so, we return to Friday, November 22, 1963.

3:10am Nine Secret Service agents assigned to the Presidential detail are still partying at "The Cellar Door" Bar in Fort Worth.[355] Secret Service Agent Clint Hill is not among them because he left about an hour earlier.

6:30am* Oswald is in Ruth Paine's home in Irving, Texas. He awakens from a restless night's sleep. Marina is still sleeping. He has an important day ahead of him, and he is aware it can be dangerous, but he has done everything in his power by reporting everything he knows to his CIA handler, Maurice Bishop, as well as his FBI handler. In his mind, his relationship with Marina has already taken its course. They have been through many ups and downs in their short marriage. Oswald's first love is his secretive life.

He never formally says goodbye to Marina or his young daughters. He gets dressed in an old, dark, rust-brown, tweed-like shirt with buttons missing at the top, exposing his stained white t-shirt. He wears an identification bracelet with a rubber band. He wears old, torn, light grey work pants made of khaki or wool material. He puts on a blue-grey work jacket. He removes his wedding ring and places it in a cup along with $170, which he recently received as a paid FBI informant. The bills are crisp. Oswald then walks about a block to Buell Wesley Frazier's house with his lunch bag containing a cheese sandwich and an apple.

Oswald's tasks for this day are relatively simple. Go to work like normal. Pretend he does not know why there is all this fuss outside of the building by asking his co-workers what all the fuss is about. Appear and act disinterested. From noon until 12:30pm, he is to have lunch in the first-floor lunchroom. Shortly after 12:30pm, he is to receive additional instructions from Bill Shelley, his supervisor.

Oswald is to leave the Depository and board Marsalis bus #433 (route 1213) to Oak Cliff. Oswald does not normally take this bus, and certainly not at this time of the day, but these are his orders. After passing the Houston Street viaduct, Oswald is to get off the bus at the first stop and will be picked up by Officer J.D. Tippit, who will drive him to his rooming house, where he is to change into black pants. Officer J.D. Tippit will then provide a police officer's shirt for him to wear. Oswald will then be safely driven to Redbird Airport. With luck, he will be in Mexico by the weekend and eventually be reunited with Judyth Vary Baker. He believes he will also be given a duffel bag full of cash for all his efforts infiltrating a group of JFK assassins.

7:10am Oswald arrives at Frazier's house and looks in the window. He sees Frazier's sister, Linnie Mae Randall, at the sink. She is startled to see Oswald at the window. Frazier goes to the door and tells Oswald to hang loose while he finishes breakfast.

7:21am Frazier comes out of his house and sees Oswald waiting under the carport. They both enter Frazier's 1954 Chevy. Oswald places his lunch on the seat between him and Frazier. They take off for the Texas School Book Depository.

7:25am* Jack Ruby is in his apartment after about three hours of sleep. He would normally still be sleeping as his job requires him to keep long night hours. But today is very important. He showers and drives to meet John Roselli at Ol' South Pancake House in Fort Worth. He will deliver fake secret service credentials in an envelope to Roselli so that Roselli can distribute them to the other men who will be in key locations in Dealey Plaza, including the grassy knoll. He had received the envelope from David Atlee Phillips a few days before. James Files Sutton is also waiting at the Pancake House but is not seen by Jack Ruby.

7:51am Frazier pulls into the parking area north of the TSBD annex. He stays in his car, revving the engine to charge up the battery even though he had just driven thirty minutes and there is no evidence he had to jumpstart his Chevy. Oswald enters work as he normally does and is seen by co-worker Jack Dougherty as he enters the building with no long bag in his hands.

7:57am* Linnie Mae Randle sees Oswald wearing a dark grey work jacket as he begins his shift.

7:59am* Oswald places his lunch in the first-floor lunchroom and hangs up his grey jacket there. This room is also known as the domino room.

8:10am Anti-Castro activist Herminio Diaz Garcia stashes a carbine with a scope and silencer in the bottom of a large toolbox and leaves for work. He is dressed like a laborer on the construction crew putting down new flooring on the 5th and 6th floor of the TSBD. He is one of two men recently added to the crew by building owner D.H. Byrd in order to complete the work before the Thanksgiving holiday. The other man is Cuban dissident Emilio Santana. Diaz Garcia throws his toolbox in the back of an old white Ford panel truck then drives over to East 12th Street to pick up Santana. The two then make the short drive across the Jefferson Viaduct into downtown Dallas and the TSBD.[356]

8:30am Jack Ruby arrives at the Good Ol' South Pancake House and goes inside. He sees Johnny Roselli sitting alone in a booth and goes over to join him. Ruby does not see Jimmy Files Sutton sitting at the counter watching the two men as they sit and chat for about five minutes. Ruby takes the brown envelope out of his jacket and slides it over to Roselli. Then Ruby gets up and leaves, followed first by Sutton, and Roselli a few minutes later.

11:41am* Secret Service Agents Henry (Hank) Rybka and Winston Lawton are recalled (removed) from the Presidential motorcade team by Supervisor Emory Roberts at Love Field. (See picture of Rybka above.) Both of these agents were assigned to the White house detail and had gone with the President when he visited other cities, including this trip to Texas up until this time. No reason is given for recalling them. I suspect that their removal w because they had expressed affinity toward Kennedy in the past and senior Secret Service leadership intentionally wanted this detail to be light in security, so they were chosen to be recalled. Both Rybka and Lawson lived with overwhelming guilt after this fateful day.

12:15pm Arnold and Barbara Rowland see a man with a high-powered rifle in an upper window on the left-hand side of the depository (i.e., the west end), and an older, dark-skinned man, about fifty-five years old, standing on the right of the building.[357] These shooters are Mac Wallace and Loy Factor. Numerous other witnesses have varying accounts of seeing more than one shooter on the sixth floor prior to the assassination.

12:24pm Ruby Henderson sees them too. (She later pins the time down exactly to 12:24pm. That is the time that prisoners in the Dallas County Jail overlooking Dealey Plaza notice two men, 'one dark-skinned or Mexican looking' in a window on the sixth floor of the depository.) One of the men checks the telescopic sight on a rifle.[358]

12:25pm Loy Factor and Ruth Anne Martinez arrive on the sixth floor. Loy Factor sees Oswald's double, dressed in a white shirt, adjusting the scope of one of the rifles and handing it to Mac Wallace. Then Oswald's double checks the scope of another rifle.

12:26pm* Steelworker Richard Randolph Carr, working on the seventh floor of the new courthouse building on the corner of Houston Street in Dealey Plaza, sees a man on the sixth floor of the depository before the shooting. The man Carr sees is nothing like Lee Harvey Oswald. This man is wearing a hat and horn-rimmed glasses. This man is Mac Wallace.[359]

12:27pm* Ruth Anne Martinez tells Mac Wallace and Oswald's double not to stick their rifles out of the windows and to stand back away from the windows.

12:29pm* As the motorcade approaches Dealey Plaza, Lee Bowers, standing in the north tower in the Union Terminal rail yard, sees two men standing behind the picket fence overlooking the grassy knoll. One of the men is middle-aged, fairly heavy set, wearing a white shirt with dark trousers. The second man is in his mid-twenties, wearing a plaid shirt or a plaid jacket. The man in the plaid jacket is James Files Sutton, based on his own admission. Bowers also sees two parking lot attendants who were wearing uniforms. No one attempts to locate or question any of these men.

12:30pm The first shot rings out and breaks the crowd's enthusiasm. It is a signal shot to the other assassins. Seconds later, there are four shots in a cluster in the first group. The shots are fired almost simultaneously, with some shots being muffled or silenced. In the second cluster, as the limousine approaches the grassy knoll, four more shots are fired in another cluster, again, only milliseconds apart from each other, making it impossible for most humans to discern how many shots were fired. The total number of shots fired are ten (1 signal shot; 4 first cluster of shots just past the TSBD; 4 more shots near the grassy knoll).

Shot #1:

12:30pm (Z188, this is the first shot confirmed by the Dictabelt recording). The Presidential motorcade arrives at Dealey Plaza five minutes behind schedule. The President's limousine passes the TSBD. About 80 feet past the TSBD, Ruth Anne Martinez, standing in the westernmost window of the TSBD, raises her right arm, counts down ...3 ... 2 ...1 ... as she lowers her arm, then yells "fire!" Lawrence Loy Factor, kneeling close to Ruth Anne, fires the very first shot from the TSBD's western window   on   the   sixth   floor.

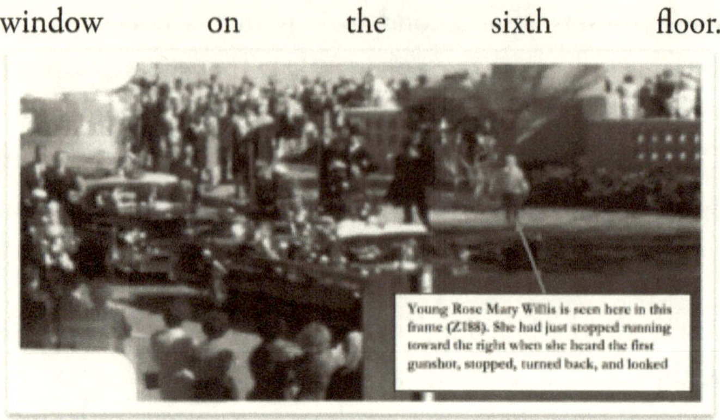

The shot's effects can be seen at approximately frame 188 of the Zapruder film when young Rose Mary Willis, in her red dress and white hooded top, stops running and turns back to look toward the Depository. This shot is a signal shot to alert the shooters in the other kill zones.

Factor uses a Mauser 7.65mm rifle.[360] The shot zips over the President's head and right shoulder, breaks through the upper left chrome upper trim (as viewed from behind) of the windshield and ricochets off the south curb of Elm, then the south curb of Main and cuts bystander James Tague in the face as he stands on the south side of Main near the triple underpass.[361]

The cheer from onlookers is eclipsed by confusion and disbelief. Many assume the loud bang is a backfire or firecracker, including Governor Connally and Nellie Connally.

Shot #2:

(approximately Z208-210; or 1 second after the signal shot; this is the second shot confirmed by the Dictabelt recording). Please note that in the Zapruder film, the Stemmons Freeway sign is largely blocking the limousine, so it is not shown here. Instead, a close-up of the Altgens6 photo is used for this illustration. Please also note that the windshield does not appear to be cracked at this time. Roscoe White, dressed in his Dallas Police uniform, shoots President Kennedy, who was looking toward the grassy knoll. Roscoe shoots from behind the northern picket fence on the grassy knoll. The shot probably passes under the Stemmons Freeway sign straight into JFK's throat from JFK's right front. White fires a pistol rifle (short Mauser) that does not pass through the President's throat.

The President, sitting straight up, grasps toward the entrance wound at the base of his throat from the frontal throat shot. (See cropped Altgens6 photo above.) This shot makes the President move to the left about three inches, and causes some forthcoming shots to miss their target. Jackie grabs JFK's left arm.

In the Zapruder film, the President is seen coming past the Stemmons Freeway sign with his elbows extended outward. Some people believe him to be in the Thorburn position – a reflex position assumed by the elbows, in an outward, butterfly position, immediately after injury to the spinal cord in the lower cervical region, but his elbows are not locked in this position and there is no injury to the spinal cord.

The doctors at Parkland hospital who see the wound in Kennedy's throat state this wound was about 4-5mm wide with rounded, inverted edges – a clear sign of it being an entrance wound. A Carcano bullet is 7.57 mm in diameter.[362] Some assassins use a sabot from high-powered rifles to slow down the bullet in order to avoid a sonic boom. The strong indication of an entrance wound in the throat is later compromised by the insertion of the tracheostomy tube at Parkland Hospital.

The President's limousine advances. Jackie leans in further to take a look at JFK and desperately tries to grasp what is happening.

Shot #3:

Clyde Foust or John Ernst, two Texas hit men hired by Mac Wallace, are situated on the grassy knoll. One of them fires and hits the Stemmons Freeway sign, making a loud clang and further contributing to the confusion. (The sign is replaced about a week later because having it exposed would indicate an additional, unaccounted bullet and thus strong indicia of a conspiracy.

Shot #4:

From the roof of the Dallas Records Building, a small diameter bullet, designed to pierce one or two inches of skin, is fired and aimed at the President's heart, but because the President has moved slightly to his left, the shot enters just to the right of his spinal cord.

Shot #5:

(Z235; 2.57 seconds after the signal shot, not heard by the Dictabelt recording). Mac Wallace, Lyndon Johnson's personal hitman, in position with his .30-06 rifle on the sixth floor. Wallace fires his first shot and hits Governor Connally. Wallace thinks that Connally is Senator Yarborough.

This is frame number 235 from the Zapruder film. The third shot from Mac Wallace hits Governor Connally in the back and the bullet exits just below his right nipple. Governor Connally is turning toward his right.

12:30pm Cliff Carter, Mac Wallace, the grassy knoll shooters, the shooter positioned at the roof of the Dallas Records building, and the shooters in the Dal-Tex building notice that the President is still alive. The limousine advances but applies its brakes as it approaches the bulk of the grassy knoll on the right.

A man with a blue shirt, a cap, and allegedly a walkie talkie in his hand steps down from the curb and onto the street. His hand is raised with a closed fist, indicating the limousine to stop or slow down. The limousine does in fact brake because many people see it slow to a crawl and see its brake lights on.

Cliff Carter gives another signal for the assassins to shoot. Another cluster of shots are fired almost simultaneously.

The man in the blue shirt has his fist raised, a signal to stop. The limousine brakes. The man next to him, known as Umbrella man, is merely a protester of JFK's father's appeasement (pro-Nazi) policies. It is a criticism of Neville Chamberlain, who famously carried an umbrella in peace talks with Hitler.

Shot #6:

(Z312, or 6.7 seconds after the initial signal shot; this is the third shot confirmed by the Dictabelt recording and has been determined to come from the grassy knoll). Either Frank Sturgis or James Files takes a shot from the grassy knoll, and many people associate it with the fatal head shot. James Files Sutton claims to have used custom-made bullets that fragment upon impact in order to cause the most damage. This assertion appears to be correct inasmuch as this shot caused a significant exit wound in the back of the President's head. (Please note that the WC never believed this shot occurred, but the 1978 House Select Committee on Assassination did believe this shot occurred when it concluded that the President was killed by a conspiracy with a man taking a shot at the President from the grassy knoll. The Committee did not find sufficient evidence, however, to assign blame to a group of individuals, such as the Mafia or the CIA.)

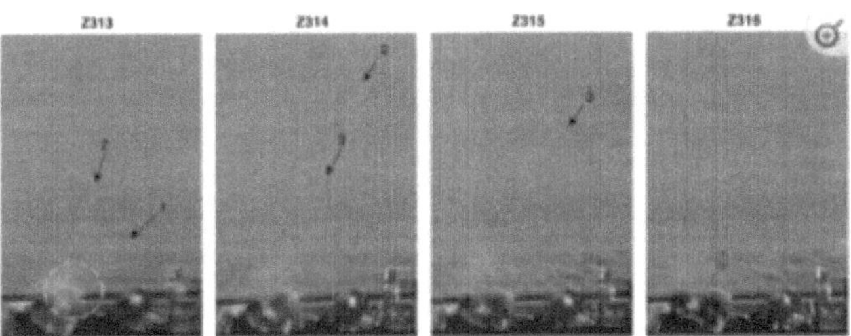

In these frames, brain and skull matter can be seen by the arrows. Courtesy of The National Library of Medicine, available at: https://www.ncbi.nlm.nih.gov/pmc/articles/PMC5934694/

The President's head jerks violently back. The motorcycle officers to the left of the limousine are splattered with blood and brain matter, whereas the officers to the right of the limousine are not splattered at all. Jackie, likewise, is splattered with blood and brain matter.

<u>Shot #7</u>:

(Z327, 0.8 seconds after the fatal headshot above, and 7.59 seconds after the signal shot. This is the fourth shot confirmed by the Dictabelt recording). Oswald's double, shooting from the eastern most window of the TSBD, takes his first and only shot, aiming at Kennedy's head. This shot enters the back of Kennedy's already fractured skull from the shot at Z313, and blood and brain matter exit the front of his face and toward the jump seats and dashboard in front of him. Governor Connally's testimony later confirms that after Nellie Connally pulled him toward her lap, he saw blood and brain matter splash over the blue interior of the Lincoln.

<u>Shot #8</u>:

(Not heard by the Dictabelt recording). Chuck Nicoletti (in the Dal-Tex second floor open window, by the fire-escape) – managed by hit team George H.W. Bush;

assisted by Jim Braden (Meyer Lanskey's mob courier from California). Nicoletti fires a shot that goes over the top of the President, slams into the limousine's rearview mirror, and cracks the windshield. Nicoletti's aim, failing to account for the slowing limo, is high and to the left of the President's head (viewed from behind). Emmett Hudson, standing on the grassy knoll steps, tells the FBI that the shots sounded as if they were *fired by someone at a position that was behind him and to his left* (emphasis added). See the famous Mary Moorman photo, above.

Shot #9:

Another shot is fired from a grassy knoll shooter, possibly a shooter located inside one of the pergolas, but the shot misses completely and continues its path in a southerly trajectory. This shot is not picked up by the Dictabelt recording.

Jacqueline Kennedy's shock begins. In a vain effort to help her husband, she climbs on top of the moving car's trunk to collect chunks of the President's brain and skull matter. Special Agent Clint Hill jumps on the back of the limousine and pushes Jaqueline back in the seat. Hill looks back to the Secret Service follow-up car and gives a thumbs down after seeing the large hole in the back of the President's head. Jaqueline never remembers climbing on the trunk. The limousine speeds off, at times as fast as 80 miles per hour, to Parkland Hospital.

Bill and Gaye Newman see the President's head explode, turn around, and throw their children to the ground. They are facing the grassy knoll because the shots came from behind them.

12:30pm Ed Hoffman, a deaf mute, is standing on the grassy knoll near the railroad underpass. Immediately after the shots are fired, he sees a man wearing a suit and tie with a rifle in his hand run along the back of the grassy knoll fence towards the underpass and toss a rifle to an awaiting accomplice dressed as a railway worker. (Several shooters had a backup to handle and dispose of a gun as part of the CIA's multi-layered redundancy or backup plans so that the actual shooter, if arrested, would not be found with a gun, and if the backup shooter were arrested, he would not have gun residue on him. The FBI later attempt to bribe Ed Hoffman so he would not tell his story.[363] (The man in the suit is suspected of being

Frank   Sturgis.)

A wave of people run toward the grassy knoll, including Dallas police officers. One of them is Officer Joe Smith, who smells gun smoke in the air and is confronted by a man with a sports jacket. Smith has his revolver drawn, but the stranger reassures him that there is nothing noteworthy here, flashing his secret service badge.

Eight other people smell gun smoke near the grassy knoll, including Senator Ralph Yarborough, who is sitting with LBJ and Lady Bird.

Within 15 to 20 seconds after the shooting, Dorothy Garner, a supervisor working on the fourth floor, runs toward the northwest stairwell and remains there as she sees Victoria Adams and Sandra Skyles go down the stairs. Adams and Skyles do not see or hear anyone else in the old, wooden stairwell or using the freight elevator.

12:31pm* Adams and Skyles reach the first floor. They notice Billy Lovelady and Bill Shelley in the rear of the building. Adams tells them that she and Skyles think the

President has been shot. Lovelady and Shelley are unmoved by this information.

Dallas police officer Joe Marshall Smith and Deputy Sheriff Seymour Weitzman are the first law enforcement officials to arrive in the parking lot between the TSBD and the grassy knoll. Smith says: "This woman came up to me and she was just in hysterics. She told me, 'They are shooting the President from the bushes.' So, I immediately proceeded up there ..... There was some deputy sheriff with me (Weitzman), and I believe one Secret Service man when I got there .... . I pulled my pistol from my holster ..... [and] just as I did, he showed me that he was a Secret Service agent."

Deputy Sheriff Seymour Weitzman is with Smith when they confront the man who told him that everything was under control and displayed Secret Service credentials. (Weitzman later says the man was of medium height, with dark hair, and wearing a light windbreaker. Years later Weitzman is interviewed by author Michael Canfield and shown a photograph of Bernard Barker (a future Watergate burglar along with Hunt and Sturgis). Weitzman says, "Yes, that's him," and identifies Barker as the man who showed him Secret Service credentials on the grassy knoll.)

12:31pm* Officer Marrion L. Baker runs into the Depository and finds Supervisor Truly, who takes Officer Baker to the northwest stairwell, passing the nearby passenger elevator for unknown reasons. Officer Baker notices two white men, who are probably Billy Lovelady and Bill Shelley. One man is standing next to the building's electrical panel near the northeast portion of the building. The other man is near the northwest stairwell. Baker and Truly run to the freight elevators on the north side of the building. Truly calls both elevators. Neither one moves. Truly notices the lights are out. Truly and Baker then take the wooden northwest stairwell and head upstairs.

12:31pm* On the second floor, Baker, with his gun drawn, catches a glimpse of a person who has his back turned toward Baker. Baker moves closer to him while Truly continues going up the stairs. Baker yells at this person, "come here." It is Oswald. Oswald calmly turns around and walks toward Baker. By this time, Truly realizes Baker was not behind him and returns down the stairs to where Baker and Oswald are on the second floor near the doorway to the lunchroom. Oswald is emotionless even though Baker is pointing a gun at him. Baker asks if he works here and Truly confirms that he does. (Baker later states he was wearing a *dark-brown jacket and white t-shirt underneath*. Oswald confirms this encounter during the interrogation with Captain Fritz.)

12:32pm* Richard Randolph Carr sees three men exiting from the northeast part of the TSBD and enter a Nash Rambler. He notices the man he saw in a sixth-floor window before the shooting. He is wearing a distinctive, tan-colored sports coat and is hurrying away with two other men on the sidewalk. They get into a grey Rambler station wagon and are driven away.[364] This man in the tan-colored jacket is Mac Wallace. The other man is Frank

Sturgis. A third man, the driver, is a dark-skinned Latino-looking man with a thick neck.

12:33pm* Dorothy Garner, still standing by the northwest stairwell on the fourth floor, sees Officer Baker and Supervisor Truly run past them.

12:33pm* Radio Programmer, Pierce Allman, speaks briefly with Oswald in the TSBD lobby, asking Oswald where the pay phone is and later describes him as being totally calm. Oswald does not say anything but merely points to the area of the pay phone.

12:35pm* NBC news correspondent Robert MacNeil comes running from the grassy knoll. He returns to the TSBD to use the pay phone. As he enters the lobby, he encounters three exceedingly calm and relaxed men in the lobby of the TSBD. One of these people is Oswald, who is wearing his rust-brown shirt with the sleeves rolled up. The other two men are probably Bill Shelley and Billy Lovelady.

12:35pm* Across the street from the TSBD, Mrs. Louis Velez and two co-workers probably of McKell's Women's Sportswear with offices in the Dal-Tex building and future mayor Wes Wise see Jack Ruby walking up and down the street by the main entrance of the TSBD.

12:35pm* Bill Shelley tells Oswald to go to his rooming house and then meet his contact at the Texas Theater. Shelley gives him a dollar bill torn in half that will be confirmation of his contact in the theater. Oswald will be driven from the theater to the airport once he meets with his contact.

12:36pm* Oswald walks out of the TSBD from the north end where a loading dock was located, walks down Houston Street, and heads east upon arriving at Elm Street. Just as Oswald turns east, he is unexpectedly confronted by Jack Ruby. Ruby stands very close to Oswald. Lucy Lopez, Mrs. Louis Velez and her two co-workers know both Ruby and Oswald and see Ruby give Oswald a revolver. The revolver has a bent firing pin, but Oswald does not know that; Ruby does. The purpose of the revolver is to incite a deadly shootout where Oswald would be killed. Oswald is getting suspicious that he is being set up. He already knows something happened to the President and he was just given a revolver by Jack Ruby.

12:38pm Police officer D.V. Harkness goes to the back of the TSBD (the north end) and, he testified to the WC, "There were some Secret Service agents there. I didn't get them identified. They told me they were Secret Service." As we learn later, no Secret Service agents were officially assigned to the Dealey Plaza area.

12:40pm Deputy Sheriff Roger Craig, along with five other witnesses,[365] sees Oswald's double running from the back of the TSBD annex, over the grassy knoll, and into a double-parked Nash Rambler station wagon with a chrome luggage rack. This Rambler is owned by Clay Shaw. Oswald's double shrill whistles at the Rambler as he runs towards it. The car is driven by a dark-skinned Latino man. Oswald's double is seen wearing a white shirt. One witness, Helen Forrest, later remarks prophetically: "If it wasn't Oswald, then it was his identical twin."

12:40pm Oswald boards Cecil McWatter's bus about five blocks east of the TSBD on Elm Street. The bus is stuck in slow-moving traffic.. Oswald bangs on the door to get the driver's attention. A blonde-haired lady follows him onto the bus. The bus is the "Marsalis-Ramona-Elwood" bus on the "1213" route. Oswald pays his 23-cent fare. He is seen by his former landlady, Mary Bledsoe, and she describes Oswald as wearing a brown shirt with holes in the elbows and ragged, grey work pants.

On CBS, the soap opera, "As the World Turns," is interrupted and viewers receive the first national television report of the shooting from CBS News Anchorman, Walter Cronkite.

12:43pm The President's limousine arrives at Parkland Hospital. The President is motionless, and his head is on Jaqueline Kennedy's lap. She hovers over her husband and refuses to move. She does not want people to see her Jack in this way. Special Agent Hill understands. He removes his jacket and places it over the President's head. Jacqueline finally lets go of her dying husband. In her hand are three pieces of his skull and brain matter, which she later gives to a hospital nurse.

12:44pm Oswald, after only advancing two blocks in the bus because of heavy traffic, obtains a transfer, gets off the bus, and decides to walk to the nearby Greyhound bus terminal to find a cab. The blonde-haired lady that followed Oswald onto the bus also gets off at the same time as Oswald.

12:46pm* Captain Westbrook and Sergeant Croy board the bus Oswald was just on. They are there to kill Oswald as part of Plan A. They know Oswald has a revolver with a bent firing pin, but Oswald is not on the bus. They search all passengers for weapons. It is the only bus searched in this manner after the assassination. (Please also note that the bus was approaching the TSBD, not riding away from it.) After the quick search, traffic subsides, and the bus continues on its regular route to the Oak Cliff neighborhood.

12:47pm* The Rambler, driven by a dark-skinned, Latino-looking man with Mac Wallace, Frank Sturgis, and Oswald's double arrives at a safe house on Holland Avenue. The Latino-looking man, Mac Wallace, and Frank Sturgis get off here. Oswald's double comes to the driver's seat and drives to the Tidy Lady Launderette.

12:48pm Oswald boards William Whaley's cab. The same blonde-haired lady also attempts to board the same cab as Oswald. Oswald offers up the cab to the lady. She refuses and walks away. Oswald asks to be taken to the 500 block of North Beckley. Oswald's rooming house is two blocks away, on the 700 block of North Beckley. Oswald needs time to think about what is going on. Ruby just gave him a revolver for no known reason and he is being followed by a blonde-haired woman. Unbeknownst to Oswald, someone also is taking pictures of the bus Oswald was just on. (Taxicab driver Whaley later describes Oswald as wearing a dark shirt with white spots and grey khaki pants. He tells the WC that Oswald's shirt was "open three buttons down" and that he wore a t-shirt underneath that was "a little soiled around the collar." He also says that Oswald was wearing "some kind of a jacket that almost matched the grey pants.")

12:50pm Kennedy arrives at Parkland Hospital with approximately 25% of his brain missing. The doctors at Parkland Hospital conclude that Kennedy's wounds are too severe for medical intervention. (This would be true even with today's medical advances.) JFK is pronounced dead; however, the time of death is delayed so that he can be given the last rites by a local Catholic priest.

Officer J.D. Tippit, at the GLOCO gas station, sees Cecil McWatter's bus pass the Houston Street viaduct without stopping at the intersection of Zang and Marsalis, but instead, keeps going. Tippit begins to panic. He follows the bus.

12:53pm Oswald is dropped off a few blocks from his rooming house by taxicab driver Whaley.

12:54pm Tippit reports his location at Lancaster and Eighth Street.

12:58pm Captain Fritz arrives at the TSBD. By this time, Dallas PD officers and Sheriff's deputies are on every floor of the TSBD.

12:59pm Oswald arrives at his rooming house and is, for the first time, in a rush. He is expected at the Texas Theater at 1pm. Earlene Roberts, the rooming house's housekeeper, notices Oswald is in a rush and does not see him with a jacket on. Oswald says nothing and goes into his room.

While in his room, Oswald removes his long-sleeved, button-down, reddish-brown shirt and his grey pants. He puts them in the lower drawer of his dresser. He puts on dark grey dress pants and a long-sleeved, reddish-brown shirt similar to the one he wore to work except without white flakes or spots and wears it over his dirty white t-shirt. He is not wearing a jacket.

1:00pm President John F. Kennedy is officially declared dead. All domestic television networks are interrupted.

Michael Paine places a collect call from his work to Ruth Paine's home in Irving and says he feels sure Oswald has killed the President but does not feel Oswald is responsible. Paine then tells his estranged wife, "We both know who is responsible." The call is overheard by the operator. (The WC made this call appear as if were made on November 23, 1963, in order to bury the issue.)

Oswald's double arrives at the Tidy Lady Launderette.[366] He is seen by John Wesley and Oda Pennington. Oswald's double enters the launderette, places a call on the pay phone, and speaks Spanish. Oswald's double then leaves the launderette and walks toward Jefferson Boulevard, abandoning the Nash Rambler.

1:01pm* While Oswald is in his room changing his clothes, Earlene Roberts notices a Dallas Police Department patrol car with two uniformed officers in it. The driver honks the horn twice. Then the patrol car slowly goes around the corner. The officers are Captain Westbrook and Sergeant Croy.

1:03pm* A frantic Tippit enters the Top Ten record store and asks to use the phone. He dials a number, but no one picks up. Tippit then leaves the record store hurriedly.

Earlene Roberts sees Oswald exit his room and walk to the nearest bus stop, just to the right of his rooming house. A bus stopping where Oswald is standing would be heading north, yet the Texas Theater is south.

1:04pm* Captain Westbrook and Reserve Sergeant Croy, now having gone around the block, see Oswald. They drive him to the Texas Theater, where they hope Plan C will take place—shoot Oswald dead as an armed cop killer and assassin of the President.

1:05pm* Oswald's double is seen passing a barber shop located at 620 East Tenth Street. He is walking west. Tenth and Patton, where Officer Tippit will soon be killed, is only four blocks away.

1:06pm* Oswald enters the movie theater, purchases a ticket at the kiosk, and enters the movie theater on the first floor.

Captain Westbrook and Sergeant Croy, after dropping off Oswald at the theater, then drive toward Tenth and Patton, about seven blocks away.

1:07pm Movie patron, Jack Davis, sees Oswald on the first-floor rear of the movie theater. Jack Davis distinctly remembers the time and seeing Oswald because the credits and advertisements prior to the movie, "War Is Hell," are displayed on the screen. The main feature would start at 1:20pm. Davis notices that Oswald changes his seat several times and sitting next to people even though there are only 24 people in a 900-seat theater. Oswald is looking for his contact and that contact will be confirmed if he or she matches the other half of his half-torn dollar bill.

1:08pm* Oswald's double, still dressed in a white shirt and light tan jacket, is approached by Officer Tippit at Tenth and Patton. Oswald's double places his left palm on Officer Tippit's closed passenger window. They have a calm conversation. Officer Tippit exits his vehicle, leaving the driver's door ajar, and walks toward the front of his vehicle. Oswald's double also walks toward the front of Tippit's car. As Tippit approaches the front of his car, near the right front wheel, Oswald's double shoots him three times. Tippit drops to the ground. Oswald's double then walks quickly toward the left rear of Tippit's car, turns back around, leans over Tippit, places his palm over Tippit's left front chrome bumper, and fires one shot into Tippit's right temple, ensuring his death. The fingerprints on the window and bumper are recovered and do not match Oswald's prints.

After the shots are fired, bystander Domingo Benevides raises his head from his truck. He sees Oswald's double unload the spent cartridges one at a time.

Sergeant Croy is given or plants a wallet at the scene of Tippit's murder that has Lee Harvey Oswald's identification, along with a selective service card in the name of Alek J. Hidell. No one calls in those names or a description of Lee Harvey Oswald as a potential suspect in the shooting of a fellow officer.

1:15pm Two hulls or empty shells are found at the sniper's nest in the TSBD. There are no latent fingerprints on these hulls. (Reports are later altered to show three hulls to imply three shots had been fired.)

1:22pm Loy Factor's German Mauser is found in the southwest area of the sixth floor.

1:30pm* Oswald's double walks .7 miles from the scene of the Tippit murder to the block where the Texas Theater is located.

1:32pm* Officers find a Mannlicher-Carcano rifle in the fifth-floor stairwell of the TSBD.

1:33pm* Johnny Calvin Brewer, an employee at Hardy's Shoe Store, claims he heard broadcasts of Officer Tippit being shot and then sees Oswald's double acting suspiciously near the vestibule of the shoe store. Radio broadcasts of Tippit's murder will not be made until 1:55pm. Brewer abandons the shoe store, leaving it without an employee, to track Oswald's double. Brewer is an accomplice to this criminal scheme.

1:36pm* Oswald's double enters the Texas Theater, pays for a ticket, and goes upstairs to the balcony where he is seen smoking a cigarette.

1:38pm A teary-eyed Walter Cronkite announces to the world that President Kennedy has died. The world is in disbelief. Then grief and sadness overcome their disbelief. (Millions of Americans remember exactly where they were when they hear the news of Kennedy's death. For many, the charismatic, young President embodied hope for a better world. That hope died upon his death. Many of those Americans knew that Johnson would not have the spark of hope that Kennedy had and that Johnson would return things to normal. They were right.)

1:45pm Johnny Brewer cannot locate Oswald (or his double). At the behest and urging of Johnny Brewer, Julia Postal, the theater employee at the ticket kiosk, calls the police to report that someone just entered the theater without paying for a ticket. Both Oswald and his double have entered the theater by paying for a ticket. The Dallas Police Department dispatcher then receives about another 6 calls from anonymous individuals about a person entering the Texas Theater without paying for a ticket. Oswald's time is running out.

1:49pm Although a fellow officer and the President of the United States have just been murdered, a swarm of Dallas police officers decides to respond to calls about a person not paying for a 93-cent movie ticket. They arrive in the front and rear entrances of the Texas Theater.

1:51pm Lee Harvey Oswald is arrested by the swarm of Dallas police officers. Oswald was expected to be killed by officers encountering an armed individual that had just shot one of their own, but Oswald averts being killed by yelling "I am not resisting!" and "Police brutality!"

Oswald has thus averted two attempts to kill him. Now Jack Ruby must act. Oswald has less than 47 hours to live.

Oswald's double is also arrested, taken to the rear alley of the theater, and quickly released.

2:38pm Judge Sarah T. Hughes rushes to Air Force One. Vice President Lyndon Baines Johnson is sworn in aboard Air force One as the 36th President of the United States. Between the time of his swearing in, until this writing, a cover-up concerning the assassinations of JFK, Oswald, and Tippit is actively maintained.

President John F Kennedy was killed because he wanted to disrupt cronyism and he stood in the way of others that did not want a disruption to their way of life and their income. Arguably, Kennedy was also imputed to be a peace president and weak on communism, but the reality was that Kennedy took the strongest stance against communism of most modern presidents. Finally, Kennedy was killed because he stood in the way of Johnson's desire to be President. More importantly, Johnson had to become President to rid himself of investigations into his numerous criminal schemes. Cronyism and corruption had a victory on November 22, 1963 and we suffered because of it.

The End

Endnotes

[i] The now-famous photo was published by Life magazine in February 1964, showing Oswald holding a rifle with a scope. In other international publications, the photo shows the rifle without a scope. The news outlets claimed they retouched the photo, and by doing so, inadvertently altered the appearance of the photo. I do not believe the photo was intentionally altered to implicate Oswald. Instead, I believe that Oswald was instructed to take a photo of this type in his mission to infiltrate pro-Castro groups, and it was later used to set Oswald up and demonstrate his pro-communist affinities.

[ii] Gunshot residue was found on Oswald's palm, but false positives from this test are far more common than false negatives because gunshot residue may last forever and anyone who has visited a firing range, yet never fired, could have gunshot residue on their skin. Additionally, Oswald worked with textbooks that had ink which, at that time, was composed of particles that would give a positive result. The FBI officially stopped relying on the paraffin test in 2006.

[iii] One Parkland Hospital surgeon, Dr. James Carraco, also noticed a large head wound on the front top portion of the President's head as he laid on the stretcher. *See* The Memory Hole, *LBJ: "I Can Believe Oswald Pulled the Trigger But I Don't Believe He Acted Alone,"* Oral History 2003, video at time stamp 17:20, accessed Dec. 4, 2022, available at: https://youtu.be/0vQfXAp4sF4.

[iv] Frazier began working at the TSBD only a month before the assassination and Ruth Paine got him the job there. More evidence of puppet mastery. Frazier claims that he remained with his car after arriving at the TSBD that morning to charge his batter because he was driving in tow and the battery was weak. He had just driven for thirty minutes. He had a four-door Chevy sedan and was not towing anything. Frazier claims he was charging the battery so that it would be strong enough to start at the end of his workday, but again, he had just driven 30 minutes. The story is problematic. Some people assert that it was Frazier that brought the rifle into the Depository after Oswald had entered the building and without being seen by others. I am reluctant to draw this conclusion. Frazier was arrested as an accomplice to the murder of JFK and was grilled by the Dallas Police Department. He was only 19-years old at the time. I am confident that Frazier,

along with his sister, were coerced into saying that Oswald brought in a long bag, allegedly curtain rods. Frazier also testified that Oswald carried this bag under his armpit and held it up with the palm of his hand. This is impossible to do with a 40" rifle even if Oswald were a professional basketball player. The average male arm length is 25" and Oswald had a relatively small stature. Incredulously, the Warren Commission then concluded that this bag was the Mannlicher-Carcano and not curtain rods. Again, more puppet mastery.

Fifty years later, in Frazier's book, *Steering Truth: My Eternal Connection to JFK and Lee Harvey Oswald,* he said that he saw an immaculately dressed man with a fedora and a rifle near the TSBD. In short, I seriously doubt Frazier brought the rifle into the TSBD, but I am confident Frazier was coerced by the Dallas police officers, the FBI, and the Warren Commission. The rifle was probably planted by hired co-conspirators working to repair the rotting floors on the fifth and sixth floors of the TSBD.

[v] The Presidential race between Nixon and Kennedy was the closest since 1916. When Kennedy won, he seemed ill prepared to fill many Executive branch positions, and some people were carried over from the prior, conservative administration. This problem was a contributing factor for Kennedy's demise as President, but will not be covered in this book.

[vi] In this book, I give numerous examples of the CIA's arrogant and rogue nature, but the CIA today is not the CIA of yesterday. Congress and numerous executive orders have significantly limited the CIA's authority, almost to the point of making it a benign agency with a huge budget. The last well-known instance of CIA malfeasance was in the form of renditions just after the 9/11 attacks. Renditions involuntarily transferred 9/11 suspects to countries that were known for employing torture techniques, but these renditions were authorized by the White House. Today, the CIA does not rely primarily on human assets, but instead, relies on technology.

[vii] E. Howard Hunt made it very clear that he wanted to be compensated for his confession and that he wanted the sponsors of any royalties from his confession to pay any legal fees that may arise from the confession, such as a defamation claim. Hunt always seemed to be hungry for money. He allegedly tried to blackmail President Nixon to keep his mouth shut about the Watergate scandal. Years after the Watergate incident, Hunt also sued Liberty Lobby for libel in the amount of one million dollars because it ran an article claiming that Hunt was associated with the assassination of JFK. Hunt initially was successful against Liberty Lobby at

trial, but the decision was reversed on appeal. In the new trial, and with Warren Commission and magic bullet theory critic Mark Lane serving as defense co-counsel for Liberty Lobby, Hunt lost, with one of the central issues being whether Hunt was in Dallas at the time of Kennedy's assassination. By the time of his deathbed confession, Hunt was keenly aware of making sure someone else paid for any legal fees to defend his assertions; otherwise, he would be held liable and would lose any of his putative winnings, as he did when he sued Liberty Lobby. Ultimately, Hunt did not reach an agreement with his sponsors and simply went forward with his deathbed confession, which is another reason why I believe it.

[viii] Kilgallen's columns featured mostly show business news and gossip, but also ventured into other topics, such as politics and organized crime. She wrote front-page articles for multiple newspapers on the Sam Sheppard trial and, years later, events related to the John F. Kennedy assassination, such as testimony by Jack Ruby. On November 8, 1965, Kilgallen was found dead in her Manhattan townhouse located at 45 East 68th Street. Her death was determined to have been caused by a combination of alcohol and barbiturates. The police said there was no indication of violence or suicide. According to New York City medical examiner James Luke, the circumstances of her death were undetermined, but emphasized that "the overdose could well have been accidental."

[ix] Babysitting is an espionage term. It means to protect, watch, or surveil. The CIA babysat Cuban General Almeida's brother in order to ensure that General Almeida completed his promise to kill Castro at his palace. George De Mohrenschildt babysat Lee Harvey Oswald until he turned him and Marina over to Michael and Ruth Paine. *See* Spy Museum, *Language of Espionage,* accessed Nov. 12, 2022, available at: https://www.spymuseum.org/education-programs/spy-resources/language-of-espionage/.

[x] Any interesting legal issue arose in Jim Garrison's prosecution of Clay Shaw, and it is featured in the movie, *JFK.* When Clay Shaw was arrested and was being booked, he was asked if he used any other names and he responded, Clay Bertrand. Bertrand was the name he allegedly used with other co-conspirators, so it was important to introduce evidence that he used this name. By the time of this trial, Garrison was obstructed significantly from obtaining probative records from the FBI and CIA despite him suing them for such information. As a matter of fact, the CIA stated they had no contact with Clay Shaw, which was later shown to be a lit. Clay Shaw was on the Domestic Contacts list of the CIA because of his foreign travel and business ties abroad, including business in Italy.

When Jim Garrison attempted to introduce the book-in sheet, the judge ruled it was inadmissible. Years later, the U.S. Supreme Court ruled that suspects that are booked into a jail have diminished or no expectation of privacy, including the right to have an attorney present because the government has a legitimate safety interest in properly identifying suspects by taking their fingerprints and other bio-metric data. Any aliases used by the person arrested is part of this process.

[xi] I am aware of the mind-altering techniques used by the CIA, particularly Project MKUltra, active from 1953 to 1973. Even David Ferrie, Carlos Marcello's pilot and the person I believe was slated to fly Oswald from Houston to Mexico, was a hypnotist and many suspect that Ferrie put Oswald under hypnosis with someone near Oswald on November 22, 1963 using "key words" to activate Oswald so he would kill Kennedy and Tippit. I do not believe Oswald was under hypnosis. In fact, I assert that Oswald's personality type made it impossible for him to be hypnotized. Nevertheless, I do recognize the popularity of hypnosis throughout the 50s, 60s, 70s, and early 80s. Today, the efficacy of hypnosis in medicine has been heavily curtailed and is often used as an adjunct to treat pain, stress, and anxiety, but not as a mind-altering treatment. Likewise, the CIA has abandoned the use of hypnosis for mind altering, probably because it does not work for this purpose.

[xii] Earlene Roberts was asked by WC Senior Counsel Ball whether she was working at the rooming house in November of 1963. She responded, "yes, to my sorrows." When asked why to her sorrows, she said, because Lee Harvey Oswald lived there "and I was put through the third degree by the FBI, the Secret Service, Captain Fritz, and [Sheriff] Decker." *Warren Commission Report, supra,* at 435-436. This is a small indication of how these witnesses' lives were disrupted, inconvenienced, and negatively impacted. Roberts had a very difficult time finding and keeping employment after this incident. So did Wesley Buell Frazier. Roberts also testified that Oswald came home around 5pm and never went out. Ibid., at 437 and 442.

[xiii] Sheriff Deputy Roger Craig testified that the Rambler had out-of-state plates. Carr testified that the Rambler had Texas plates. I believe Roger Craig as officers are trained to focus on license plates and have significantly more experience with the.

[1] Murdoch, Robert. *Ambush in Dealey Plaza: How and Why They Killed President Kennedy* (LookBack Publications, 2014) *The Fourth Shot hit Connally,* location 503-508.

[2] House Select Committee on Assassination, *Report of Activities After Assassination,* dated April 11, 1978, accessed on Jan. 24, 2023, available at: chrome-extension://efaidnbmnnnibpcajpcglclefindmkaj/ https://www.archives.gov/files/research/jfk/releases/docid-32268213.pdf

[3] Ibid.

[4]Weisberg, Harold, *Post Mortem: JFK Assassination Cover-Up Smashed,* (The Mary Ferrell Foundation, 1975) 437.

[5] Nelson, Phillip F., *LBJ: The Mastermind of the JFK Assassination,* (Skyhorse Publishing, 2013), 412.

[6] Shenon, Philip, *A Cruel and Shocking Act,* (Henry Holt & Co, 2013) 41.

[7] Ibid., at 60.

[8] JFK Library and Museum, John F. Kennedy and PT109, accessed on January 2, 2023:

https://www.jfklibrary.org/learn/about-jfk/jfk-in-history/john-f-kennedy-and-pt-109.

[9] Ibid.

[10] Hornberger, Jacob G., *The Kennedy Autopsy 2: LBJ's Role In the Assassination* (The Future of Freedom Foundation, 2019) 22.

[11] Wecht, Cyril H., *The JFK Assassination Dissected,* (McFarland, 2022) 38.

[12] **New York Times article dated Sept. 24, 1964, Autopsy Showed 2 Bullet Wounds, accessed Dec. 29, 2022, available at: https://www.nytimes.com/**

1964/09/28/archives/autopsy-showed-2-bullet-wounds-shot-through-brain-fatal-medical.html.

[13] City of Allen – ACTV, *Uncut Interview – JFK's Emergency Room Doctor: Dr. Robert McClelland,* April 20, 2017, video at time stamp 10:17 accessed Feb. 12, 2023, available at: https://youtu.be/lQ435lMaCng,

[14] Ibid., at time stamp 13:27.

[15] Bugliosi, Vincent, *Reclaiming History: The Assassination of President John F. Kennedy,* (W.W. Norton Co. 2007) 383-384.

[16] *The Warren Report: The Official Report on the 1963 Assassination of President John F. Kennedy,* (GPO 1964) Vol. 2, 361 (hereinafter referred to as the Warren Commission).

[17] Davis, *supra,* at 67.

[18] Ibid.

[19] Ibid., at 126.

[20] Ibid.

[21] Lifton, David, *Best Evidence: Disguise and Deception In The Assassination of John F. Kennedy* (MacMillan 1980) 615.

[22] Hornberger, Jacob G., *The Kennedy Autopsy 2: LBJ's Role In the Assassination* (The Future of Freedom Foundation, 2019) 59. *See also,* Washington Post, *Ford's Editing Backed 'Single Bullet Theory,'* July 3, 1997, accessed on Jan. 24, 2023, available at: https://www.washingtonpost.com/archive/politics/1997/07/03/fords-editing-backed-single-bullet-theory/9054d41d-40e2-4e7f-8a52-fd8489aee9e5/

[23] Nelson, *supra,* at 444.

[24] Wecht, *supra,* at 127.

[25] Ibid., at 126.

[26] Hornberger, *supra*, at 23.

[27] Wecht, *supra*, at 126.

[28] Ibid.

[29] On the day after the assassination, a medical student named Billy Harper was walking in Dealey Plaza, where he found a bone fragment about 5 x 7 centimeters. He took the bone to his uncle, who happened to be a pathologist at Methodist Hospital in Dallas. His uncle had the hospital medical photographer take a picture of the fragment. He also pulled together a small team of pathologists to analyze it. They concluded that it was occipital bone, which made sense, given that the wound was located in the occipital region of the skull. That bone fragment, which ultimately disappeared after it was sent to federal officials in Washington, D.C., became known as the Harper Fragment. Hornberger, *supra*, 24.

[30] Ibid., at 24.

[31] Warren Commission, *supra*, at 765 (emphasis added). *See also,* Davis, *supra*, at 31.

[32] Ibid.

[33] Davis, *supra*, at 31-33.

[34] Nelson, *supra*, at 520. *See also,* Lifton, *supra*, at 687 and 721.

[35] Wecht, *supra*, at 125.

[36] Nelson, *supra*, at 526.

[37] Ibid., at 492 (The FBI Report was drafted by Special Agents Silbert and O'Neill).

[38] Ibid., at 666.

[39] Ibid.

[40] Ibid., at 665-667.

[41] Ibid., at 673.

[42] Ibid., at 667.

[43] Ibid., at 576 (emphasis added).

[44] Barret Jackson Auction for a 1963 Pontiac Bonneville ambulance (used to transport Kennedy's ornate and flag-drapped casket and the immediate Kennedy family to Bethesda Medical Center. Accessed on January 15, 2023. https://www.barrett-jackson.com/Events/Event/Details/1963-PONTIAC-BONNEVILLE-JFK-AMBULANCE-202029.

[45] Lifton, *supra*, at 668.

[46] Ibid.

[47] Ibid., at 675.

[48] Ibid., at 691.

[49] Nelson, *supra,* at 514.

[50] Ibid., at 515.

[51] Hornberger, *supra*, at 18-19.

[52] Wecht, *supra*, at 72.

[53] Ibid.

[54] Stone, *supra*, 238 (emphasis added).

[55] C-Span, *John Connally on JFK Assassination*, accessed on Dec. 12, 2022, available at: https://youtu.be/hSKcOoQH8bc (emphasis added).

[56] Twyman, *supra*, at location 2505, (*"The Puzzle Comes Together,"* emphasis added).

[57] Ibid., at 72.

[58] Wecht, *supra*, at 278.

[59] Ibid.

[60] Ibid., at 278.

[61] McClellan, *supra*, at 270-271. *See also*, The Baltimore Sun, *The Fateful Politics of Nov. 23, 1963,* Nov. 23, 2013, accessed on December 15, 2022: https://www.baltimoresun.com/opinion/bs-xpm-2013-11-22-bal-jules-witcover-the-fateful-politics-of-november-22-1963-20131121-story.html (noting that [t]he principal story line about the visit was whether a feud between liberal Texas Sen. Ralph Yarborough and Gov. John B. Connally, a close Johnson friend, could be smoothed over, to assure Kennedy's re-election in 1964).

[62] Nelson, *supra,* at last page of acknowledgements section.

[63] Nelson, *supra*, at 300.

[64] Hughes-Wilson, John. *JFK—An American Coup: The Truth Behind the Kennedy Assassination* (Read How You Want, 2015) 159.

[65] Ibid.

[66] Ibid.

[67] Minutaglio, *supra*, at 299.

[68] Nelson, *supra*, at 385.

[69] Ibid., at 384.

[70] Ibid., at 385-386.

[71] Ibid.

[72] Reston, James, *The Lone Star: The Life of John Connally,* (Harper Collins, 1989), 270.

[73] Sample, *supra*, at 141 (emphasis added).

[74] Minutaglio, *supra*, at 307.

[75] Ibid.

[76] Davis, *supra*, at 153.

[77] Ibid., at 155 (emphasis added).

[78] Ibid., at 156-157.

[79] Ibid., at 157.

[80] Murdoch, *supra*, at location 1374 (Kindle Edition).

[81] Marina stated "she couldn't identify it positively but she said it looked like the rifle that he had, but she couldn't say for sure" (quoting from the Warren Commission Report). Davis, *supra*, at 138.

[82] Lane, Mark, *Commission Exhibit 399, Last Word—My Indictment of the CIA in the Murder of JFK,* (Skyhorse Publishing, 2011) *location* 260 (Kindle Edition).

[83] Ibid., at 264.

[84]Twyman, *supra*, at location 2491-2564 (Kindle Edition) (citing to the Warren Commission: Warren Commission Exhibit showing two empty cartridges on sixth floor of the Texas School Book Depository Building. The cartridge in the lower circle appears to be a crude attempt of forgery to conceal that it was live ammunition as apparently shown in Exhibit 10-14. (citing to the Warren Commission Report, Volume XVII,p. 223 Commission Exhibit 512).

[85] Ibid.

[86] Murdoch, *supra*, at 1527-1532 (Kindle Edition).

[87] Ibid.

[88] Ibid.

[89] Epstein, *supra,* at 38.

[90] *See, e.g.,* Mallon, Thomas, *Mrs. Paine's Garage: and the Murder of John F. Kennedy,* (Harvest Books, 2003).

[91] The Mary Ferrell Foundation, *The Twelve that Built the Oswald Legend,* accessed on Jan. 25, 2023, at: https://www.maryferrell.org/pages/ Essay_-_Oswald_Legend_12.html.

[92] Davis, *supra*, at 272.

[93] Ibid.

[94] Warren Commission, *supra*, at 149 (Kindle Edition).

[95] Ibid., at 153.

[96] Harvey and Lee, *Mail Order Rifle,* accessed Jan. 7, 2023, available at: https://harveyandlee.net/Mail_Order_Rifle/Mail_Order_Rifle.html.

[97] Armstrong, *supra*, at 832.

[98] Ibid., at 834.

[99] *See, e.g.,* Goldsmith, Jack L., *In Hoffa's Shadow: A Stepfather, a Disappearance in Detroit, and My Search for the Truth,* (Farrar, Straus, Giroux, 2019) (claiming Hoffa was not involved in JFK's assassination).

[100] Marrs, Jim, *Cross Fire – The Plot That Killed Kennedy*, (Basic Books, 2013) 223 (stating that he was told by the FBI "If you didn't see Lee Harvey Oswald in the School Book Depository with a rifle, you didn't witness it").

Marrs, *supra,* at 223.

[101]Belzer, Richard, Hit List: An In-Depth Investigation into the Mysterious Deaths of Witnesses to the JFK Assassination (Skyhorse Publishing, 2016).

[102]Bartlow, John Martin, *Third Oral History with Bobby Kennedy,* John F. Kennedy Library, April 30, 1964, *available at:* https://www.jfk-assassination.net/vietnam.htm

[103]*See* JFK Presidential Library and Museum, Dulles, Allen W, June 1959—Nov. 1962, available at: https://www.jfklibrary.org/asset-viewer/archives/JFKPOF/029/JFKPOF-029-021

[104]Dulles, Allen W, *Oral History Interview*, John F. Kennedy Library, Dec. 5, 1964, *available at: https://www.jfklibrary.org/sites/default/files/archives/JFKOH/Dulles%2C%20Allen%20W/JFKOH-AWD-01/JFKOH-AWD-01-TR.pdf*

[105] As I assert, LBJ was the missing link to perfect the CIA, the Mafia, and Cuban exiles' ire with Kennedy. Ostensibly, LBJ was seen as someone that supported Kennedy's policies, and some say, went even further than Kennedy with his Great Society reforms. Even the accused assassin, Oswald, for example did not see a distinction between Kennedy and LBJ. During his interrogation on the Sunday morning he was killed by Jack Ruby, Oswald was asked if his beliefs regarding Cuba played a role in the assassination. Asked by Secret Service inspector Thomas J. Kelley if Kennedy's assassination would have any effect on the US policy toward Cuba, Oswald replied, "Will Cuba be better off with the President dead? Someone will take his place, Lyndon Johnson, no doubt, and he will probably follow the same policy." Marrs, Jim, *Cross Fire – The Plot That Killed Kennedy*, (Basic Books, 2013) 149. Only a small group of people knew that Johnson sanctioned the hit on Kennedy.

[106] Sample, Glen; Collom, Mark, *The Men on the Sixth Floor: The "Must Have" JFK Assassination Book for the Serious Researcher,* (Sample Graphics, 2010) 95-97.

[107]Nelson, *supra,* 347.

[108]Stone, Roger, *The Man Who Killed Kennedy* (MJF Publishing, 2013), inset photos.

[109]Hunt, Howard E, *American Spy* (Turner Publishing, 2007) 2363-2488 (Kindle Edition: Chap. 12: The Assassination of President Kennedy).

[110] Hunt, Saint John, *Bond of Secrecy,* 48, available at: chrome-extension://efaidnbmnnnibpcajpcglclefindmkaj/https://cryptome.org/2012/07/bond-hunt.pdf

[111] Ibid.

[112] Ibid.

[113] Hunt, Howard E., *supra,* at 2405 (Kindle Edition: Chap. 12: The Assassination of President Kennedy).

[114]Hunt, E. Howard, *supra,* at 2585.

[115] Davis, Mike, *The JFK Assassination Evidence Handbook: Issues, Evidence & Answers* (Self Published, 2018) 27.

[116] Ibid.

[117] Ibid.

[118]Political Dictionary.com, entry for *Plausible Deniability,* available at: https://politicaldictionary.com/words/plausible-deniability/.

[119] McClellan, Barr, *Blood, Money, and Power – How LBJ Killed JFK,* (Skyhorse Publishing, 2011) 192.

[120]Sample, *supra,* at 150-153.

[121]Ibid·

[122]Ibid., at 159.

[123] Twyman, *supra*, at location 10022 (Kindle Edition: Going Into Business).

[124]Stone, *supra*, at 23.

[125]Caro, Robert, *The Path to Power—The Years of Lyndon B Johnson, Vol. I* (Vintage Publishing, 1990) 100.

[126]Nelson, *supra*, at 3.

[127] McClellan, *supra*, at 93.

[128]Joesten, Joachim, *The Dark Side of Lyndon Baines Johnson,* (Iconoclassic Books, 1968) 17-18

[129] McClellan, *supra*, at 139.

[130] Ibid., at 140.

[131] Ibid., at 120-121.

[132] McClellan, *supra*, at 191.

[133] Sample, *supra*, 121.

[134] Ibid., at 125-126.

[135] Joesten, *supra*, at 135.

[136] Ibid., at 135-135

[137] Sample, *supra*, at 168.

[138] McClellan, *supra*, at 190-191.

[139] Sample, *supra*, at 120.

[140]McClellan, *supra*, at 236.

[141] Ibid., at 237.

[142] O'Sullivan, Shane, *"The Watergate Burglars—Nixon, Dirty Tricks, and the CIA,"* (Skyhorse Publishing, 2018) 67.

[143] Stone, *supra*, at 153.

[144] Ibid. (internal citations omitted).

[145] Nelson, *supra*, at 171.

[146] Thomas, Ralph, *Wall Of Secrecy—Inside The JFK Assassination: - How James Angleton & William Harvey Set Up An Assassination Team Inside The CIA,* (Self-published, 2018) 5.

[147] USA Today, *JFK Files: Controversy Surrounding CIA Counterspy Chief Fed Assassination Conspiracies,* dated Nov. 13, 2007, accessed on Jan. 15, 2023, available at: https://www.usatoday.com/story/news/politics/2017/11/13/jfk-files-controversy-surrounding-cia-counterspy-chief-fed-assassination-conspiracies/857616001/

[148] Thomas, *supra*, at 1.

[149] Some claim that Angleton was not in the house on the very same day Mary Meyer died, but a few days later. Regardless, he was not expected or called.

[150] National Records, *"Chronology of William Harvey,"* undated, but from the year 1975, accessed Dec. 12, 2022, available at: chrome-extension://efaidnbmnnnibpcajpcglclefindmkaj/ https://www.archives.gov/files/research/jfk/releases/2022/ 157-10014-10102.pdf

[151] Ibid.

[152] Minutaglio, Bill, and Steven L. Davis, *Dallas 1963* (Twelve, 2013), 332-333.

[153] History News Network, *Brown & Root, a Company with a History,* dated Dec. 24, 2003, accessed on Jan. 25, 2023 available at: https://historynewsnetwork.org/article/2851.

[154] Minutaglio, *supra,* at 333.

[155] Nelson, *supra,* at 477.

[156] National Archives, *Report of the Reaction of Soviet and Communist Party Officials to Kennedy Assassination,* dated Dec. 1, 1966, accessed on January 2, 2023, available at: https://www.archives.gov/files/research/jfk/releases/docid-32204484.pdf.

[157] Nelson, Phillip F., *LBJ: The Mastermind of the JFK Assassination,* (Skyhorse Publishing, 2013), 378-380.

[158] Texas Monthly, *Death of a Fixer,* Nov. 1992, accessed Dec. 2, 2022, available at: https://www.texasmonthly.com/news-politics/death-of-a-fixer/.

[159] McClennan, *supra,* at 32.

[160] Some say the thunderstorm and rain had subsided significantly by the time Ferrie and his two friends started their journey. Regardless, they drove 400 miles in about six hours or less, thus averaging 67 miles per hour assuming they did not stop.

[161] Wecht, *supra,* at 191.

[162] This is how Frank Sturgis spelled his name under oath before the House Select Committee on Assassinations. I have seen others spell it as Fiorini.

[163] Hearings Before the Select Committee on Assassinations, *Testimony of Frank Sturgis,* dated March 20, 1978, accessed on Feb. 1, 2023, available at: chrome-extension://efaidnbmnnnibpcajpcglclefindmkaj/ https://www.archives.gov/files/research/jfk/releases/2018/docid-32252529.pdf.

[164] Meskil, Paul, "Ex-Spy Says She Drove To Dallas With Oswald & Kennedy 'Assassin Squad,'" New York Daily News p. 5, Sept. 20, 1977.

[165] The National Security Archive, *JFK and the Diem Coup,* posted Nov. 3, 2003, accessed Jan. 30, 2023, available at: https://nsarchive2.gwu.edu/NSAEBB/NSAEBB101/index.htm

[166] Armstrong, John, *Harvey & Lee—How the CIA Framed Oswald,* (Quasar Ltd, 2003) 885.

[167] Ibid.

[168] There is also evidence in the form of pictures that Bill Shelley is with Oswald in New Orleans as Oswald passes out *Fair Play for Cuba* literature. *See* https://harveyandlee.net/TSBD_Elevator/TSBD_elevator.html

[169] Armstrong, *supra,* at 812.

[170] Waldron, Lamar, *Ultimate Sacrifice,* (Carroll & Graf, 2005) 283-284, 323, 325.

[171] Marrs, *supra,* at 341.

[172] Ibid., at 342.

[173] The Portal to Texas History, *Affidavit of Seth Kantor,* dated Dec. 4, 1963, accessed Feb 23, 2023, available at: https://texashistory.unt.edu/ark:/67531/metapth339044/m1/1/.

[174]Ray, Pamela J. Primary Target: JFK—How the CIA Used the Chicago Mob to Kill the President, (Authorhouse, 2020), 93.

[175]Ibid.

[176] Stone, *supra,* at 143-144.

[177]Nelson, *supra,* at155-156.

[178] Stone, *supra,* at 145.

[179] Ibid.

[180]Moldea, Dan E., *The Hoffa Wars* (Charter Books, 1978)

[181]Twyman, Noel H., Bloody Treason: The Assassination of John F. Kennedy, (Laurel Publishing) 164.

[182] Wecht, *supra*, at 260.

[183]Warren Commission, *supra*, 439.

[184]Ibid., at 449 (Several witnesses testified that Lee Oswald was not aggressive).

[185]Waldron, Lamar, *Ultimate Sacrifice* (Carroll & Graf, 2005) 440.

[186]Warren Commission, *supra*, at 737-738.

[187]Ibid.

[188] Oswald, Robert L. *Lee: A Portrait of Lee Harvey Oswald by His Brother* (Coward-McCann, 1967).

[189] Warren Commission, *supra*, at 30.

[190] Epstein, Edward Jay, *Legend: The Secret World of Lee Harvey Oswald* (Eje Publications, 1978), 74.

[191] Ibid.

[192] Ibid., at 75.

[193]Warren Commission, *supra*, at 677.

[194] Ibid., at 678.

[195] Epstein, *supra*, at 76.

[196] Warren Commission, *supra*, at 677 (emphasis added).

[197] Ibid.

[198] Ibid. (emphasis added).

[199] Ibid., at 450.

[200] *See* Frontline.com Article: 8 Things You May Not Know About Lee Harvey Oswald, dated Nov. 19, 2013, https://www.pbs.org/wgbh/frontline/article/8-things-you-may-not-know-about-lee-harvey-oswald/ (accessed December 5, 2022)

[201] Wecht, *supra*, at 264.

[202] Warren Commission, *supra,* at 679.

[203] Waldron, *supra,* at 441.

[204] Ibid·

[205] Senator Richard S. Sweiker, a member of the subcommittee on intelligence, is quoted as stating "[w]e don't know what happened, but we do know Oswald had intelligence connections. Everywhere you look with him, there are the fingerprints of intelligence."

[206] The terrorist attacks of September 11, 2001 were also a result of a lack of coordination of intelligence among agencies. The intel about individuals learning how to fly planes with the goal of using them as projectiles to fly into buildings in U.S. cities was not shared, particularly, with then Immigration and Naturalization Services, which could possibly have deported them or otherwise averted the events by detaining them. Accordingly, Congress created the Department of Homeland Security, a conglomeration of 22 agencies with the goal of further coordinating intelligence efforts, among many other goals.

[207] Wecht, *supra*, at 223.

[208] History Matters, *Oswald's 201 File*, accessed Jan. 4, 2023, available at: https://www.history-matters.com/archive/contents/cia/contents_cia_oswald201_thru_11-21-63.htm

[209] Waldron, *supra*, at 94-100.

[210] Ibid., at 95.

[211] Ibid.

[212] **USA Today, "U.S. Planned a 261,000-troop invasion force of Cuba, Newly Released Documents Show," Oct. 30, 2017, accessed on Jan. 25, 2023, available at:**

https://www.usatoday.com/story/news/politics/2017/10/30/u-s-planned-261-000-troop-invasion-force-cuba-newly-released-documents-show/813376001/

[213] Ibid.

[214] Marrs, Jim, *supra,* at 4.

[215] Ibid. (emphasis added).

[216] National Archives Release of JFK-related documents about assassination plans, accessed on Jan. 24, 2023 : https://www.archives.gov/files/research/jfk/releases/157-10004-10147.pdf

[217] *See* Spy Museum, Host: Jonna Mendez, former CIA Chief of Disguises, accessed Feb. 23, 2023, available at: https://www.spymuseum.org/host-an-event/spy-speaker-series/jonna-mendez/#:~:text=Jonna%20Mendez%20served%2027%20years,retiring%20as%

[218] **Harvey and Lee, "Lee Harvey Oswald: The Legend and the Truth," by James Norwood, accessed April 2, 2023, available at: https://harveyandlee.net/J_Norwood/Legend.html**

[219] Epstein, Jay, *"The Legend—The Secret world of Lee Harvey Oswald,"* (Eje Publ. 1978) 159.

[220] Memo is available at: https://harveyandlee.net/Comrade/Hoover.jpg.

[221] Harvey and Lee, *"John Armstrong's Documented History of the CIA's 'Oswald Project,'"* accessed March 15, 2023, available at: https://harveyandlee.net/.

[222] Ray, *supra*, at 60.

[223] Ibid., at 54.

[224] Lucky Bean Tours, *Lee Harvey Oswald in New Orleans,* Jan. 15, 2017, accessed March 3, 2023, available at: https://www.luckybeantours.com/lee-harvey-oswald-in-new-orleans/.

[225] For additional background about Oswald's double, I recommend the video "Who Impersonated Lee Harvey Oswald?" by MrChrillemannen, accessed on Feb. 1, 2023, available at: https://youtu.be/LMAc7WKMP2c. The video interviews John Armstrong, author of the book, *Harvey and Lee.*

[226] Davis, *supra*, at 335.

[227] Murdoch, *supra*, at 721-738 (Kindle Edition).

[228] Davis, *supra*, at 275.

[229] Armstrong, *supra*, at 848.

[230] Marrs, *supra,* at 338.

[231] Ibid.

[232] Warren Commission, *supra*, at 437.

[233] Ibid., at 438.

[234] Pictures of jacket courtesy of Gil Jesus, on the Education Forum at: https://educationforum.ipbhost.com/topic/27458-oswalds-jacket/

[235] Ibid., at 343.

[236] Ibid.

[237] Davis, *supra*, at 333.

[238] Ibid.

[239] Warren Commission, *supra*, at 568.

[240] The Portal to Texas History, *Crime Scene Search Report of Captain W.R. Westbrook,* dated Nov. 22, 1963, accessed on Feb. 12, 2023, available at: https://texashistory.unt.edu/ark:/67531/metapth339366/?q=H%20R%20Westbrook.

[241] Warren Commission, *supra*, at 569.

[242] Ibid., at 333.

[243] Ibid., at 334.

[244] Ibid.

[245] Armstrong, *supra*, at 856.

[246] Ibid., at 857 (emphasis added).

[247] Armstrong, *supra*, at 841-842.

[248] Ibid., at 849.

[249] Summers, Anthony, *"Not in Your Lifetime—The Assassination of JFK,"* (Headline, 2013) 109.

[250] Ray, *supra*, at 255.

[251] Ibid.

[252] The Education Forum submission of Greg Doudna, *Shasteen Barber Shop Customer Was Not Oswald,* dated Feb. 17, 2021, at: https://educationforum.ipbhost.com/topic/27009-shasteens-barber-shop-customer-was-not-oswald/.

> Mr. Shasteen lives at 2214 Fairfax in Irving, Texas. He is owner and operator of Clifton's Barber Shop located at 1321 South Storey in Irving, Texas. He has lived in Dallas for twenty years. He testified that

in the course of looking at television on the afternoon of November 22, 1963, he saw on the screen the man said to be Lee Harvey Oswald and it occurred to him immediately that the man was the fellow who had come into his barber shop to have his hair cut. While looking at television some more "it finally dawned" on him where he had seen him; "I knew where he lived." The witness also volunteered that "actually, I knew where the station wagon was that was parked that I saw him and this lady in." So he allegedly took out to run to "the house." He testified that he drove "up there" and he couldn't get within four blocks of that house. He knew then that he was not mistaken. When he got back to the shop, they began to talk about it. He testified that all three barbers had cut Oswald's hair, but he had cut it more than the others. He cut Oswald's hair three or four times. The boy in the middle chair cut it a couple of times and the boy in the front chair cut it once. Oswald was always disgruntled.

He then related an occasion when the man he thought was Oswald had come into the shop wearing a pair of yellow house shoes which the witness admired. The customer said they had only cost a $1.50 and he obtained them in Old Mexico. He added that when next he was down there, he would pick up a pair for Shasteen. This was the only time the customer was pleasant.

While Doudna, the person that submitted the write-up by Mr. Shasteen concludes that Mr. Shasteen is obviously imagining things, I have come to the conclusion that there was an Oswald double based on the evidence. Mr. Shasteen was not imagining things.

[253] Armstrong *supra,* 861.

[254] Warren Commission, *supra*, at 36 (Kindle Edition)

[255] Ibid.

[256] HSCA, *supra*, at 356.

[257] Waldron, *supra*, at 466.

[258] Ibid., at 467.

[259] Ibid.

[260] Marrs, *supra*, at 242.

[261] Ibid.

[262] Giancana, Sam, Giancana, Chuck, *Double Cross*, (Skyhorse Publishing 1992) 94.

[263] Ibid., at 95.

[264] Ibid.

[265] Ibid., at 96.

[266] Ibid.

[267] Huey Long—The Man, His Mission and Legacy, accessed on Jan. 2, 2023, available at: https://www.hueylong.com/life-times/assassination.php

[268] Ibid.

[269] Hughes-Wilson, *supra*, at 119-122.

[270] Ibid. (citations in original omitted).

[271] Ibid.

[272] Stone, *supra*, at 87.

[273] Ibid., at 88.

[274] McClelland, *supra*, at 240.

[275] Ibid., at 242.

[276] Ibid., at 243.

[277] **RR Auction, Jack Ruby Handwritten Letter from Jail Identifying LBJ as the Kennedy Assassination Mastermind, accessed Jan. 12, 2023, available at:**

https://www.rrauction.com/auctions/lot-detail/33049970417260-jack-ruby-handwritten-letter-from-jail-identifying-lbj-as-the-kennedy-assassination-mastermind

[278] Stone, *supra*, at 82.

[279] The Education Forum, *Life Magazine, LBJ, and the JFK Assassination*, submission by then Chief of Time/Life Editorial Services, posted Nov. 4, 2009, accessed Feb. 12, 2023, available at: https://educationforum.ipbhost.com/topic/14966-life-magazine-lbj-and-the-assassination-of-jfk/.

[280] Waldron, *supra*, at 295.

[281] Ibid., at 294.

[282] Ibid., at 295.

[283] Ibid.

[284] Ibid., at 296.

[285] Ibid., at 297.

[286] Southwell, David, *The Kennedy Assassination, The Truth Behind the Murder of America's 35th President,* (Future, Issue 4) p 26.

[287] **El Paso Times, Ex-CIA Contract Pilot had Front Row View of the JFK assassination, Served on Team to Prevent it, Met Oswald, dated Nov. 12, 2013, accessed Jan. 24, 2023, available at: https://www.elpasotimes.com/**

story/news/local/blogs/border-cafe/2013/11/22/ex-cia-contract-pilot-had-

front-row-view-of-the-jfk-assassination-served-on-team-to-prevent-it/

30957221/.

[288] The Daily Mail, *JFK's Assassin, Lee Harvey Oswald, was Trained at a Secret CIA Camp Preparing for Invasion of Cuba and Sniper Who Taught Him Insisted After That There Was No Way Oswald Had the Marksmanship To Kill the President,* dated Oct. 29, 2021, accessed January 25, 2023, available at: https://www.dailymail.co.uk/news/article-10145399/JFKs-assassin-Lee-Harvey-Oswald-trained-secret-CIA-camp-says-family-FBI-informant.html

[289] Holy, Chauncey M., *Self-Portrait of a Scoundrel,* (Trine, 2013).

[290] Nelson, *supra,* at 810.

[291] The JFK Truth Matters, *Symptoms of Foreknowledge,* dated Mar. 28, 2021, accessed Jan. 27, 2023, available at: https://thejfktruthmatters.wordpress.com/.

[292] Ibid.

[293] Sample, *supra,* at 143.

[294] Armstrong, *supra,* at 808.

[295] Ibid., at 838.

[296] The Portal to Texas History, *"Affidavit of Seth Kantor,"* dated Dec. 4, 1963, accessed Feb. 16, 2023, available at: https://texashistory.unt.edu/ark:/67531/metapth339044/m1/1/.

[297] Marrs, *supra,* at 341-342.

[298] Photo courtesy of Harvey & Lee, *Westbrook and Croy,* accessed on Jan. 7, 2023, available at: https://harveyandlee.net/WandC/Westbrook_and_Croy.

[299] Many have spelled Baker's first name as "Marion," with one "r," but the Warren Commission wrote his name as "Marrion," so that is how it will appear throughout this book.

[300] Warren Commission, *supra*, at 613 (emphasis added).

[301] The Portal to Texas History, *Affidavit by Billy N. Lovelady*, undated, but based on other indications, it was made on Nov. 22, 1963, accessed Dec. 9, 2022, available at: https://texashistory.unt.edu/ark:/67531/metapth338698/m1/1/.

[302] Lifton, *supra,* at 412.

[303] Warren Commission, *supra*, at 24 (Kindle Edition).

[304] Ibid. *See also,* Davis, *supra,* at 232-233.

[305] The Portal to Texas History, *Affidavit of Officer Marrion L. Baker,* dated Nov. 23, 1963, accessed Nov. 1, 2022, available at: https://texashistory.unt.edu/ark:/67531/metapth337201/m1/1/.

[306] Warren Commission, *supra*, at 24 (Kindle Edition).

[307] Lifton, *supra*, at 410.

[308] Warren Commission, *supra*, at 592-593, available at: https://www.aarclibrary.org/publib/jfk/wc/wcvols/wh7/pdf/WH7_Baker_aff.pdf.

[309] Warren Commission, *supra*, at 24 (Kindle Edition) (stating that the total time elapsed *"was not more than two minutes since the shooting."*) (emphasis added).

[310] Davis, *supra,* 226.

[311] Ibid.

[312] Sample, *supra*, at 191.

[313] Murdoch, *supra*, 921 (Kindle Edition "Witnesses: And the ring of truth").

[314] 22 November 1963, *Carolyn Arnold's Statements to the FBI,* accessed on Feb. 3, 2023 at: http://22november1963.org.uk/carolyn-arnold-witness-oswald.

[315] Murdoch, *supra*, 947 (Kindle Edition "Brennan does not pick out Oswald from a line-up").

[316] Warren Commission, *supra*, 696.

[317] Sample, *supra*, 56-57.

[318] Ibid.

[319] Ibid., at 64.

[320] Ibid., at 67.

[321] Ibid., at 57-61.

[322] Ibid., at 41.

[323] Ibid., at 44 and 60.

[324] County of Dallas, *Supplemental Investigative Report of Sheriff Deputy Luke Mooney,* dated Nov. 23, 1963, accessed on Jan. 22, 2023 at: https://www.jfk-assassination.net/russ/testimony/mooney1.htm (emphasis added).

[325] The Portal to Texas History, *Report on Officer's Duties by R. M. Sims and E. L. Boyd RE: the President's Murder #1,* undated but probably typed days after the assassination, accessed Jan. 23, 2023, at: https://texashistory.unt.edu/ark:/67531/metapth339596/m1/1/?q=Luke%20Mooney%20school%20book%20depository.

[326] Ibid.

[327] The Portal to Texas History, *Affidavit of Seymour Weitzman,* dated Nov. 23, 1963, accessed on Nov. 25, 2022, available at: https://texashistory.unt.edu/ark:/67531/metapth338815/m1/1/.

[328] The Portal to Texas History, *Report on Officer's Duties by R. M. Sims and E. L. Boyd RE: the President's Murder #1,"* undated but probably typed days after the assassination, accessed January 23, 2023, at: https://texashistory.unt.edu/

ark:/67531/metapth339596/m1/
1/?q=Luke%20Mooney%20school%20book%20depository.

[329] Warren Commission, *supra,* at 235.

[330] Sample, *supra,* 56-57.

[331] Ibid.

[332] Ibid., at 64.

[333] Ibid., at 67.

[334] Ibid., at 57-61.

[335] MacKenzie III, Roderick, *The Men That Don't Fit In,* (Self-Published, 2016) 109.

[336] Harvey and Lee, *Mail Order Rifle,* accessed on F. 1, 2023, available at: https://harveyandlee.net/Mail_Order_Rifle/Mail_Order_Rifle.html

[337] Ibid. Please note that Oswald was fired from this job because of excessive absences, but on this particular day, he was at work.

[338] Ibid.

[339] Photo courtesy of Harvey and Lee, *Harvey and Lee Depart the TSBD,* accessed on March 2, 2023, available at: https://harveyandlee.net/Leaving/Leaving_the_TSBD.html

[340] Armstrong, *supra,* at 823.

[341] Holland, Max, *Lie That Linked the CIA to the Kennedy Assassination,* Studies in Intelligence, Vol. 45, No. 5 (2001) 4.

[342] Ibid.

[343] Photos courtesy of Harvey and Lee, *Harvey and Lee Depart The TSBD*, accessed on Feb. 20, 2023, available at: https://harveyandlee.net/Leaving/Leaving_the_TSBD.html

[344] The Portal to Texas History, *Letter Concerning Arrest of Lee Harvey Oswald*, dated Nov. 23, 1963, accessed Dec. 14, 2022, available at: https://texashistory.unt.edu/ark:/67531/metapth340311/?q=lee%20oswald%20arrest.

[345] Armstrong, *supra*, at 864.

[346] Ibid.

[347] Ibid.

[348] Ibid., at 865.

[349] Ibid.

[350] To better illustrate the level of confusion, here is the most comprehensive list of eye and earwitnesses and what they heard that day:

Witnesses who testified to hearing three shots: Victoria Adams (CD5, p.39); Danny Arce (CD205, p.7); Virgie Baker (CD5, p.66); Police officer Marrion Baker (WCHE, v.24, p.199b); Secret Service agent Glen Bennett (WCHE, v.18, p.760); Jane Berry (CD5, p.42); Deputy Sheriff Eugene Boone (WCHE, v.19, p.508); Lee Bowers (CD5, p.43); Charles Brehm (WCHE, v.22, p.837b-838a); Police officer E. V. Brown (WCHE, v.6, p.233); Dallas mayor Earle Cabell (WCHE, v.7, p.478); Elizabeth Cabell (WCHE, v.7, p.486); Vice-presidential aide Cliff Carter (WCHE, v.7, p.475); Governor Connally heard the first and third shots, and felt the second shot hit him. (WCHE, v.4, p.132-133); Nellie Connally (WCHE, v.4, p.147); news photographer Malcolm Couch (CD5, p.18); Deputy Sheriff Roger Craig (WCHE, v.19, p.524); Police chief Jesse Curry (WCHE, v.12, p.28); Mrs. Joseph Eddie Dean (CD5, p.44); Deputy Sheriff Harold Elkins (WCHE, v.19, p.540); Deputy Sheriff Jack Faulkner (WCHE, v.19, p.511); Police officer J. W. Foster (WCHE, v.6, p.251); Secret Service agent Will Greer, who was driving the Presidential limousine (WCHE, v.2, p.118); Postal inspector Harry Holmes (WCHE, v.7, p.291); Emmet Hudson (WCHE, v.19, p.481); Police officer Douglas Jackson who rode alongside the Presidential limousine (FBI 62-109060 JFK HQ File, Section 181, pp.94); News photographer Robert Jackson (CD5, p.15); James Jarman (CD5, p.335); Secret Service agent Lem Johns (WCHE, v.18, p.773-774); Ladybird Johnson (WCHE, v.5, p.565); Deputy Sheriff C. M. Jones (WCHE, v.19, p.512); Secret Service agent Roy Kellerman (at least 3 – WCHE, v.2, p.76); Secret Service agent Sam Kinney (WCHE, v.18, p.732); Secret Service agent Jerry Kivett (WCHE, v.18, p.778); Domyths Kounas (CD5, p.68); Patricia Ann Lawrence (CD5, p.51); Secret Service agent Winston Lawson (WCHE, v.4, p.353); Deputy Sheriff C. L. "Lummie" Lewis (WCHE, v.19, p.526); Billy Lovelady (WCHE, v.24, p.214b); Police officer B. J. Martin (WCHE, v.6, p.291); Secret Service agent William McIntyre (WCHE, v.18, p.747-748); Austin Miller (WCHE, v.19, p.485); Mary Ann Mitchell (WCHE, v.6, p.176); Deputy Sheriff Luke Mooney (WCHE, v.19, p.528); Mary Muchmore (CD735, p.8); Harold Norman (CD5, p.26); Presidential assistant Lawrence O'Brien

(WCHE, v.7, p.464); Presidential assistant Kenneth O'Donnell (WCHE, v.7, p.448); Eddie Piper (WCHE, v.6, p.385); Presidential assistant David Powers (WCHE, v.7, p.473); Frank Reilley (CD205, p.29); Texas Highway Patrol officer Joe Henry Rich, who drove the Vice-presidential follow-up car (WCHE, v.18, p.800); James Romack (WCHE, v.6, p.280); Arnold Rowland (WCHE, v.26, p.166a-b); William Shelley (WCHE, v.24, p.226a); James Simmons (WCHE, v.22, p.833a); Deputy Sheriff L. C. Smith (WCHE, v.19, p.516); Secret Service agent Forrest Sorrels (WCHE, v.21, p.548); Pearl Springer (WCHE, v.24, p.523a); Deputy Sheriff Allan Sweatt (WCHE, v.19, p.531); James Tague (CD205, p.31); Secret Service agent Warren Taylor (WCHE, v.18, p.782-783); Roy Truly (WCHE, v.24, p.227b); Police officer Buddy Walthers (WCHE, v.7, p.545); Sheriff's Department radio operator Watson (WCHE, v.19, p.522); Deputy Sheriff Harry Weatherford (WCHE, v.19, p.502); Deputy constable Seymour Weitzman (WCHE, v.24, p.228a); Otis Williams (CD5, p.64); Linda Kay Willis (WCHE, v.7, p.498-499); Phillip Willis (WCHE, v.7, p.495); Deputy Sheriff John Wiseman (WCHE, v.19, p.535); Mary Woodward (WCHE, v.24, p.520a); Secret Service agent Rufus Youngblood (WCHE, v.18, p.768)

Witnesses who reported hearing four or more shots: Robert Edwards (4) (WCHE, v.19, p.473; v.6, p.205); Amos Euins (4) (CD205, p.12), Ronald Fischer [3 in his statement to the Sheriff's office (WCHE, v.19, p.475); 4 in his deposition (WCHE, v.6, p.195)]; Ruby Henderson (4) (WCHE, v.24, p.524a-b); Jean Hill (4 to 6) (WCHE, v.6, p.207); S. M. Holland (4) (WCHE, v.19, p.480; v.6, p.244); A. J. Millican (8, in three separate volleys) (WCHE, v.19, p.486); Mary Moorman (3 or 4) (WCHE, v.19, p.487); Jesse Price (5 or 6) (WCHE, v.19, p.492); Royce Skelton (4, including 1 that hit the pavement) (WCHE, v.19, p.496; v.6, p.238); Carolyn Walther (at least 4) (WCHE, v.24, p.522b); James Worrell (4) (WCHE, v.16, p.959; v.2, p.193)

Witnesses who reported hearing fewer than three shots: Howard Brennan (2) (WCHE, v.3, p.144); John Chism (at least 2) (CD205, p.38); Marvin Faye Chism (2) (WCHE, v.19, p.472); Jack Dougherty (1) (WCHE, v.6, p.379), Police officer Bobby Hargis, whose motorcycle was traveling at the left rear of the President's car (2) (WCHE, v.6, p.294); Charles Hester (2) (WCHE, v.19, p.478); Secret Service agent

Clint Hill (2) (WCHE, v.2, p.139), Jacqueline Kennedy (2) (WCHE, v.5, p.180); Secret Service agent Paul Landis (2) (WCHE, v.18, p.754-7555); F. Lee Mudd (2) (WCHE, v.24, p.538a); Thomas J. Murphy (2) (WCHE, v.22, p.835b); Jean Newman (2) (WCHE, v.19, p.489); Emory Roberts (2 or 3 per his report of 11/22/63 (WCHE, v.18, p.739); 3 in his report of 11/29/63 (WCHE, v.18, p.734)); Bonnie Ray Williams (2 in his affidavit to police (WCHE, v.24, p.229a); 3 in his testimony to the commission (WCHE, v.3, p.179)); Abraham Zapruder (2) (WCHE, v.7, p.571)

Witnesses who reported hearing four or more shots: Robert Edwards (4) (WCHE, v.19, p.473; v.6, p.205); Amos Euins (4) (CD205, p.12), Ronald Fischer [3 in his statement to the Sheriff's office (WCHE, v.19, p.475); 4 in his deposition (WCHE, v.6, p.195)]; Ruby Henderson (4) (WCHE, v.24, p.524a-b); Jean Hill (4 to 6) (WCHE, v.6, p.207); S. M. Holland (4) (WCHE, v.19, p.480; v.6, p.244); A. J. Millican (8, in three separate volleys) (WCHE, v.19, p.486); Mary Moorman (3 or 4) (WCHE, v.19, p.487); Jesse Price (5 or 6) (WCHE, v.19, p.492); Royce Skelton (4, including 1 that hit the pavement) (WCHE, v.19, p.496; v.6, p.238); Carolyn Walther (at least 4) (WCHE, v.24, p.522b); James Worrell (4) (WCHE, v.16, p.959; v.2, p.193).

Davis, Mike. *The JFK Assassination Evidence Handbook: Issues, Evidence & Answers* (Self Published, 2018) 194-195.

See Davis, *supra,* at 192-195.

[351] For an excellent video with the digitally remastered Dictabelt recording over the Zapruder film, please see Drew Techner, *Zapruder film with Dictabelt Records 1,* accessed Feb. 25, 2023, available at: https://youtu.be/TUZFsvCmJHE

[352] MacKenzie III, Roderick, *The Men That Don't Fit In,* (Self-Published, 2016).

[353] Ibid., at 1262 (Kindle Edition, *"Confessions of a Paradox Man"*).

[354] Armstrong, *supra*, at 809-811 (Miss Geneva Hine worked at the credit desk of the TSBD on the second floor and described events as the Presidential motorcade approached the TSBD. She told the Commission, "I was alone until the lights all went out and the phones became dead because the motorcade was coming near us ...... "Moments after the shooting Geneva Hine watched from her second-floor office window as people ran across Elm Street. She then left her office and hurried down the hall to the office of Lyons and Carnahan, room 201, to see if she could get a better view from the front windows. She knocked on the door, but when nobody answered, she hurried to the west end of the hall and knocked on the door of Southwestern Publishing, Room 203. She saw a woman through the opaque glass, heard her talking on the phone, and continued knocking on the door, but the woman never answered. The woman was Mrs. John L. Carol Hughes, a 27-year-old employee of Southwestern Publishing, who was alone in the office during the shooting. She was not interviewed by the Commission and was not questioned about her phone conversation or her refusal to answer the door. The fact that telephone service to the TSBD office was interrupted while phone service to Southwest Publishing on the same floor of the building was not interrupted, strongly suggests that the interruption of telephone service at the TSBD office was deliberate).

[355] Even today, the Secret Service has a history of "thoroughly enjoying" jaunts to cities Presidents visit both domestically and abroad. *See, e.g.,* USA Today article dated Oct. 18, 2012, *"ABC: Secret Service Agents had Hookers Before Colombia,"* accessed Jan. 3, 2023, available at: https://www.usatoday.com/story/news/ondeadline/2012/10/18/abc-prostitution-secret-service-colombia-obama/1642559/.

[356] The Girl Who Shot JFK, *The Big Event,* accessed on Feb. 3, 2023, available at: https://www.thegirlwhoshotjfk.com/the-big-event/.

[357] Hughes, *supra*, at 158.

[358] Ibid.

[359] Ibid.

[360] While Factor claims he did not shoot that day, I disagree, and I support the theory, as did Glen Sample and Marc Collom, authors of "*The Men on the Sixth Floor,*" that he fired one shot and he intentionally missed the president.

Factor was initially paid $2,000 and then $8,000 on the day of the assassination. *See* Sample, Glen; Collom, Mark. *The Men on the Sixth Floor: The "Must Have" JFK Assassination Book for the Serious Researcher* (Sample Graphics, 2010) 67. When Factor relayed to Sample and Collom that he denied being involved in the shooting despite being paid $10,000 by Wallace (or about $97,000 in today's money), Sample and Collom tried to give Factor a way out by suggesting he did, in fact, fire, but he intentionally missed in order to appear to fulfill his contractual obligation, but Factor again denied shooting. *See* Ibid., at 57-61.

[361] "Bullet hit curb 260 feet from president's limousine; piece of concrete hit James T. Tague on cheek, drew blood. Twyman, Noel H. *Bloody Treason: The Assassination of John F. Kennedy* (Laurel Publishing, 2010). *See also*, MacKenzie, Rod; *et. al. The Men That Don't Fit In* (E-book 2016) 1872-1873. "Loy Factor had to shoot because Mac Wallace and Ruth Anne Martinez, who stood right next to Mac, had already paid Loy 2 grand, and so Loy fired over the President's head in order to collect his 8-grand balance."

[362]Ibid·

[363] Hughes, *supra*, at 166.

[364] Ibid.

;

[365] Those witnesses are Marvin Robinson, Roy Cooper, Richard Randolph Carr, Helen Forrest, and James Pennington.

[366] Armstrong, *supra,* at 831.

About the Author

I became a lawyer and worked initially as a prosecutor for the Department of Justice, and then the Department of Homeland Security. I was diligent and hard-working. I rose quickly within the federal government, earning and maintaining a Top Secret-SCI (secret compartmented information) clearance, the highest clearance anyone can get. For almost twenty years, I handled national security cases, human persecutor cases, class-action cases, and media-interest cases. I was a counselor to two political appointees of one of the largest law enforcement agencies in the world. As I rose up in the federal government, my exposure and expertise in various legal fields increased. They included criminal law and procedure, immigration, naturalization, customs, habeas corpus, labor and employment, and tort law. I worked with many federal, state, tribal, and local agents and officers from numerous law enforcement and intelligence agencies, both domestically and internationally, in both civil and criminal matters. I was able to see how federal agencies work and how law enforcement agencies collaborate and compete with each other. I also provided advice abroad to national police and prosecutors that resulted in hundreds of arrests of human traffickers and smugglers in a multi-nation, multi-agency operation.

I have always enjoyed reading true crime stories and I decided that my first book would be about the JFK-assassination because I have been fascinated with it since I was a teenager. I hope to write more true crime books in the near future.